To Vietnam in Vain

To Vietnam in Vain

*Memoir of an Irish-American
Intelligence Advisor,
1969–1970*

EDWARD A. HAGAN

McFarland & Company, Inc., Publishers
Jefferson, North Carolina

LIBRARY OF CONGRESS CATALOGUING-IN-PUBLICATION DATA [new form]

Names: Hagan, Edward A., 1947– author.
Title: To Vietnam in vain : memoir of an Irish-American intelligence advisor, 1969–1970 / Edward A. Hagan.
Other titles: Memoir of an Irish-American intelligence advisor, 1969–1970
Description: Jefferson, North Carolina : McFarland & Company, Inc., Publishers, 2016 | Includes bibliographical references and index.
Identifiers: LCCN 2015042569 | ISBN 9780786499670 (softcover : acid free paper)
Subjects: LCSH: Hagan, Edward A., 1947– | Vietnam War, 1961–1975—Military intelligence. | United States. Army—Officers—Biography. | Irish Americans—Biography. | Vietnam War, 1961–1975—Personal narratives, American.
Classification: LCC DS559.8.M44 H28 2016 | DDC 959.704/38—dc23
LC record available at http://lccn.loc.gov/2015042569

BRITISH LIBRARY CATALOGUING DATA ARE AVAILABLE

ISBN 978-1-4766-2368-9 (ebook)

On the cover: Edward Hagan in Can Tho, November 1969; U.S. Military Assistance Command (MACV), Vietnam Veteran patch; Vietnam map (Thinkstock)

Printed in the United States of America

McFarland & Company, Inc., Publishers
  Box 611, Jefferson, North Carolina 28640
  www.mcfarlandpub.com

For 2nd Lieutenant John P. Goggin (1946–1969).
Xavier High School, 1964.
Fordham College, 1968.
Military Assistance Command Vietnam Advisory Team 56, 1969.
Killed in Action, September 11, 1969,
Thuan Trung District, Phong Dinh Province, Republic of Vietnam.

Table of Contents

Acknowledgments

Colleagues, friends, and fellow former soldiers helped me to research and write this story.

I spent several weeks in the National Archives in College Park, Maryland, where the records of Advisory Team 56 are housed in great abundance. I was greatly assisted by Martin Gedra, a librarian on the staff there. I had the help of Carrie G. Sullivan and Lauren Hammersen at the U.S. Army Center of Military History at Fort McNair, D.C., where many hours of recorded interviews with members of Advisory Team 56 are housed. I must mention the valuable help of Kristen J. Nyitray, in the Special Collections and University Archives, Frank Melville, Jr. Memorial Library, Stony Brook University, where the papers of Senator Jacob Javits are housed. I am indebted to Rosalba Varallo Recchia at the Seeley G. Mudd Manuscript Library of Princeton University, who helped me find my letters from Vietnam to Congressman William Fitts Ryan, whose papers are archived there. Joanne Elpern helped me to find numerous sources through her work in interlibrary loan at the Ruth Haas Library of Western Connecticut State University. Laurel Richards of Western's Department of Writing, Linguistics, and Creative Process, helped me with the preparation of the final draft of the text. Peggy Stewart and Erin Manion of Western's Publication and Design Department assisted me greatly with the photos and illustrations. I am indebted also to Western Connecticut State University for two Connecticut State University/American Association of University Professors (CSU-AAUP) research grants that financed my travel and research at the National Archives.

Numerous readers of drafts of the book offered perceptive comments and suggestions: Ray Baubles, John Bergstrom, Christopher Booth, Kevin Boylan, John Briggs, Bob Burns, Doug Hemphill, Denis Hynes, Jay Jackson, Herb Janick, Bob Lowery, Rich Lundy, John Malone, Cecilia Miller, Andrew Milward, Jerry O'Gorman, Malachy O'Neill, Jim Pegolotti, and John Sullivan. I made many changes based on their recommendations; all of them helped me sort out the story. I do have to single out John Briggs for his special help in this project. He has helped me to "brew" it since 1987.

I thank my fellow soldiers who gave me permission to use their real names in the writing of this memoir: Robert Alderson, John M. "Mac" Ball, Mark Barrett, Steven Black, Brendan Brophy, Bob Burns, Frank Dursi, Lucas Carpenter, Gerry French, Doug Hemphill, Peter Katopes, Ron Marksity, Brian McMahon, Neil Meoni, Ben Nelson, Larry Quasius, John Thompson, and Troy Yarbrough. Francine L. Talbert gave permission to use the name of her deceased husband, Henry Talbert. Gloria Ormandy Murria gave permission to use her late husband Miguel C. Murria's name. Other soldiers below the rank of colonel have been given pseudonyms, either because they are deceased or I could not find them or their heirs to ask permission to use their real names.

I must mention also the support of other friends and colleagues who believed that I should write this story and helped in one way or another: Oscar De Los Santos, Jack Dunn, Brian Heller, Patrick Hicks, Chris Kukk, Ben Lambert, Eric Lewis, Eugene O'Brien, S.J., Bill Perry, Sean Reynolds, Jim Rogers, Linda Vaden-Goad, and Bob and Donna Zachariasiewicz.

I have been blessed with loving family members, and I am grateful to them. I thank my cousin, Paul Hagan, for providing the photo of my grandfather. My wife, Denise Lepicier, encouraged me for years to write this memoir, and my son, Peter, and my daughter, Christine, are unfailingly enlightening and keep my humility in good shape.

Preface

The present work is primarily a memoir of my service in Vietnam from October 1969 to October 1970 as a member of a U.S. Army province advisory team—Advisory Team 56 in Phong Dinh Province in the Mekong Delta. There have been great Vietnam memoirs such as Philip Caputo's *A Rumor of War*, Michael Herr's *Dispatches*, and Tim O'Brien's *If I Die in a Combat Zone: Box Me Up and Ship Me Home*. No book, however, documents the advisor's experience on a province advisory team in the depth of *To Vietnam in Vain*.

There are books on the role advisors played in the Vietnam War, but almost all of them report the experiences of advisors who worked with Army of the Republic of Viet Nam (ARVN) main force units, i.e., infantry divisions. Province advisors worked with the local militias—the Regional and Popular Forces, who were recruited for duty near their home villages and hamlets. Often disparaged, these units nonetheless contended with local Viet Cong guerrillas for control of local communities. The ARVN divisions, like American divisions, sought "big battle" confrontations with Viet Cong and North Vietnamese main force units. Province advisors were both civilians and army personnel, and they were often engaged in community building projects and local government initiatives. Consequently, province advisors saw much of the sometimes well-meaning and well-intentioned, but often sordid, efforts of our Vietnamese allies. The story of these efforts offers a distinctly different understanding of the war from that of the average American who served in an American unit and actually knew few Vietnamese.

Irish-Americans of my generation served in Vietnam in very high numbers. Being an Irish-American male has defined coming-of-age as service as an American soldier since the Revolutionary War. The definition still holds. My story explains how military service grows out of growing up Irish in America, as I did in New York, the son of Irish immigrants. No previous book has spoken to the Irish-American experience in Vietnam in any depth.

As my title suggests, the memoir is the ambivalent story of my year in Vietnam as a U.S. Army officer intelligence advisor in the Mekong Delta. I grew up in the largest Irish neighborhood in New York during the 1950s and '60s, and I was raised to be a Catholic American patriot— to be idealistic polit-

1

ically, patriotically, and religiously. The memoir records my coming to awareness of the paradoxes and difficulties of that identity. My service in the Vietnam War offered little outlet for idealistic behavior. As a U.S. army advisor on province Advisory Team 56, I worked entirely with Vietnamese military personnel and discovered almost every day the difficulties of supporting the corrupt structure of the Government of Vietnam. The memoir also records what it has meant to live the rest of my life with vivid memory of my year in Vietnam. This is not a coming-of-age story unless my maturity comes only in my late 60s. The memoir is a report of the evolution of my consciousness from youth to retirement age: it avoids chronology as its structure. The memoir is written to reflect the muddle of my consciousness (and perhaps also the consciousness of the country itself) about the war that continues to define how Americans think of themselves and of the meaning of patriotism to their country.

I became an army officer upon graduation in 1968 from Fordham University where I was a member of the Army Reserve Officers Training Corps (ROTC). Assigned to the Military Intelligence Branch of the Army, I was sent in early 1969 to the U.S. Army Infantry Officers Basic Course at Fort Benning, Georgia; subsequently I was sent to the Tactical Intelligence Officers Basic Course at Fort Holabird, Maryland. After spending a few months in the Intelligence Branch of 5th Army Headquarters at Fort Sheridan, Illinois, I was sent to Vietnam in October of 1969. The memoir focuses on my one year, nine months, and ten days on active duty in the Army. I should mention that 5th Army Headquarters coordinated the army's participation in the quelling of the riots in Chicago that accompanied the Democratic National Convention in 1968. Much of the activity of 5th Army Headquarters during my three months there was focused on threats of civil disorder in the wake of the 1968 riots. It was odd to be at the epicenter of the army's readiness preparations for using troops at home on the streets of the midwestern United States.

But I went on a "short, unaccompanied tour" to Vietnam (they call that a "deployment" now), and I tell that story here.

Preamble

For a thousand years in thy sight
are but as yesterday when it is past,
or as a watch in the night.
Thou dost sweep men away; they are like a dream,
like grass which is renewed in the morning:
in the morning it flourishes and is renewed;
in the evening it fades and withers.
So teach us to number our days
that we may get a heart of wisdom.
                        —Psalm 90, Verses 4–6

I went to Vietnam as a U.S. Army officer in October 1969 and was assigned as an intelligence advisor. At that point U.S. advisors had been in Vietnam since 1950. Later I found out that the Tay Do I Viet Cong battalion had been fighting in the Mekong Delta since World War II. Hell, the French established "French Indochina" in 1887. In 1965 President Johnson had greatly increased the size of the American military presence in Vietnam when he added about 160,000 servicemen, including Marine and Army infantry units, in that year alone. I arrived in 1969, a year and a half after the Tet Offensive of 1968 had led Johnson to withdraw from the 1968 presidential race. The war was well along, but American soldiers entered the war in the middle, a period that lasted roughly from 1965 to 1973. We all joined a war in progress; it kept right on going after each of us left.

When I left in October 1970, while progress was claimed, the war was much the same as it was when I arrived. The Viet Cong were subjected to intense American firepower, but they were still fighting when I went home. Four and a half years later, on April 30, 1975, Saigon fell to the Communist forces. I had long since "zoned out" of the war.

But I really never have.

I have thought about the war, however briefly, almost every day since. I joined the war in mid-stream, and I'm still in the stream. Did the stream start with my grandfather in the Boer War or my father in World War II? I can't tease out a neat, logical timeline. Doing so distorts the entanglements of my consciousness and the consciousness of the entire country.

The one-year tour created a false chronology for the war. My goal, upon arrival, was to go home a year later. I wasn't really motivated to win the war; moreover no one really defined what winning would look like. So in short, I had a beginning—my arrival, a middle—my year on duty, and an end—my return home—built into my consciousness. Those moments in time were strictly my own, shared only by a few others who arrived on the plane with me, were not assigned to my unit, and went home a year later too. All of us joined units that had been operating in Vietnam for some time, years even. But hardly any member of any unit had been around for the entire duration of the war. The story of the war, as experienced by most U.S. service personnel, is too often told as the closed-ended narrative of a year.

The real story was quite a different matter. We began our tours of duty without any knowledge of what had happened in the previous week, month, year, ten years, or even since 1950. We were thrust into the middle of an already existing situation. America continues to make such thrusts—in Iraq, Afghanistan … hell, we're sending advisors to Nigeria to hunt down Boko Haram.

So when I set out to write this memoir, I realized that I could not tell the truth of my Vietnam experience except by suggesting its "middleness." James Joyce begins several of his short stories in *Dubliners* by using a pronoun without an antecedent. He plunges his readers into a stream already flowing; we have to get our bearings by figuring out who the "him" is in the first line of the first story. I had to figure out the antecedents of my war in Vietnam, mostly by myself, because hardly anyone knew what they were or even deemed them important.

A memoir of that war, and maybe the story of any war, must dispense with the false consciousness of "once upon a time there was Pearl Harbor," and "they lived happily ever after when the Japanese signed the surrender on the battleship *Missouri*." In between, the boys fought on D-Day and at Guadalcanal. In truth, the Americans arrived in the middle of the Indochina Wars and left before they were over. And we still fly the POW-MIA flag everywhere. I write to reveal fake demarcations and suggest personal and national entanglements. Failure to recognize the middleness of the Vietnam situation makes its story false when it insists on allegiance to conventional narrative. I hope my readers will appreciate being disoriented; I hope to reward them with a more realistic experience of the war as lived by this former soldier. I was disoriented by my service: it comes back in a rush. The rush beats stuffing your head with fake war stories.

Introduction

My first few months inside [the stockade at Ft. Knox], I spent a lot of time trying to piece the war into a pattern. I developed the habit of making a mark on my cell wall when I remembered a particular event, thinking at some later date I could refer to it and assemble all the marks into a story that made sense.... Eventually, ... I realized that the marks could not be assembled into any kind of pattern. They were fixed in place. Connecting them would be wrong. They fell where they had fallen. Marks representing the randomness of the war were made at whatever moment I remembered them: disorder predominated.[1]—John Bartle, the central character in Kevin Powers' *The Yellow Birds*

"A great deal of intelligence can be invested in ignorance when the need for illusion is deep," the novelist Saul Bellow *once wrote. We should keep that in mind as we consider the lessons from the wars in Iraq and Afghanistan—lessons of supreme importance as we plan the military of the future.[2]*—Major General H.R. McMaster, Commanding Officer, Fort Benning, GA, Home of the Infantry School. "The Pipe Dream of Easy War." July 21, 2013. *New York Times*

For this people's heart has grown dull, and their ears are heavy of hearing, and their eyes have closed, lest they should perceive with their eyes, and hear with their ears, and understand with their heart, and turn for me to heal them.—Matthew 13:14–5

A 2008 episode of PBS Television's program, *Nature*, records the reintroduction of wolves into Yellowstone National Park after 70 years of absence. *In the Valley of the Wolves* tells the story of the Druid Wolf Pack with melodramatic anthropomorphic flair: "Like all dynasties, however, the Druids were destined for a fall." Clichéd, suspenseful music plays in the background as heavy-voiced narrators tell the story of "survival of the fittest." We Americans like bravado—perhaps because we're insecure about whether we'll measure up to tight situations when we're actually faced with them.

And like most people, Americans like to think well of our ancestors: their survival testimony to strength of will and character. (Since we have their blood in our veins, we like the implied compliment to ourselves—a too-clever bit of narcissism.) We like illusions and dreams of fortitude. We like teleologies and tales with meaningful endings. I have found no way to craft either a meaningful ending or beginning for this memoir. I can't cut out my war story from whoever I was at age 22 and age 23 from what I was at age 10 or what I am now at age 68. One idea associates freely with another. My memoir makes me the star of my show, but I haven't been suckered by its narrative into thinking my show tells the whole story. At best it offers a glimmer of what the big picture might be. There is no master narrative possible, and I can't promise to re-introduce a post–World War II, pre-and post–Vietnam War consciousness into the current Yellowstone of our minds.

Now, dear reader, I warned you in the Preamble that you're likely to want me to impose a logical narrative framework on my "middle-muddle." Don't be insulted. You, like me, would like a bit more certainty in our lives, but we're not dead yet. There will never be a time when all of America's enemies are defeated. I can't give the Vietnam War an ending that it lacks. There's an Irish legend that at the Battle of the Valley of the Black Pig, all of Ireland's enemies will be defeated. The battle never happens, but the idea of its coming arises in moments of crisis. It's a desire for a finality that we can't have. We're stuck only with the dream of such a battle.

For the American soldier in Vietnam, there was no discernible way to create an ending such as the capture of the enemy's capital city or its leaders. Body count was invented as a measure of progress, but no one notified the Viet Cong that when a certain number had been killed, they were to accept that they had lost. The war, as I came to know it during my year in Vietnam, was virtually identical in terms of its "progress" when I left as when I arrived. We made matters worse by ignoring Vietnamese history and by adopting a goalless mode of fighting the war.

I was trained as an intelligence officer: I'm given to looking for patterns in people's behavior and clues to their intentions that I know others miss. I became a college professor and literary critic after the war: There is a real correlation between being an intelligence officer and being a literary critic. I read closely and surmise much. I hope I'm not conceited. Sometimes I'm dead wrong, but I like the game of figuring out what's going on. When I notice a colleague, especially a junior one, suddenly become chummy, I don't always accept the friendliness at face value. I ask why the behavior has changed. I've served on my university's Promotion and Tenure Committee (P&T) for four years and will probably serve for at least a couple more. I draw a line between the sudden collegial friendliness and my service on P&T. Am I cynical? No. I like people and like to promote and tenure them; no junior colleague needs to butter me up. But maybe butter goes well with bread.

As I wrote this memoir, I discovered that the calendar's movement is often not meaningful although the reader will notice that I'm a stickler about dates even when their specificity seems unnecessary. In 1977 Michael Herr ended his Vietnam memoir, *Dispatches*, with "Vietnam, Vietnam, Vietnam, we've all been there."[3] We're all still there. The current date is always 1969 or 1970. Vietnam is deeply imbedded in the American unconscious. The black POW/MIA flag is still ubiquitous, and flies everywhere—on town halls, in Yankee Stadium, on every public building on the Massachusetts Turnpike, on the official flag poles of Middleburgh, New York, outside the post office in Brewster, New York, inside the Vet Center in Danbury, Connecticut. But then ask the young what it represents: few know, but all have seen it. George W. Bush and Bill Clinton are still draft-dodgers as they were in 1968 although their importance has faded in the current national consciousness. Triage, as refined by the war in Vietnam, is now Standard Operating Procedure (SOP) in most American hospital emergency rooms.

But there is a much deeper consequence of the war: We learned to ignore evidence. We seemed to prefer lies to truth, and maybe we always have. We seem now to have given up on any pretense of seeking for truth. In my research into my year in Vietnam, I went to the National Archives in College Park, Maryland, where the records of my unit, Military Assistance Command Vietnam (MACV) Advisory Team 56, are stored. I also found that a spring 1969 U.S. Army military history project, now stored at the U.S. Army Center of Military History at Fort McNair, contains recorded interviews with many of the people I came to know in October 1969. I have made extensive use of these interviews. I was pleasantly surprised at how much truth the lieutenants, captains, majors, and civilians on Team 56 were putting into writing and stating on tape even as they tried hard to establish a Government of Vietnam (GVN) worth having and to limit the appeal of Vietnamese communism. Their skepticism about the war effort is amazing: Even when loyalty and "can do" spirit seem to make them claim things in general are improving, they offer detailed evidence that much is not going well.

I am impressed by the military history team's ignorance of history. The questions on the tapes reveal that the interviewers knew very little about Phong

Dinh Province in IV Corps, the Mekong Delta. They might as well have been interviewing an advisory team in I Corps. There is no hint that they were aware of an M.A. thesis on Phong Dinh by Howard Maxwell Potter, which had been completed in the previous year, and Potter was teaching at West Point in the spring of 1969. A U.S. Army military history detachment ought to have known about a study of Phong Dinh in 1964–65 conducted by a West Point history professor. The questions are focused on the functionality of the advisory team— in particular, its combination of civilians and military advisors. The assumption is that history is a study of the machine's production. There is no need to know what the situation was like five, ten, fifteen years previously; present functioning is all that matters. And then it is also obvious that only a few of the interviewed advisors even know what happened in the province a year previously.

So the military history project was consistent with the way the U.S. was fighting the war in general: bad history describing bad strategy. We were making history then, as the Bush administration was to proclaim after 9/11 and went into Iraq and Afghanistan blissfully ignorant of the histories of those countries. On the highest levels, there was and is studied ignorance. Truth is hard; lies are easy. Very junior and mid-level officers were working hard and telling the truth in Phong Dinh; their senior leaders were taking it easy.

So we've been doing ever since. Mostly we've become content with lies, with a dissociation of reality into disparate parts about which we can tell nicely formed, conclusive lies. Such lies are whoppers. We seem to want whoppers on the highest level. Promotion to high rank means that we have to put a smile on prognostications, no matter how much at odds they are with the Edsel we were making on the Mekong factory floor.

Universities are now directed almost entirely by people who do not teach. And it is a good bet that many university administrators started out as professors and did not like teaching (or the pay), yet they do try to dictate what is going on in the classroom. Their thinking becomes highly theoretical; they often ballyhoo the latest fad in education. They bloviate in abstractions and do not value the classroom teacher's views.

Business has the same affinity for trends in management. Gurus of one sort or other turn up with some regularity, and businesses re-invent themselves in accord with those theories. Tom Peters' book, *In Search of Excellence*, was all the rage in business management in the ten years after it was published in 1982. Businesses scurried to employ Peters' eight common themes of successful businesses. The themes were actually fairly pedestrian common sense (stay close to the customer; stick to the knitting), yet they seemed like manna from heaven to companies lost and wandering in the desert. They wanted profits and thought Peters a prophet.

All of this suggests gross insecurity about whatever these organizations are attempting to accomplish. Team 56 was trying to make Phong Dinh Province a functioning bureaucracy, yet the junior officers and civilians were writing about the futility of key efforts. In large part, they were ignored.

We can establish cause and effect by focusing on part of any situation. Advanced scientists these days are openly calling into question the whole concept of cause and effect. There appear to be uncaused causes; effects appear to be uncaused on the quantum level. I'm reminded of undergraduate philosophy courses in which we struggled with Deist concepts of God as the Unmoved Mover. I remember thinking then that immanence and transcendence were really the same. Those committed to transcendental views of reality were often denying the truth of their immanence in ordinary reality. God is part of and inherent in his own creation; the numinous is not separate from the material. Years later, when I read Thomas Carlyle's chapter on "Natural Supernaturalism," I thought he understood the vapidity of abstract transcendentalism. When I read the work of contemporary postmodern scholars, I think that, while posing as materialists, they are almost completely ungrounded and wholly committed to abstraction and even the denial of the possibility of truth. That such scholarship started as part of the New Left opposition to the Vietnam War does not surprise me. The materialism of these characters is mere know-it-all posture— an outgrowth of abandoning hope of any holistic view of reality. Their posture is really a belief system, and, as Paul Simon's song, "The Boxer" conveys, "we believe what we want to believe and disregard the rest."

I'm trying not to disregard the rest—as impossible as that is. All writing is a process of selection. I try to show how entangled my memories, thoughts, and observations are with everything else. The American War in Vietnam is not *sui generis*. So this memoir meanders, gives dates, gets specific, and then tries to show how the dates set up *post hoc, ergo propter hoc* fallacies. Like Lawrence's Bedouin, I'm entangled with God, and I can't untangle myself from the all. Heck, why would I want to?

Progress

As a first rule of thumb ... you can tell a true war story by its absolute and uncompromising allegiance to obscenity and evil.[4]—Tim O'Brien, "How to Tell a True War Story," *The Things They Carried*

Like my father and my grandfather, I went to war. I'll try to make sure that I follow Tim O'Brien's dictum for telling true war stories and tell what I know about our service with maximum allegiance to its obscenity and evil. I might point out that "war story" in soldiers' parlance implies exaggeration, even lying. War stories are like fish stories. So a true war story is a kind of true lie. And a "true lie" is an irony. So irony is truth.

My true war story lacks the usual rising action, the denouement, the conclusion, the theme. My war sprawls and flows in uncontrolled directions. There's not much derring-do. Above all, I don't find any moral improvement in what we did. Or do. When I used my Veterans Administration ID card to get 10 percent off at Home Depot recently, the cashier looked me in the eye intently and said fervently, "Thank you for your service." Huh? What did I do?

Andrew Bacevich, a retired West Point-educated career army officer, a Boston University professor, and a staunch conservative, has commented at great length on this current empty adulation for veterans. He was particularly incensed about the staged return of a female U.S. Navy sailor from Afghanistan during a July 4 game in 2011 at Fenway Park. In discussing his book, *Breach of Trust*, he told Phil Donahue that the Red Sox and the military

> ... are manipulating the American people. And they are encouraging the American people to think that to go to the ballgame on the 4th of July and sing the national anthem and clap for the troops that are on the field, and then to react emotionally to this contrived reunion—all of that is intended to persuade the American people that they have acquitted their responsibility to the troops.... I go to the ballgame. I clap. I get teary-eyed. Then when they say, "Play ball," I buy a beer and basically forget about the episode ... that's not good enough.... That's an exercise in what Dietrich Bonhoffer called "cheap grace."—grace you award yourself without having

earned [it]—grace that enables you to feel that you are virtuous when, in fact, you are complicit in wrong-doing.... Our first obligation to those we love, to those we care about, is to protect them, to preserve them, to keep them out of harm, and therefore if indeed we love the troops, ... then we would all want to make sure that they were only sent in harm's way when absolutely necessary.... Since 9/11, they have been abused.... And I think that that's wrong. I think that's undemocratic. I think it's immoral. And I think that the American people need to be called on it.[5]

So I'd like to call that Home Depot cashier on that "thank you." I was hardly heroic.

I went to my war in October 1969 as an intelligence advisor in Phong Dinh Province, but I was mostly a bureaucratic warrior. I put my initials, "E.A.H.," on the memos that crossed my desk every morning; about one-fourth of my afternoons or evenings I buckled myself into the back seat of an olive-drab UH-1D or Huey helicopter, put on a headset and plugged in a Y-cord so that I could talk to the pilots with the din of the egg beater blades muted. From 1,500 feet, I mostly studied the shack-type, palm frond-roofed-and-sided, one-room "hootches," houses that most farmers inhabited, the milk-chocolate brown water in the elaborate, rectilinear canal system, and the sometimes green rice paddies of the Mekong Delta. We did fly much lower at times—able to see the concealed Viet Cong grey sampans and the fishing nets strung across the canals on crisscrossed poles. In the weeks following defoliation by a Huey equipped with 55-gallon drums of Agent Orange, I could see right down to the canal banks that previously sheltered the VC with shade palm and cajeput trees. Mostly, I remember what a sergeant looked like the night after he flew on the defoliation helicopter: his fatigues had been bleached almost white from the blow-back of the defoliant into the helicopter, and he was shaking at the Team House bar because the helicopter had been blasted by a tree-top mine designed to go off when a helicopter flew low overhead. I remember that he was from Pennsylvania, and he had seen a ghost and looked like one himself.

Drinking Pabst Blue Ribbon at the bar in the evening after swooping like the Coney Island Cyclone roller coaster above the canal banks seemed impossible even when the beer was cold. To get on a helicopter at the air field, we had to drive a jeep through Can Tho City's chaotic traffic; the streets were usually busy with motor scooters, bicycle-or motor scooter-propelled cyclos (armchair taxis in which Americans were forbidden to ride in Can Tho), and other military vehicles. Pushcart stands on corners sold French bread in the mornings. The city seemed unaware that combat was going on a short distance away—ten kilometers distant and sometimes less. We passed restaurants, bars that catered to GIs, and other shops fitted into the gaps between the sandbagged and guarded entrances to government and military buildings. MPs and QCs (Vietnamese MPs) patrolled the bar area; the MPs occasionally even set up radar speed traps on the road between the Tactical Operations Center (TOC) in downtown Can Tho and the air field on the outskirts of the city. Women were either dressed like peasants, usually with straw conical hats, a floral print top, and black pajama-type pants, or fashionably outfitted in pastel-colored silky dresses called ao-dais, slit to the waist, and worn with black pants, although the pants were sometimes the same color as the dress itself. Many young women were very beautiful, groomed impeccably. Most men were dressed raggedly, especially if they were workers in the city and certainly if they were farmers out in the country. It was not unusual to see a water buffalo (a living tractor) being led through the streets, often by a young boy. Almost all the men between 20 and 40 seemed to be in Vietnamese army fatigues although standard non-military attire was a collared white shirt and dark pants. Young boys frequently wore white shirts and short royal blue pants—school uniforms perhaps. Everyone seemed to be busy in one way or another although men would sometimes stand around with their hands linked behind their backs—much like the British do. And the Vietnamese generally ignored us. On some level we weren't there.

The environment reinforced the strong sense of a divided consciousness in my daily life that was a function of my military duties. I can remember how cautious I felt when I landed in Can Tho for the first time: I wondered whether I needed to be ready that night to deal with the VC. Specialist Larry Quasius, the S-2 clerk typist, picked me up at the airport and drove me into the city. Quack, as we called him, was a great talker from Sheboygan, Wisconsin; he was so friendly and relaxed that he put me at ease. I quickly discovered that life in Can Tho would not be more scary than parts of the South Bronx. While I had a cushy job, I saw the bullets fly with some regularity, and some of them occasionally came in my direction. I came to know how possible it was for a chopper to be hit by enemy fire although mostly we simply sat and looked out at a flat, alien, mostly yellow-brown world—nothing like the hilly deciduous virgin forest in the park in my neighborhood in New York City.

Phong Dinh covered 651 square miles—a little smaller than Westchester and Putnam Counties in New York put together and a little larger than Fairfield County, Connecticut. The province was as flat and wet as most of central Florida; rice paddies covered every inch outside the market towns of Phong Dinh; the province seat was also the capitol city of the Mekong Delta—Can Tho. The French, a century before, had created a system of canals, so the paddies were often drawn like the figures in my high school geometry book—squares, rectangles, triangles of all sorts, even parallelograms. Some canals radiated out of district towns like the spokes on a wagon wheel. The imprint of human organization rested heavily on the landscape. Foreigners had been re-making Vietnam for several centuries. A seventeenth-century French Jesuit, Alexandre de Rhodes, even created a way to write the language by the use of the Latin alphabet as opposed to *chữ nôm*, a script that used Chinese-type characters.

I lived in a three-story house in Can Tho for a year; we could sit on the roof and see buildings featuring brightly painted, red and gold animated dragons and mythological animals common to Buddhist architecture. But there were many Spanish tile roofs and French balconies with black grillwork on the many two-and three-story buildings in the city. There were many smaller homes with a variety of pitched and flat roofs; the roofing was often corrugated sheets of metal. The outside stucco walls were pastel-colored. Inside almost all buildings the floors were composed of ten-inch square ceramic tiles, many with floral patterns and often outlined in primary colors. At night when it was quiet, I could hear the haunting, alluring sound of female Vietnamese singers who seemed to crack their voices when they abruptly changed pitch throughout their songs. Our neighbors must have had recordings or radios tuned to the same female vocalist. I was reminded of the sounds of various kinds of ethnic music on radio stations back in New York.

My war wasn't hell. Most of the time it was like the Limbo described by medieval theologians—a temporary netherworld for unbaptized infants, happy but bereft of the beatific vision on tap in Irish pubs in New York; at other times it was downright Purgatorial—a temporary state of hell. I lived through some temporary hells, so I wasn't fully a REMF—a Rear Echelon Mother F. But I didn't want to go on any of the missions to which I was assigned: I'd have been happy to be a full-fledged REMF.

There was one mission in August 1970 that I wanted to go on, and I know that sounds like an empty boast. The operation never happened—a mission to rescue American Prisoners of War (POWs), based upon intelligence as good as any I saw in my year in Vietnam. I don't know why the response to the intelligence was so lackadaisical although I suspect a rescue mission in Phong Dinh lacked political capital. It did not appeal to the contemptible bastards running our military and the politicians who actually launched a raid on an empty POW camp in North Vietnam in November 1970—just three months after they dithered with far superior intelligence in Phong Dinh Province. The POW-MIA issue became President Nixon's way of keeping the war going for several years while he faked real interest in the fate of the POWs. Yeah, I do think he was that callous.

I couldn't fight corruption at home, but I tried twice to fight the corruption of the Vietnamese military. On one of the two occasions, February 28, 1970, to be exact, a Vietnamese captain, Dai-uy Liem, confided in me that the Thuan

Nhon District Chief was stealing from and gouging the people of Thuan Nhon, one of the seven districts into which Phong Dinh Province was divided. Liem paid for his whistle blowing by being sent to the Seven Mountains area on the Cambodian border—a VC stronghold where the possibility of his early death was higher than in Thuan Nhon. Then, on July 19, 1970, at 9:00 a.m., the Viet Cong (VC)—maybe—bumped off the Province Chief, Colonel Nguyen Van Khoung, in a well-executed ambush in broad daylight. Colonel Harold Van Hout, the Province Senior Advisor and Khoung's counterpart, expressed doubt that Khoung was killed in a military encounter. Writing soon after the event, Van Hout actually said "it is not certain that the act was perpetrated by the Viet Cong."[6]

Van Hout may have been aware of American attempts or those of friendly, responsible Vietnamese to replace the Province Chief. In any event, the Province Chief's death was not lamented; I do remember that all the Team 56 officers went to Khoung's wake. A portly man with deeply creased jowls, he was laid out in an open coffin in his dress uniform adorned with multi-colored military decorations that seemed somehow inappropriate to me. Mostly I remember that we didn't know how to act and that there was a whole stalk of bananas laid at his feet. I wondered what the meaning of that stalk was although I guessed that it offered some assurance that Khoung would be able to eat the most popular Vietnamese fruit in his new state. There were cut flowers and burning joss sticks—incense that gave off a pungent, burning-wood odor that an American wouldn't actually call a fragrance unless you like the smell of cigarette smoke. The odor was common in Buddhist Can Tho; the Vietnamese believe that the fragrance creates a spiritual connection with their ancestors. The spirituality was surely lost on the Team 56 officers; I, for one, wasn't sure what to make of our *pro forma* mourning since Khoung was viewed with some skepticism by the advisors.

All the senior advisors seemed delighted with the new athletic-looking, handsome Province Chief, Colonel Le Vang Hung, so the VC were improving the GVN in Phong Dinh through well-executed and well-informed ambushes. Could it be possible that someone tipped the VC as to the Province Chief's itinerary? Not impossible at all. In his end-of-the-year letter for 1970, Colonel Van Hout wrote: "Colonel Hung, this year is rapidly drawing to a close. I can only state that I wish the whole year had been as satisfying and rewarding as the last half that I served with you. Because I will be leaving soon on a holiday with my family, I will wish you, your family, and your staff a 'Merry Christmas and a Happy New Year.'"[7] Now I rather suspect that Colonel Hung was not a Christian, but that would probably not have bothered Van Hout. Still, his statement is an outright expression of his disgruntlement with the bumped-off chief.

I was the editor of the Province Monthly Report for about ten of my twelve months in Phong Dinh. This duty was one of my most important jobs every month. It also gave me license to chill out a bit. I could sip a can of Schlitz in my room at the Team House and edit away to any *New Yorker* editor's content. There were 44 provinces in South Vietnam, and I was always told that the Province Monthly Report actually went to the president, i.e., Richard Milhous Nixon. Well, I never quite believed that, but the Report consumed several days each month. Virtually every senior military and civilian person on the team had a section that he was supposed to write and submit to me. Then there was the opening paragraph—a summary entitled "Overall Status of the Pacification Effort." Well, the truth was that I wrote that paragraph during most months. Get this—a 22-and 23-year-old, wet-behind-the-ears (with floppy lobes) lieutenant was making the overall assessment of, in New York Mayor Ed Koch's phrase, "how I'm doin.'"

I did the writing because many of the army officers and Foreign Service Reserve (FSR) civilians could not write a satisfactory sentence in the English language. (I also became the *sub rosa* editor of several efficiency reports of officers superior in rank to me. I remember Majors Jackson and Yarbrough slipping damning reports to me for "fixing." I learned that writing skills are powerful: I gained in stature because I had a rep as a writer.) I remember an FSR graduate of the University of Pennsylvania who had little idea what a subject and a verb were. As a Jesuit-educated snob, I was impressed by his "little Latin and less Greek." I put my knowledge of the ablative absolute, the passive periphrastic, the aorist tense, and the middle voice to work, and by the time July 1970 rolled around, the Colonel expected me to write the paragraph. Usually he just let it go as I wrote it. And I shudder today that I spoke of "tappable resources" and "deleterious factors" and that I thought that "an atmosphere of progression" existed. Maybe I didn't want to call what I was reporting "progress." In the June 1970 report I actually wrote, "Progress is being made, but it is barely noticeable at this time."[8] I was a budding and unwitting satirist.

The hit on the Province Chief struck me as a major setback for pacification, so I set out to write some purple prose on his demise. I searched among all the books that were lying around for some funereal poetry. Finally I found Walt Whitman's elegy written in 1865, right after the assassination of Abraham Lincoln. (Just think about it: I found old Walt lying around in Can Tho about 28 years before Bill Clinton gave Monica Lewinsky a copy of Walt's *Leaves of Grass*.) The first six lines of "When Lilacs Last in the Dooryard Bloom'd" seemed to hit the right note:

> When lilacs last in the door-yard bloom'd,
> And the great star early droop'd in the western sky in the night,
> I mourn'd—and yet shall mourn with ever-returning spring.

O ever-returning spring! trinity sure to me you bring;
Lilac blooming perennial, and drooping star in the west,
And thought of him I love.[9]

Now I knew I was being a wise guy, pushing the military pouch, you might say, by putting poetry in the mouth of this grizzled warrior, as "Tiger" Van Hout apparently fancied himself. I looked forward to discussing the concept of the trinity in the poem—lilac, star, and thought—and its fitness to sum up our deep sense of loss at the Province Chief's demise.

Well, Van Hout looked me in the eye and said, "The poetry goes." But, for the first time, Van Hout discussed the content of the "Overall Status" paragraph with me. We actually negotiated somewhat. I suspect that, as the Province Senior Advisor, he was concerned about how he would look if he said the death of his counterpart was a crushing blow. Would some general ask a tough question like "Why didn't Van Hout stop the Province Chief from making that trip?" Or better: "Why wasn't Van Hout with the Province Chief when he was killed?" Now I doubt anyone asked those questions, but I do think Van Hout was always worried about being second-guessed from above and always considered how radioactive the Province Monthly Report might be. In any event, we had a case of "Lieutenant Truth" making for "Colonel Think." Van Hout knew we had to see the death of the Province Chief as very serious. His arrogant ghost writer lieutenant made him feel that the July report was a hot L-Z and he had better put his flak jacket on.

The paragraph, in final form, does suggest that all was not going well in Phong Dinh—the model province for war tourists in the Mekong Delta. The paragraph reads, in part:

> The mixed success that was reported in June has since been determined by the latest HES [Hamlet Evaluation System] ratings to have been a regression since about 2% of the population now live in D, E, and V hamlets that were formerly rated as C. The month of July can be described as one without progress, but a completely honest appraisal would indicate a further regression. Territorial forces continued to conduct stereotyped, ineffective, and poorly executed tactical operations. A particular low point for the month was the killing of the Province Chief, BG [Brigadier General—promoted posthumously] Nguyen Van Khuong, in an apparently well planned and executed ambush along Highway 31 in Thuan Nhon District. This event must be recognized as the most noteworthy and disruptive incident in Phong Dinh during the recent past. While it is not certain that the act was perpetrated by the Viet Cong, the ambush was certainly not an extremely difficult military achievement. However, its immediate effect was to cause temporary inactivity on the GVN side due to the loss of a leader. Yet the appointment of Colonel Le Vang Hung, 35-year-old former Commanding Officer of the 31st Regt, 21st ARVN Division, as the new Province Chief has provided both GVN

officials and U.S. Advisors with a new impetus to implement pacification plans previously moribund.... It is hoped that the appointment of Colonel Hung will provide a deterrent to this deterioration in security. He has embarked immediately on a vigorous schedule of activities and has led several GVN province-level chiefs to privately express hope in the potential of the new Province Chief to pursue their programs.[10]

Initially Van Hout had been unwilling to suggest that we had regressed. Eventually he seemed to understand that the ability of the VC to whack the Province Chief did not look like progress, but the Province was in better hands after Khoung's death, thanks to those reliable VC hit men. I was happy too: since the Province Chief was the guy who had sent Dai-uy Liem to the Seven Mountains, Liem gained a reprieve, courtesy of the VC who, after all, were opposed to GVN corruption.

Corruption in Thuan Nhon was no secret. Colonel Lester M. Conger, Van Hout's predecessor, used the Province Monthly Report on several occasions to point to the hopelessness of improving Thuan Nhon as long as the current District Chief, Major Bon, remained in charge. In the January 1970 report, Colonel Conger (with me as his ghost writer) used very strong language: "Thuan Nhon remains the one sore spot in pacification and development in Phong Dinh.... It can be explained in no other way than by the complete ineptness and continued malpractice and power abuse of the Thuan Nhon District Chief."[11] On February 23, 1970, the commanding general of Delta Military Assistance Command, the IV Corps top American, Major Gen. Hal D. McCown, paid a pointed visit to Phong Dinh and visited Thuan Nhon only. He asked for a briefing from Major Bon; both Conger and Colonel Khoung were present. The American advisors were showing their concern at the highest level. I have to think that Liem was emboldened by the general's visit to make his full disclosure of the details of the corruption, four days later—on February 28, 1970, secretly, in my room at the Team House. Bon was transferred to a province somewhere north on March 16. Rumor had it that he was promoted— to ease the pain of the loss of income.

I have to believe that Colonel Conger, Colonel Van Hout, John Paul Vann,[12] Ambassador William Colby, and General McCown wanted to see Colonel Khoung replaced as Province Chief. A report on October 19, 1970, stated that a VC proselytizing agent named Ban had managed to recruit the father-in-law of the late Colonel Khoung. I wonder if the father-in-law suspected that his son-in-law had been bumped off by his own people, and so he was ready to switch sides. Perhaps the family was already playing a double game. It is tantalizing to consider that Khoung's incompetence and corruption might have actually been motivated by playing simultaneously on both sides in the ball game. On July 23, 1970, four days after Khoung's death, Lieutenant Colonel Jack L. Young, the Team 56 Chief of Staff, wrote about the difficulties his Vietnamese counterpart had faced under Colonel Khoung: "The former Province Chief obviously trusted him [Lieutenant Colonel Nguyen Than Nhon] but misused him from all indications. It is believed that Col. Khoung required him to attend to many of his personal business affairs which left him only a minimum amount of time for his primary military tasks."[13]

Corruption apparently flourished under Colonel Khoung. Captain Neil Meoni was the S-4 advisor—a logistics position that enabled him to see how equipment was being misused and misappropriated. A soft-spoken and serious Italian-American graduate of City College of New York, Meoni had written on July 18, just five days before the Province Chief's death, to explain that the new, promising commander of the Equipment Center was in a difficult position with

> ... the previous center commander having been relieved for embezzlement. These officers resent his [the new commander's] lack of "obligation" to them and his refusal to do "personal favors." Additionally, many of the officers and men assigned to the Center have relatives in fairly influential places who constantly call Major Dams [the new commander's superior] and complain any time he counsels or punishes one of these men.[14]

Meoni was merely echoing the words of Colonel Conger who wrote in his Completion of Tour Report on April 15, 1970:

> In this province, however, the Chieu Hoi Service has had a record of poor administration, mismanagement and corruption. There have been 3 service chiefs during my tour. The first two were vile. They should have been relieved and criminally prosecuted long before they were ultimately removed. The first one was given a better, higher paying position within the service, serving notice on his replacement that he too could be corrupt and get away with it which he promptly proceeded to do for many months. His present station is unknown but it is a certainty he is not in jail though he should be. No doubt both of these are prime examples for the present incumbent who is beginning to give some signs of condoning and getting involved in some financial manipulations too.[15]

So while Dai-uy Liem gained a reprieve after the assassination of Colonel Khoung, it took Khoung's death, not the discontent of the Colonel and the General with corruption, to bring Liem back from the VC staging area on the Cambodian border. One afternoon in late July 1970, Liem came to the S-2 office and sat on my lap and stroked my leg while a rooster crowed just outside our office and our 10th Mountain Division World War II veteran sergeant, a wiry man in his 50s, looked on with utter amazement. Sergeant Nguyen Tan Thong, our interpreter, was translating for Liem, and I understood that Liem had been told specifically that he would pay for cooperating with the Americans.

It helps to imagine this scene when you realize that I was nearly 6'4" tall and about 215 pounds. Liem was about 5'2" and about 100 pounds. I tried to listen with an air of seriousness, but Liem and Sergeant Thong kept giggling—a sure sign that they knew the scene they were creating. After Liem left, Sergeant First Class Arthur Bush puffed on a Newport menthol cigarette, smiled wryly, and told me that all Vietnamese men were queer because they held hands, and now he was worried about me. Well, I didn't worry about Sergeant Bush's perspectives on homoeroticism, but I sure had been worried about Dai-uy Liem when he disappeared after we had reported the chicanery of his District Chief in great detail. He was told specifically that he was going to be "fixed" for cooperating with the Americans. Terrific guys in charge, eh?

Liem's situation had festered with me for three months when I finally wrote to my Congressman, William Fitts Ryan—a leading anti-war spokesman. I told Ryan that "knowledge of the District Chief's corruption was widespread, but squelched due to the fact that the District Chief was known to have relatives in high places in the Saigon government." I went on: "I do not feel that any effort was expended by the upper echelons of command on this advisory team to see that this man was not transferred."[16] I actually told Ryan how he could legitimately find the details of the story; Ryan did indeed make some attempt to find the reports. He wrote to Defense Secretary Melvin Laird and asked for them. I only found out what he did recently. Ryan was an honorable man and a World War II veteran: may he rest in peace.

Oplan Missouri: Harry's Funeral

We had our terrific guys too, and they kept the bodies flowing to Vietnam. (General Westmoreland prepared for his role as Commanding General by attending Bakers' School in Hawaii and no command and general staff schools.) I remember being in a sort of trance during the summer of 1969 when I was stationed at 5th Army Headquarters at Fort Sheridan, Illinois, just north of Chicago. I was living in an apartment on Winthrop Avenue in the North side of Chicago and driving north every day through the tony suburbs, towns like Evanston, Wilmette, and Highland Park. I was getting used to playing basketball in the gym at the base and working on Oplan Missouri, the secret plan for the burial of Harry Truman.

I actually arranged for aerial photography of Independence, Missouri—a mission carried out with maximum secrecy so as not to alert Truman's daughter Margaret as to what we were up to. The brass apparently thought she would muck up Oplan Missouri if she could. I had the impression that some senior officer invented a task for me to accomplish: I wasn't sure that anyone really wanted the aerial photography to plan the route of the funeral cortege. I did learn that the army liked bureaucratic busy work. I talked a National Guard unit into taking on the job—a somewhat irregular maneuver as I wasn't using normal channels. But I got the job done, and when Truman died on December 26, 1972, I was living on Decatur Avenue in the Bronx and wondering if the photos mattered at all when world leaders converged on Independence.

The bureaucratic inefficiency kept me hoping that the army would forget to put me in the pipeline to Vietnam and leave me to crucial matters of national security like Oplan Missouri. A schoolmate of mine from grade school, high school, and college was an enlisted draftee assigned to the Personnel office of the Continental Army Command at Ft. Monroe, Virginia. In early August, he alerted me that the office that controls military intelligence officers had sent a message saying that there were five lieutenants in the 5th Army area ready for assignment to Vietnam. And, sure enough, I received an advance warning that I would be getting orders to Vietnam in October. Meanwhile the Pentagon sent my pal, Mac Ball, to peaceful Korea before someone could get the bright idea to send him to Vietnam. I was happy for Mac. He says he was just lucky, but I like to think he had figured out how to send himself to Korea. There was always a great thrill in subverting the army.

Pacification

> *Defenceless villages are bombarded from the air, the inhab-*
> *itants driven out into the countryside, the cattle machine-*
> *gunned, the huts set on fire with incendiary bullets; this is*
> *called pacification.*[17]—George Orwell. "Politics and the
> English Language"

While Mac was lucky to avoid Vietnam, I could have fared much worse. I was very lucky to be assigned to the S-2 advisor's office in Phong Dinh Province where, on October 29, 1969, in Can Tho City, I went to work in the pacification effort for Captain Bob Burns—a political scientist who went on to a distinguished career at South Dakota State University. (The S-2 was the Province's Intelligence officer; Bob was Dai-uy [Captain] Minh's counterpart.) Bob was a prince—a sophisticated, decent man who understood that the war was a charade. Bob's eyes twinkled with ironic merriment, and his flat Midwestern humor mocked his own amazing 60-pound weight loss as well as our screwy mission. We hit it off quickly and have stayed in touch for all the years since. He actually wrote the report of my interview with Liem.

But an Advisory Team? I was one member of a team of about 150 army and civilian advisors. The army advisors were mostly junior officers (lieutenants and captains) and career non-commissioned officers—the sergeants. There were about ten majors on the team, but most of them were senior advisors at the district level; I was assigned to the province level in Can Tho. There were few low-ranking enlisted men—clerk-typists and radio-telephone operators (RTOs) mostly. The civilians were mostly Foreign Service Officers, and a few were Filipinos—Third Country Nationals, as they were termed. Together we were supposed to help the GVN create a bureaucracy and a local army responsive to the people's needs, especially an environment secure from Viet Cong control. This was a task for Rube Goldberg, not raw and dopey lieutenants like me.

The concept of an advisory team was preposterous, especially in my case: I was 22 years old when I arrived in Vietnam—a recent college graduate but surely not well-schooled in military matters and not very sophisticated about how to offer advice to Vietnamese officers at least ten to fifteen years my senior. I must say that I was better prepared for my role than a very pleasant, recently promoted captain I met toward the end of my year. He had spent the preceding two years as a stalwart on the U.S. Army Ski Team, but in late 1970 he was being sent to the field as an infantry officer to lead a Mobile Advisory Team (MAT). He confessed to me that he barely knew how to fire a rifle, but he sure could teach the Vietnamese how to ski.

As I think back on such brilliant assignments, I realize how condescending we were to lord it over the Vietnamese as we did. I actually don't remember ever giving any advice to my counterpart. That was OK by him and by me, too. Mostly we hung out together at a few parties, but I can't remember any conversations about the military situation. I remember a promotion party for Dai-uy Minh in January 1970 at which the Vietnamese roasted an entire carcass of beef over an open fire. They sliced the meat right off the carcass: it was very tasty—an amazing feat of cookery. On July 20, 1970, we all submitted written evaluations of our Vietnamese counterparts that were classified as "Confidential Noforn," i.e., No Foreign Nationals. When I read that report now, I think that I was a brash young man, ungrateful for the roasted beef, and I'm surprised that the 22-year-old version of me actually wrote this:

> Dai-uy [Captain] Chau is a lazy and a somewhat less than intelligent individual. Offering advice to Dai-uy Chau is a very frustrating experience as he will always nod and agree with whatever advice is given to him. His primary interests appear to be extracurricular activities as he spends little time in the office. He almost never solicits advice on any subject and on the rare occasions that he does, his questions are so incredibly simplistic that one is led to wonder whether he could be serious about his questions. It is impossible to judge what influence my advice has upon him because of his seemingly total acceptance of whatever I say. Dai-uy Chau's whole concept of action is inaction, so it matters little whether he understands what I say since he probably wouldn't do anything anyhow.[18]

No one disagreed with my opinion of Dai-uy Chau, yet somehow I was supposed to accomplish something with him. My guess now is that Chau was not such a lazy and stupid guy as I thought then; he had other "business" to manage. (There were rumors about seedy businesses downtown.) Bob Burns laid out no agenda for me, probably because no one above him did either. We were just supposed to advise and make "things" better. I learned quickly that Advisory Team 56 was part of a bureaucracy, and bureaucracies have no goals but their own continuance. I was a big fan of Joseph Heller's *Catch-22,* so I understood very well that we all owned shares in Milo Minderbinder's M & M Enterprises, and, since we all owned a share, whatever was good for the syndicate was good for us.

Winning

Cynicism was high among the captains and lieutenants on Team 56. It was common for G.I.s to greet one another with the two-finger peace sign, and junior officers as well as enlisted men flashed the sign. Doing so wasn't outright sedition, but it showed a general skepticism toward the whole American enterprise in Vietnam that we were part of. When *M*A*S*H*, the movie, came out, it attracted more than the usual interest when it was shown at the Team 56 House. Some critics have argued that the rebellious mentality of the central characters befits the Vietnam War, more than the Korean "Conflict." And clearly the members of Team 56 in Vietnam were delighted with the irreverence for the military that makes the movie funny. Inspired by the general disaffection for the entire enterprise, my roommate and I cut out a 12-inch peace sign and posted it on our wall. Senior officers saw the symbol often enough, but no one ever objected. The U.S. was losing the propaganda war with its own most loyal troops. Military experts have said that American infantry divisions had become dysfunctional by 1971. I can believe it.

John Thompson from St. Paul, Minnesota was one of my roommates during my year in Phong Dinh. John played the guitar and composed seditious songs that the junior officers sang with heartfelt gusto. I remember how he changed a line in a Kingston Trio song, "Greenback Dollar," to "I don't give a damn about Nguyen Van Thieu." Since Thieu was the GVN president, we especially enjoyed voicing our disdain for him and his government that we were "advising." Sedition bubbled over one day in early October 1970, a few weeks before I went home. After a night of singing and drinking, all the junior officers (and the majors too) poured out on the street in front of the team house, dressed in gym shorts and flip-flops, and put on a mockery of close order drill—all for the amusement of the enlisted men who couldn't quite believe what they were seeing. The incident seemed innocent, but I think now it was symptomatic of our soul-sickness with the emptiness of our duties, i.e., promoting the "pacification" charade. We were not greatly afraid that we might get in trouble with senior officers. We used the well-worn wisdom of the soldier in Vietnam: "What are they going to do? Send us to Vietnam?" That wisdom still works: when other people worry about paper tigers (especially academic administrators), I say to myself, "What are they going to do with me? Send me to Vietnam? I've been there."

I can remember Bob Alderson, who had a booming voice, bellowing close-order drill commands that we executed with maximum imprecision on that night of officer "riot." Bob told me that the riot was repeated after I left, and everyone got into trouble. But what kind of trouble? I looked up Bob on Google recently. He seems to have survived handily any censure he faced for mocking close order drill—a remnant of 19th century battle movements—while on duty in a war in which drill had no relevance. Bob's performance did not keep him from becoming the CEO of Kirkland's, Inc., a large retail store chain. I have to think that he gets people to do stuff with greater precision now than he did then, and I'm betting he has not been worried overmuch about the consequences of periodic irreverence for false gods. Kirkland's appears to have won its battles in recent years.

Winning the war was never spoken of although, in his military history interview in March 1969, Captain James Pederson stated baldly and presciently that we would lose the war—if the Vietnamese didn't change their ways of operating and we our ways of advising. "Pacification" was the key buzz word: we were to promote the "pacification effort." Fortunately I had read Caesar's *Commentaries* in high school Latin class and understood what it meant to pacify Gaul and Britain. *Gallia est pacata*, as Caesar reported to the Roman Senate, meant that Gaul had been subdued. "Pacify" sounds so much more, well, pacific, euphemistic. I also remembered Tacitus' famous lines about the pacification of the Britons: "*Ubi solitudinem faciunt pacem appellant*," or "Where they make a desert, they call it peace." And, boy, we were making desert out of one of the most fertile places on the planet—the Mekong Delta: its rice paddies were pockmarked everywhere with craters—ten to twenty feet wide—from 500-pound bombs that could not have been militarily effective. Sometimes a paddy about the size of a football field would have three or four of these craters.

And we didn't know how to play football in Vietnam. Vince Lombardi's famous words did not fit into my war in Vietnam: "Winning isn't everything; it's the only thing." When Lombardi died on September 3, 1970, I found out about his death when my ears perked up at the playing of "The Ram"—the marching song of my alma mater, Fordham University. I was listening to AFVN, the Armed Forces Radio Network outlet in Vietnam, while lying down for our daily two-hour siesta from noon to two o'clock. (The war stopped for two hours every day; Vietnam was hot and humid—no point in killing anyone when it is so hot.) It was haunting to hear "The Ram" in Vietnam, but a tribute to Vince Lombardi might logically start with his days as a member of the legendary Seven Blocks of Granite—Fordham's great line of the 1930s. The stirring ren-

Above and opposite: Typical rice paddies in the vicinity of Can Tho in early 1970. Note that the paddies are pockmarked with craters created by bombs and rockets.

dition of the song seemed so out of place, yet oddly commonplace in Vietnam. Lombardi's death from cancer, after all, was an ordinary event.

We had brought America to Vietnam and were trying to re-create it there—all without a well-conceived plan or even good reason to do so. Actually our plan called for a revolution in Vietnamese society that really wasn't much different from the VC plan: the Vietnamese had to create a post–French, equitable society. But we mapped no realistic way to make that change. Advisors would talk about reaching some sort of accommodation with the Communists, but by 1970 no one was talking about winning—only what would happen after some sort of agreement was reached in Paris. And it is really important to understand that the junior officers I served with were not unwilling to fight or face the VC. We had not gone to San Francisco with flowers in our hair. (It was cut off in the barbershop.)

Six months before I arrived, Major Philip S. Kim, the senior RF/PF advisor, felt that he had to make an important point at the end of his military history interview. He obviously was alarmed by the attitudes of the junior officers. He called for

> a good TI [Traditional Instruction] class on why we are here. Junior officers in particular that have a great deal to look forward to but are coming over here

2

because they wear the green, because they took the oath, finding themselves losing a leg, losing an arm, losing life and the question always comes up, "Why was I here? Why did I lose my leg? I don't see any advancements in the war effort. I don't see any advancements in the RD [Revolutionary Development] effort." I think we're falling down on our selling of why we are here.[19]

Kim's statement is stunning: he recognized that the lieutenants and captains had begun to find the war pointless and not worthy of their blood. He seems to have been worried that the young officers might be thinking that they should have been in San Francisco.

About ten years later, I saw Arnold Brackman, a seasoned reporter of the wars in Southeast Asia, proudly sporting a T-shirt that said, "SOUTHEAST ASIA WAR GAMES, 1956–1975— UNITED STATES—SECOND PLACE." And Brackman still insisted that the war in Vietnam had been worth fighting. I guess the Lombardi spirit didn't work out so well, but the irony of a second place finish in war offers a salvation that we ought to have accepted before we settled for more second place finishes in other places like Iraq and Afghanistan. Losing wars should lead to self-analysis. We have successfully avoided it.

The first-place finishers, the Viet Cong, had a holistic vision for a communist Vietnam. A few months ago, I bought a pair of work gloves at Home Depot. They were made in Vietnam. Those Asian communists are much more flexible than the Soviets ever were although the Vietnamese authorities cracked down on Internet use in 2013. I noticed that Secretary of State Hillary Clinton made nice with the Vietnamese "communists" in 2012 and President Obama welcomed President Truong Van Sang to the White House on July 25, 2013— a signal to the Chinese "communists" that the United States is a Pacific power. The oil reputed to be in the Spratly Islands off the coast of Vietnam is a probable reason for making nice.

On April 30, 1985, I walked into a freshman writing class at Western Connecticut State University, and, after taking attendance, it occurred to me that it was exactly ten years since the North Vietnamese tanks rolled into Saigon and re-named it Ho Chi Minh City. I had written the date, 4/30, down as the date of absence of a few students, so it was in my head. Before I began class, I mentioned that it was ten years exactly since the fall of Saigon. The twenty students looked at me blankly; only then did I realize that they didn't know what I was talking about. So I probed a bit. I asked what I was referring to. After a while one student raised his hand gingerly and asked, "Is that in Vietnam?"

I was jolted by the ignorance of Saigon. The class seemed unmoved by my disbelief that they didn't know where Saigon was. Their attitude was simply, "We were only ten years old in 1975. Why should we know?" (Those students are now close to 50 years old: I wonder what they know now about Iraq and

Afghanistan.) I realized also that, ten years after the war was over, I was still mentally alert to any Vietnamese reference.

Over the years I've been keenly aware that Americans stopped talking about Vietnam, yet it still affects daily life. Urban legends have grown up about the war. Despite the fact that apparently no verifiable evidence exists that any veteran was ever spat upon when he came home from the war, the legend of spitting on veterans is widely believed.[20] Think about how absurd the scenario is: a vet fresh from the battlefield in peak physical condition gets spat upon by a hippie. Does the vet turn away meekly? Where are the reports of toothless hippies? How many hippies were medevaced to emergency rooms after being coldcocked by spat-upon vets?

Gross ignorance about the facts of the war accompanies the urban legends. Many contemporary students think that the war was always unpopular; the polls only began to show lack of support after the Tet Offensive of 1968. Many Americans continue to believe that the war was worthwhile, even heroic. I have buddies who say we achieved our strategic goals in Vietnam: we halted the spread of communism. When the My Lai massacre of several hundred South Vietnamese civilians was revealed by Seymour Hersh in November 1969, public opinion polls supported the Americal Division's actions. Americans refused to believe that our boys were capable of killing women and children although the *Cleveland Plain Dealer* published pictures of dead bodies lying in rows along a canal bank. *Time* reported the results of a Lewis Harris poll on January 12, 1970: "By a substantial 65% to 22%, the public shrugs off My Lai, reasoning that 'incidents such as this are bound to happen in a war.' It also rejects by a margin of 65% to 24% the charge that My Lai proves that U.S. involvement in the war has been morally wrong all along."

And in the years that followed, college students routinely misidentified who was shooting whom in one of the most famous photos of the 1968 Tet Offensive.[21] A still photo and NBC cameras recorded the summary execution of a Viet Cong guerrilla in Saigon by the police chief. When asked, college students would say that the shooter was a communist who was shooting a friendly Vietnamese man. Americans simply don't want to imagine that we and our allies are not always angels.

And, then, we hear that Americans cannot point to a map and say where Syria, Iraq or Afghanistan are even though they may sport bumper stickers that say, "Support our Troops." I always want to add a line to that sticker, "But don't draft me." Polls of college students less than ten years after 9/11 revealed overwhelming belief that at least some of the hijackers were Iraqis. None were.

I'm disturbed by all this, but not many of my fellow citizens appear to share my concern. Their attitude seems only to suggest that I'm making too much of a fuss about this matter. Yet almost no day has passed since I returned in October 1970 during which I have not thought about Vietnam. And I know it's prominent in the consciousness of my fellow veterans. So we go around thinking about the war when, let's say, the Yankees beat the Red Sox three out of four games in Fenway Park just before the All-Star break. Or I think about Vietnam when a university vice-president says at a meeting that no one knows what our veterans have been through. (This actually happened on Veterans Day, Friday, November 11, 2011, at 1:45 p.m.: I sat quietly and chuckled to myself. It was, after all, a true statement even if I had been "there.")

We compartmentalize reality when actually it is more fluid than it seems. It flows in, through, and around the barriers we set up. And we actually thought that we could solve the Vietnam puzzle as we might a real board puzzle, i.e., by grouping similar pieces into piles and then by fitting them together. We created administrative structures, conducive to the American way of war. We supported Vietnamese bureaucrats, well-conditioned to manipulating bureaucracy for private ends by the French. Jaime Concepcion, the civilian New Life Development Advisor, said that the bureaucracy was completely in thrall to Saigon. Local officials needed to get the "green light from Saigon"[22] for even the smallest initiatives. Some thought the slow pace resulted from the exacting of kickbacks for any approvals. That may have been the case, but it's also true that the Vietnamese were very bureaucratic. They wrote on graph paper and always had handy rubber stamps and red ink pads that made the graph paper "official." They learned this from the French, who are skilled practitioners of what they term *paperasse*, or unneeded paperwork. The British term for such paperwork is "bumf"—a derivative of "bum fodder." Clearly the British term offers a much more vivid visual and olfactory image. While the British term is superior to the French, the Brits lack the French talent for bureaucracy. It's amazing that right-wing Americans today despise the French. The Pentagon is a "perfect" French institution.

History Lesson

The Pentagon's Military Intelligence Office of Professional Development, in its wisdom, saw the need for my professional development and gave me orders to Vietnam one day in August 1969. On Sunday, October 19, 1969, I took a charter airplane from Travis Air Force Base in California to Vietnam. I know we stopped in Hawaii for an hour, on to Guam, then the Philippines, and finally we landed in Saigon in the Republic of Vietnam. I disembarked from the plane at each stop, and the weather was hot and humid at each location. Saigon, especially, was a lot like New York on a hot and humid summer day. So New York's dog days of summer had prepared me for Vietnam.

The airplane was your standard airline plane, equipped with comely flight attendants who pleasantly served standard airline meals and made all the usual in-flight announcements. No one said, "Don't you dumb bastards realize that you're headed to a war zone, and we're giving you a last touch of saccharine American 'normality' before you encounter the VC."

Everyone acted civilly, and we behaved. No one expressed his fears. Some guys were going back for second and third tours. For them, all this seemed routine. I had planned to study the booklets from the Infantry School at Fort Benning on how to adjust artillery, not having paid a lot of attention while instructors there had droned on about the mathematics of artillery. I do remember reading Andre Malraux's *Man's Fate* during nuclear weapons class. I had concluded that following up a tactical nuclear detonation with an infantry assault was madness, so I deliberately did not learn the mathematics of measuring the back blast from the nuke. Malraux's depiction of the conflict between the individual and the political and military authorities who seek to govern the individual's life seemed like the right antidote. Yet, on the way to Vietnam, I was sweating my inattention to artillery class, as that seemed like some necessary military knowledge. I had banked on the lazy convenience that a military intelligence (MI) officer would not really need to know how to adjust artillery, much less follow up a tactical nuke detonation. Yet every MI officer earned the 1542 Military Occupational Specialty (MOS)—Infantry Platoon Leader. He could have been assigned to lead an infantry platoon in a pinch—an ouch that few of us wanted. I went to the Infantry Officers Basic Course (IOBC) at the home of the Queen of Battle, the Infantry, at Fort Benning, Georgia. (The Queen? Huh? Almost sounds British…)

But I couldn't concentrate on artillery. I was struck simply by the oddity of what I was doing. I was on a plane loaded with strangers. Like most soldiers I went to Vietnam as an individual; I had no military buddies with whom to face the impending danger. My seat companions were not talkers; I went to war somewhat anonymously. I was just a body to replace a body that probably traveled home just as anonymously.

When we landed in Saigon at Tan Son Nhut Air Base, the terminal bustled with servicemen who all seemed to know where they were going and what they were doing. I felt quite lost. Someone told me to go with the MACV people, and I got on a bus that drove through the busy streets of Saigon. The bus had wire mesh on the open windows to prevent a casual dropping of a hand grenade through a window. Finally I arrived at the transient barracks and was told to grab any bunk. The barracks looked familiar; they were almost identical to the barracks on most army posts in the States. I got my first taste of the Americanizing of Vietnam.

It hit me: I was in Vietnam although no one in authority had ever told me why. I received an "in-country" series of briefings at MACV headquarters, near Tan Son Nhut airbase. Part of that briefing included an explanation of the MACV patch that was affixed to my left shoulder.

I have never forgotten that explanation as the patch itself reveals the political absurdity of the war. The two castellated devices on the left and the right of the patch represent the Great Wall of China, but there is a break in the wall through which the tide of Communist aggression is flowing. The sword of American military assistance stands in the breach (like the little Dutch Boy, I suppose) damming up the tide.

The Military Assistance Command Vietnam (MACV) patch.

The patch's edge and the two castellated devices are yellow;

except for the white sword blade, the rest of the patch is red. Red and yellow are the colors of the flag of the Republic of Vietnam.

Now that was a thrilling, fantastic explanation. Even then I knew a tiny bit about Vietnamese military history: the major enemy of the Vietnamese has always been the Chinese (the French were a temporary problem for about a century) until numbskull American policy made the Vietnamese and the Chinese into pals for about 20 years. And it is well to recall that as soon as Saigon fell to the Communists in 1975, the Vietnamese went right back to hating the Chinese and fought a small war with them in 1979. There were limits to the international communist brotherhood.

This explanation was part of a 45-minute briefing on the political purposes of the war. The officer delivering the lecture seemed almost sheepish about it. If memory serves me correctly, he was a graduate of Georgetown University and was manifestly embarrassed to be delivering such pabulum. He might actually have blushed slightly as he told us, apologetically, why we were fighting. To his credit, his briefing was not delivered with any conviction. He said simply that we were there to fight communism. I don't recollect his saying a word about SEATO or other legal covers for the fighting. I don't recollect reference to the Gulf of Tonkin resolution. In short, fighting godless communism was supposed to be enough of a reason—and maybe it was for many Americans. In Buddhist Vietnam the godlessness of communism seemed to be entirely a non-issue. The implications for the Cold War were mentioned, but no ironclad case was made.

By the time 1969 had arrived, Americans were thoroughly committed to not remembering history. It is singular that the Cold War had inured Americans to thinking about how events came to transpire. As I arrived in Saigon, I was not given to understand the full sweep of events, even since 1965. Only the Tet Offensive of 1968 was mentioned: it was the only recent historical event, and the Army was claiming complete victory. The VC had come out into the open and had been decimated. When I arrived in Phong Dinh, no briefing or reading materials educated incoming officers on the history of the province, on its people, its religions, its culture, its agriculture, and the war to-date. Occasionally I'd hear a rumor: a captain told me one evening a few weeks after I arrived that it was predicted that the big final battle of the Vietnam War would take place in Can Tho. He didn't tell me who was doing the predicting, and a big, final battle in Can Tho didn't sound then like a conclusion. But it's noteworthy that the rumor reflects the American idea that at some point there will be a big stand-off battle. Well, I guess there was a big final battle although it does seem that Hanoi simply drove its tanks to Saigon in early 1975. It is true that some ARVN Divisions resisted gallantly, but mostly the GVN simply collapsed.

Tet '68: We Won

> *The moral basis of the war doesn't seem to interest soldiers much, and its long-term success or failure has a relevance of almost zero.*[23]—Sebastian Junger, *War* (regarding the state of mind of combat soldiers in the 173rd Airborne Brigade Combat Team in Afghanistan in 2007–2008)

We were not given much historical perspective on the war although we were entering a zone that had been almost continuously at war since World War II. Why was no one in MACV smart enough to think that it would help advisors to understand Vietnamese history? Americans seem to live in an eternal now, almost like children, and that now might be OK if its eternity were consubstantial with the past and the future. Indeed it would be ideal; instead "now" was conceived as *sui generis*—unattached, unaffiliated, and untroubled by the past or the future. We weren't told to concern ourselves about how the war had evolved, and we were given no plan to end it.

Instead my in-country briefing moved hastily to claiming that Tet of '68 was a disaster for the VC, that they were severely disabled by the losses they took when they came out and fought. This was standard army doctrine during my year there: The VC had blundered seriously in Tet of '68, and we had destroyed them. Most historians now suggest that the VC won the war where it mattered—back in the States when the American people began to think that their government was lying to them about the light at the end of the tunnel.

The assessment of Tet that I heard at the in-processing briefing may have been true, especially in Phong Dinh Province. The briefing officer went on to claim that the VC were severely handicapped from promoting the war. And it's important to remember that it was the North Vietnamese army that invaded in 1975 and rolled their tanks into Saigon—not a guerrilla army indigenous to South Vietnam. The war was actually decided by conventional ground warfare. The ARVN generals were probably awful. Thieu gave up half the country and did not oppose the attack in most of I and II Corps—the northern half of

South Vietnam. I suspect he thought he could get America to come back. Not a chance…

But in October of 1969 all that was to come. I was not surprised by the 1975 outcome although I did watch the Communist takeover with strong feelings of disgust and embarrassment for the failure of Americans to take care of the Vietnamese people we had compromised by their cooperation with us and our dopey policies and the intellectual sloppiness evident in the MACV patch—reasons for both me and the in-country briefer to blush.

He did go on to give us a worthwhile sociological lecture on the habits and customs of the Vietnamese. He told us not to finish our plates when we ate at a Vietnamese house: doing so would indicate that the host had not been generous enough. He told us not to beckon to the Vietnamese with our index fingers as that was how they called their dogs. He told us not to take photographs of Vietnamese people without their permission; he claimed that some Buddhists felt that a camera could steal their souls. He did also say that offering a few piasters in payment would likely ease the danger to the pious Buddhist's soul. Hmmmmm … this sure sounds like an American panacea.

And he did address the moral turpitude of racial bias. But I had been present in Captain Ron Marksity's class in the Intelligence School when he had raised our consciousness about referring to the Vietnamese as "gooks." Marksity was a terrific, riveting instructor. One day while role-playing, he assumed a role as an NCO with whom a lieutenant had to make arrangements for interpreters assigned to his unit. The lieutenant began, "Well, Sarge, we have these gook interpreters…" Marksity stopped him cold, "Sir, my wife is a gook."

Hardly any decent person could be an advisor to the Vietnamese for very long and throw around racial slurs: knowing the Vietnamese was the antidote to racism, and advisors worked closely with the Vietnamese and generally respected them. When I hear Vietnam vets talking about the "gooks," I usually surmise correctly that they served with American units that never came to know Vietnamese other than prostitutes. The closeness that advisors experienced is probably the antidote to racism in most places in America.

The Man Who Wore
a Tux to War

The unreality of my flight, some 46 years ago, seems even more unreal now as I look back on what I did in 1969. I can hardly believe that some version of me actually got on a plane and went to war. Veterans report that being in Vietnam was surreal. They referred commonly to the States as "The World," as in "back in The World." The term expressed their feeling that they were not quite sure that the war was actually happening. Vietnam was just a dream, a mirage. I always felt out of sync with the army and never got sorted. Now 46 years later, I find it hard to believe I was actually there. The person I am today does not seem like the person who apparently went to Vietnam in 1969. The comedian Robin Williams is said to have made the now famous joke about the Sixties drug culture, "If you remember the Sixties, you weren't there." My feeling about Vietnam is similar: I feel like a junkie who was there but is actually "never there." And I am some kind of war junkie; I follow the military quietly but obsessively. The war today seems just as surreal as it did in 1969 although the kaleidoscope through which I'm viewing it has shifted all the pieces into a new pattern.

A few years ago I heard a story about a guy whom I have not seen since 1968. The story has that surreal quality that Tim O'Brien reports in *The Things They Carried*. In "Sweetheart of the Song Tra Bong," O'Brien tells the story of Mark Fossie, a medic, who sent home for his girlfriend; one day she arrived on a chopper, dressed in pink culottes, with "long white legs and blue eyes and a complexion like strawberry ice cream." Lenny DeStefano cut a similarly unusual figure one day in Vietnam. He was a classmate of mine at Fordham Prep and then at Fordham College, where he was the most unlikely Classics major on campus. Lenny seemed to spend the four years of college playing bridge and poker in the cafeteria. I have to think that he cut most of his Latin and Greek classes since the card games would begin about 8 a.m. and continue into the afternoon. He was given to loud outbursts of anger over alleged cheating by his card-playing cronies. Lenny would stand up on a chair, or even on a table, to express his outrage so that the entire cafeteria crowd could hear him. He was a skinny guy, maybe 5'8", and a notorious character. He was frequently dressed in a black suit with an ornamental belt across the back, complemented by a skinny dark tie and pointy black shoes—a costume popular with many of the Italian-Americans whom I went to school with. He liked to call himself the "Cincinnati Kid" after the Steve McQueen gambler character in the 1965 movie with that title.

Lenny must have been very smart although he did a good job of hiding his smarts. I can't remember Lenny ever getting into disciplinary trouble in our Jesuit high school although surely he must have always been on the edge. He was given to making intemperate (often sexually charged) remarks in a very loud voice. He was a pal of Rich Perrotta, whom Lenny called "Dick." If separated from Rich, he'd shout, "Where's my Dick?" I also remember his affection for a buxom thirtyish woman who worked in the cafeteria. At age 16 Lenny would romance her. He'd fly into paroxysms of teenage lust whenever he saw her, and she would play along. He'd go right up to her, embrace her, and tell her how much he lusted for her. Afterwards he'd tell the rest of us who were too shy to approach even a 15-year-old girl that "Doris is a mature hump." Lenny spoke as if knowledgeably, but I'm not sure that he actually had a girlfriend.

Teachers seemed to regard him as incorrigible. I'm guessing that they probably regarded sending him to JUG (Judgment Under God), a discipline that involved walking around a mini-quadrangle for 30 minutes after school, as a waste of the Prefect of Discipline's time, not Lenny's. (I wonder if the circular movement was actually Buddhist in origin. Was it preparation for surreal service in a Buddhist country like Vietnam?) Lenny was a man of many antics. Rumor has it that he has lived on Central Park West and in Fairfield, Connecticut, both posh addresses, but I'm betting that he's still at least slightly outrageous.

Apparently Lenny was drafted right after graduation from Fordham College in 1968 and found himself in Vietnam in 1969. I have no idea what he did there, but another classmate, Gerry French, reports that he, Gerry, was in a convoy outside Saigon when he spotted a guy walking along the road. Maybe *ya hadda be there*, and it was probably tropical hot—good weather for shimmering visions and delusions. The sight of the guy was startling. Being on convoy could be dangerous, so, no doubt, French's senses were on the alert. The guy was wearing a tuxedo—black suit, ruffled white shirt, and untied black bow tie—and just shambling along. As Gerry got close enough to see the guy up close, he realized that he was looking at Lenny DeStefano.

Wearing a tux in Vietnam should have been impossible. I can't imagine that there was a store in Saigon where a G.I. could buy one. Yet Lenny DeStefano wearing a tux in Vietnam figures—though no Fordham guy would really expect to see Lenny anywhere but in the cafeteria. I never saw any male in Can

Tho in a jacket and tie although I did once, when in Saigon briefly, see Vietnamese politicians in suits. (I'm guessing that the Communists dispensed with the suits when they took over, but the politicians may now be taking them out of moth balls. A Google search reveals several tailors in contemporary Communist Vietnam willing to cut tuxes to order.) Such clothing is completely impractical in the heat of Vietnam, and there were not many formal balls and swank affairs to wear a monkey suit to. (Tim O'Brien does talk about troops on ambush imagining they are hearing a recital of the Haiphong Boys Choir, so I like to think that Lenny had attended a gala performance.) A lone walker in a tux along a dusty road in the hot humid climate of Bien Hoa is a mirage. The problem is that bombastic Lenny was very unpromising material for a mirage maker.

Gerry French did explain that Lenny was returning from R'n'R in Hong Kong. Now lots of guys went to Hong Kong for R'n'R, but not many put on a tux while there, much less wore it on their trip back to their unit. It might help to recall Klinger from M*A*S*H to understand all this. Klinger wore dresses in the hope of being sent home on a Section 8 discharge, but no one noticed that he wasn't in army fatigues. I have to guess that Lenny went back to his unit in his tux, and no one noticed—just like the Prefect of Discipline at Fordham Prep never noticed Lenny. Why, I'll bet Lenny wore the suit around for a day or two after he returned.

The Book and the Movie

So "The Man Who Wore a Tux to War" makes sense in the bizarre world that confronted American boys in Vietnam. I can't recognize myself now in that context, but I have decided that it is time to consider who that person was and what the 68-year-old version of me now thinks.

Why now? Well, I'm ready to talk about all this. I flew back on October 27, 1970, put the war aside, and have thought about it every day since. The war is always there—some horror, some pain, some beneficial experience, some good memories of great guys, much disgust with the government that sent us all there and now sends boys and girls to Afghanistan and other places that seem like Vietnam in important ways. Well-researched histories of the war and its politics have been written by Neil Sheehan and David Halberstam, and Philip Caputo's *A Rumor of War*, along with Herr's *Dispatches*, set high standards for memoirs in 1977. What remains to be said that needs to be said now? Well, I have heard about plans to leave American advisors in places like Iraq and Afghanistan where conflicts are burning out. Politicians and generals ruminate about other plans to move advisors into new situations like Nigeria and Mali and other parts of Africa. The job description, "Advisor," strikes me as a foolish euphemism for the bait that triggers the trap of more fruitless war. And euphemism is a species of lying. I'd like to speak truth about my experience of "advising" in Vietnam.

I have read widely about the American War in Vietnam and have studied the best movies and fiction to come out of the war. I'll never forget the impact that *The Deer Hunter* had on me when it first came out: I can remember leaving a movie theater in 1978 on a sunny spring afternoon and thinking that I had just seen the most meaningful depiction of the war to-date. The director, Michael Cimino, had set the war in its American mythic context: the film consciously avoids realism. Realistic scenes from the war are placed in a collage of memories; time is obliterated; Saigon is falling in 1975; the 1968 Tet Offensive is going on—apparently at the same time. The Russian roulette scenes suggest a metaphor for the war itself: the communists held the gun to our heads while we shot ourselves in the head. The result: a fractured and chastened community back in America. Would that we could have learned to sing "God Bless America" somberly rather than boisterously. Would that we had learned that "one shot"— the male ideal of deer hunting proficiency as well as the truth about his sexual limitations—offers a false confidence in a man's ability to control his world.

Nine years later Stanley Kubrick made *Full Metal Jacket*—another movie that placed the war in a mythic context. The troops march off to the city of Hue at the end of the film while singing the chorus of the "Mickey Mouse Song." I was struck then by the immaturity of our Vietnamese expedition—a willed naiveté that believed in the infallibility of American good intentions. But we were also quite mad. We thought we could re-make a country and would not tolerate anything getting in the way. I think of Jewel Bundren in William Faulkner's novel, *As I Lay Dying*. Jewel walks right through the cottonhouse to get from Point A to Point B. There's no acknowledgment that the conduct is inappropriate. The cottonhouse, in some ways, isn't really there. We were in Vietnam, but we weren't really "there": we were just walking through the Vietnamese cottonhouse.

And then there was the great fiction of Tim O'Brien, a fellow veteran, whose "novel in stories," *The Things They Carried*, seemed to catch everything that I might want to say about the war. He seemed to be answering the question, "What was it like in Vietnam?" O'Brien understood the full difficulty of offering a factual response to that question. So his narrator begins by enumerating what the soldiers carried, but that simplistic answer to the question quickly bogs down because the items aren't just items. They can't be cataloged; they can't be merely counted. We learn then how foolish it was to fight war by some abstract calculus like body count. But the war is not over: we persist in fidelity to our body count m.o. I see it daily in higher education: statistics determine what gets funded. There is no intrinsic value. We know the cost of everything and the value of nothing. This valueless American commodity culture revealed its pernicious logic during the war in Vietnam and pervades our lives today. The irony is that I am not sympathetic with the nostalgia for the good old, pre–Vietnam days when Negroes and ladies knew their places, when the Mass was said in Latin, and when Hollywood cooperated with the military in creating heroic war movies.

For some, however, the war in Vietnam was a crusade about values—respect for the individual, opposition to godless communism, and resistance to Soviet Expansion. I knew many young conservatives who read Barry Goldwater's *The Conscience of a Conservative* in the early 1960s and felt a call to duty in Vietnam in the later '60s. Hell, it wasn't just Goldwater who sent the boys "over there": Neil Sheehan has said that he first went to Vietnam because he was inspired by John Kennedy's rhetoric. Kennedy championed the army's Special Forces units—the ultimate advisors—by making the green beret the standard headgear for these elite small units. On April 11, 1962, Kennedy said the green beret was "a symbol of excellence, a badge of courage, a mark of distinction in the fight for freedom."[24] By 1968 John Wayne was using the green beret to promote the war in his comic book film, *The Green Berets*. The movie depicted Special Forces troops in heroic advisory roles against the beastly communist insurgents. As advisors, the Green Berets were charged with responsibility for bringing American values to the beleaguered people of Vietnam. Advisory Team 56's mission was similar and hopeless: the grand province-building mission (in the image and likeness of Kansas) was futile. The Vietnamese insisted on being Vietnamese. Maybe we can find values if we can see the vanity of our endeavors in Phong Dinh Province.

I have for the last two years racked my memory for details. I have remembered incidents and people. The National Archives have helped: 83 boxes are filled with about 1,200 to 1,500 documents each-all created by Advisory Team 56 from 1966 to 1973. The West Point Library helped too; it houses Potter's 1968 M.A. thesis. He was a predecessor intelligence advisor who served in Phong Dinh during 1964 and 1965 and again, briefly, in 1967. Potter wrote a really penetrating account[25] of the war in a few villages in Phong Dinh, but I didn't read his account until 2011. (Yes, you might well wonder why I wasn't required to read it in October 1969.) Maybe Potter's opinion that the VC had been darn close to winning in Phong Dinh in 1964 was not to be considered although Colonel Conger, the Province Senior Advisor when I arrived, did state in his Completion of Tour Report (that no lower-ranking member of Team 56 read) that the VC were close to victory in 1968 when he arrived. It is amazing that the press did not report how precarious the American position was until Tet of 1968 opened some reporters', notably Walter Cronkite's, hearts and minds. Doing this reading brought on some sleepless nights as I felt like I was back "in country" in 1969.

I found the names of many of my fellow soldiers on Team 56 in the files. I have Googled some of the names and discovered that some of them, like Bob Alderson, have had notable careers, and others are dead of natural causes. Still others are now in their mid–70s—a shock of sorts since I knew them when they were 35-year-old majors. I remember the junior guys well: Ben Nelson is an architect in Tinley Park, Illinois; he specializes in building churches. John Thompson, the father of six children, has been a hospital administrator for 40 years in Minnesota. Henry Talbert was the Executive Director of the Southern California Tennis Association until his death in 2013, and he was a beloved and esteemed figure in the tennis world. I'm sure he was funny right up until his death. He used to tell me that he would be getting in trouble with his Marxist-Leninist study group at UCLA if they ever found out what he was doing in Vietnam. Brian McMahon is still laughing in Indianapolis after a career selling insurance in Richmond, Virginia. Larry "L.A." Quasius has been a salesman for Hormel Foods for 40 years and lives in Springfield, Missouri. Doug Hemphill became a career officer and professor of military science at Notre Dame where he still advises business students. And he helped me discover how fraudulent the artillery logs were in Phong Dinh. These guys are frozen in my brain for a lot of reasons, most of them good. We all carry some ghosts, but we're far from the stereotype of the down-and-out Vietnam vet. But obviously the world has seemed to move on, especially Vietnam. I know people who have been tourists there.

I have not moved on; the same questions abide now as those I had when I was 19: What is my moral obligation here? Why did I go to Vietnam? Was I not really a volunteer? Is that not really the case since I enlisted in ROTC? Did my actions bring death to some in Vietnam? What do I make of this so many years later?

Models for Irish Youth

The son of Irish immigrants, I grew up in Inwood in upper Manhattan—so far north that sophisticated Manhattanites frequently thought it was in the Bronx. Social life for Inwooders often took place by crossing the two bridges out of Inwood into the Bronx. Maybe the less provincial Manhattanites thought that sophistication stopped north of 96th Street on the East Side and 116th Street on the West Side, but that calculus of urbanity doesn't explain the presence of Columbia University's Baker Field on the northern tip of Inwood, but Columbia was good at keeping us street urchins off the property. My bolder compatriots got revenge by harassing geology classes that used to come north to see Inwood limestone—a marble that still attracts geological marveling.

One of my father's favorite expressions was that I had "rocks in my head." He used it whenever I proposed some theory of how the world came to be. I had the standard upbringing of a first-generation Irish-American in the 1950s and early 1960s: we hardly had a pot for the chicken, but we were better off than Frank McCourt in Limerick, whose 1996 memoir, *Angela's Ashes*, described the abject poverty of his youth. So the rocks in my head were probably the mill that was grinding out an Irish-American cosmogony while playing on the peculiar rock formations that abounded in various spots in the neighborhood—especially in the park right across the street from Good Shepherd School. Inwood Limestone protrudes from the ground there in undulating waves. From 1947 until I reported for active duty in the army at age 21 as a second lieutenant in January 1969, Inwood was the most Irish neighborhood in New York. My parents moved into Apartment 2B in 24 Cooper Street when they married on November 23, 1941, and, as a child, I never lived anywhere else. My parents moved in July 1977 because the neighborhood was "changing." I might have spent fewer than ten nights in any other place until I was 19 years old and went to Army ROTC summer camp at Fort Knox, Kentucky. If Inwood's rocks attracted the geologists, they could also slake their thirst in any of the 73 Irish bars in Inwood in 1968, and I'm just counting those on or north of Dyckman Street. But I suspect that none of the "rockheads," as we called them, would have been comfortable in a local Irish working-class pub. They certainly couldn't look at the rocks in peace if the right neighborhood kids spotted them: It was quite a sight when a group of twenty male Ivy Leaguers in jackets and ties ran full-tilt down Cooper Street, to elude the flying stones of the locals, with the Met's repository of medieval art—the Cloisters—in the background. We were pre-medieval in our use of stones.

I'm only guessing, but I'd estimate that in the '60s Inwood was about 60 percent Irish, either Irish-born or, like my close friends and myself, first generation Irish-American. The neighborhood was also about 30 percent Jewish. There were no Jewish bars in the neighborhood although there were kosher butchers. The rarest species was a Protestant although I'd bet that the majority of Ivy League rockheads in the 1950s were Prots. There were Protestant churches in the neighborhood, but their doors always seemed locked. Church attendance on Sundays by Protestants seemed sparse, usually at only one scheduled Sunday service, while Good Shepherd Church packed congregants into about 11 masses per Sunday in two different locations. I concluded that Protestants were really not religious. (My father did like to listen to Protestant religious programs on the radio, Billy Graham in particular, but I always thought he did so to annoy my mother who was horrified that I might catch the Protestant influenza.) In any event I grew up with a strong sense of 24 Cooper Street, Good Shepherd parish, and Inwood, in general, as my home.

While I felt anchored by my community, at times it could be enchaining. The war specifically and adult experience in general have left me ambivalent about virtually every facet of life. (That might qualify me as an ideal college professor.) But I can't say that a capacity for living with ambivalence was the legacy of my youth. I can remember being required to memorize and recite Alfred, Lord Tennyson's "The Charge of the Light Brigade" in the sixth grade: the poem filled me and my fellow students with patriotic ardor. We didn't notice that in the glory of the charge, the speaker makes us conscious of its blundering foolishness:

> Not tho' the soldier knew
> Some one had blunder'd:
> Theirs not to make reply,
> Theirs not to reason why,
> Theirs but to do & die,
> Into the valley of Death
> Rode the six hundred.[26]

Instead we learned that heroic self-sacrifice was a very high call to duty. I remember too that in the sixth grade at Good Shepherd School Brother Patrick told us the story of Colin Kelly, who was reputed to be a sort of American kamikaze pilot. Brother Patrick opined that Kelly—a World War II Medal of Honor winner—had not willfully committed suicide but had heroically given up his life by plowing into a Japanese warship. (At issue was the Catholic understanding of "final despair"—the only unforgivable sin and the reason that suicides were traditionally not afforded Catholic burial rites.) Kelly was not heroically suicidal: he did try to eject from his B-17 Flying Fortress, but his parachute did not open before he hit the ground. Doubtless Kelly was courageous, but even a story, designed to promote heroic qualities, told to me quite sincerely by a good man in my youth has disappointed me when I have examined it as an adult. Maybe that's not an unusual experience, but I got the Irish-American Catholic version.

Learning the real Kelly story has been part of my life's slow unmasking of the heroic illusions and lies I believed as a boy. I grew up thinking that Cardinal Spellman was to be worshipped, right up there with the Blessed Virgin Mary; I never suspected that he might be having sex—with men. (The hypocrisy matters, not the homosexuality.) When I was a student at Good Shepherd School, where ninety percent of my classmates were Irish-American, I read Dr. Tom Dooley's books—*Deliver Us from Evil*, *The Edge of Tomorrow*, and *The Night They Burned the Mountain*—about his saintly medical heroics in Southeast Asia. Only in the last ten years or so have I learned that Dooley was probably a homosexual CIA informant. Our teachers offered Kelly, Spellman, and Dooley to us as Irish-American heroes, and we were awed by their heroic selflessness.

I did read a life of St. John of the Cross as a twelve-year-old eighth grader, and I've grown into his mysticism over the years. John of the Cross inoculated me against the rule-bound bureaucratic Churchmen who have made American Catholicism indistinguishable from American fundamentalist Christianity. I was raised as an Irish Catholic member of the Democratic Party, and I stick with that identity. I stuff my ears when priests who should be ashamed speak of homosexuals with disdain. I could not stand Bill Clinton, that philandering bastard. And I cringe on St. Patrick's Day when young guys, wearing four-leaf clover tee shirts, become boisterous and drunk. (Note: a shamrock has three leaves and legend has it that it was used by St. Patrick to explain the trinity.) I hate the sound of "When Irish Eyes Are Smiling," although I do have a soft spot for shamrocks because they annoy Irish Studies academics who deem them "tacky." Those scholars should go to Gettysburg and look at all the shamrocks that festoon the graves of fallen Irish soldiers. Talk about sources of ambivalence...

Tammany's Heirs

But change was on the way despite our faith in the 1950s that Inwood, like Ireland, would always be Inwood even when England's time was up. There were very few American Republicans in the neighborhood (paradisiacal, wasn't it?), but that was changing by the time 1970 arrived. By the 1972 general election, Jack Walsh, the long-time New York State Assemblyman from the neighborhood, through his alliance with liberal Republicans like Nelson Rockefeller and Malcolm Wilson, organized a branch of Democrats for Nixon in the neighborhood. And, by that time, the Conservative Party was posing an electoral threat to traditional Democratic hegemony among the Irish voters in the neighborhood. But from the time I became conscious of politics in the 1950s until I got married in 1975, I was immersed in Democratic politics. The election of John Kennedy was the apogee of twentieth century Irish Catholic consciousness. I remember the delight of my parents, especially my father, at the election of the first Irish Catholic president. My mother told me many times that Al Smith had lost the presidency in 1928, shortly after she arrived in America, because he was Catholic. She always seemed to be biting her lips when she told me that story.

My father's politics were more complicated. Always perverse, he supported Alf Landon for president in 1936 against FDR—an unbelievable departure for an Irish immigrant—and George McGovern for president in the 1972 election—a position good for controversy in my cousins' bar where support for Republicans was popular. My cousins used to offer to take up a collection to send him back to Ireland. My father enjoyed controversy more than politics. If he saw a weed among the flowers, he'd argue for the unique beauty of the weed. McGovern lost all but Massachusetts in the election, but Nixon went on to suffer ignominy because of the Watergate scandal. Then, when everyone including the Republicans was reviling Nixon, my father called him "a great man"—a position dictated by perversity. Morals were secondary to a good argument.

In 1960 I turned 13, and my father and I followed the Democratic primaries with great interest. The Democratic Convention was held from July 11 to 15, and we listened to it every night on the radio. We had no television—a fact that I was ashamed to admit to the other neighborhood kids who were gorging themselves on episodes of *Gunsmoke* and *Have Gun—Will Travel*. It was not cool not to know what Marshall Matt Dillon and Paladin had done last night. We also had no telephone, but that was less unusual. My sister, Winifred, graduated from high school on June 26, 1960, and within a year she had bought a television and installed a telephone with money she earned on her first job—a clerk at the Morgan Guaranty Trust Company. (Think about this: In 1960 as the number two student in her high school, my sister entertained no thoughts of college attendance. Girls should go to work and become secretaries, no matter what academic honors they had won.)

I had been an avid radio listener since 1954 when my father brought home an old Philco radio in a large, polished, wooden furniture cabinet. The radio was a remnant of the early days of radio; the cabinet was created so as to create a focal point for the living room. A few tubes were missing, so we couldn't get all the stations. But we had enough reception for me to become a fan for several years of the nightly episodes of *The Lone Ranger* that ran until 1956. Even when *The Lone Ranger* was no longer on the air, I found other passions: I watched the Yankees on the radio whenever they were playing. Mickey Mantle was my hero: I knew that he was named after Mickey Cochrane, a great catcher, and that Mickey's father put toy baseballs in Mickey's baby carriage in Commerce, Oklahoma.

Saint John
Fitzgerald Kennedy

I was ready for the broadcast of the debate between Lyndon Johnson and Kennedy on July 12, 1960. The debate was held at 5 p.m. in Los Angeles, so it was 8 p.m. in New York when my father and I both lay down for a long night of listening to the convention. It was summer, and there was no school the next day. Conventions hold no real drama these days, but in 1960 Kennedy did not have the nomination locked down before the Convention. So he accepted an invitation to debate Johnson before the Massachusetts and Texas delegations. I remember the delight of my father at the very end of the debate when Johnson said that he hoped everyone would support the nominee. Some-one, no doubt, from Massachusetts shouted, "And that'll be Jack." Oh, this was great stuff. My father leapt up in joy at the man's shout. Johnson had entered the race only one week previously as had Adlai Stevenson. To my father it seemed that the old boys weren't going to allow the Irish Catholic upstart to take the nomination.

On July 13 we listened carefully late into the evening for the roll call. Finally at 2 a.m., New York time, Wyoming put Kennedy over the top, and my father and I were deliriously happy. The neighbors were ecstatic too. When everyone's radio or television was tuned to the same broadcast, you could stick your head out the window above the alley between 24 and 30 Cooper Street and hear the sound of the radios and televisions like a public address system. Both buildings were five stories tall, and the alleyway was like an echo chamber. The neighbors were dancing in their apartments.

You could also listen to the sound of the All Ireland Gaelic Football final, every fall, on a Sunday morning. On Sunday, September 25, 1960, my father was ecstatic when County Down, one of the six Ulster counties in Northern Ireland, defeated Kerry, 2–10 to 0–8, or 16 to 8. 1960 was truly an *annus mirabilis*. The vibrato sounds of the famed announcer, Micheál [Mee—Haul] Ó Muircheartaigh, from Croke Park in Dublin rang throughout the 24/30 Cooper Street alleyway. My father, whose home county Tyrone was not far from Down, was beside himself with glee. Down had proved that the six counties were part of Ireland. And Micheál Ó Muircheartaigh would provide Telefís Éireann [Irish television] with a five-hour running commentary on the funeral of Kennedy on November 25, 1963.

On the morning following Kennedy's nomination, my mother was also ecstatic. My Republican sister was not impressed. She was the harbinger of what was to come among the working-class Irish. She and my cousins were Nixon supporters, mostly because of their anti-communism. My father loved to annoy all of them with his unflagging support for Kennedy.

Election night, November 8, was a reprise of the roll call night at the Convention. At 3 a.m. Nixon seemed to concede but actually didn't. My father made me go to sleep because I had to go to school the next day, but he turned the radio on very low after he thought I was asleep. But I wasn't, and I listened surreptitiously until the wee hours of the morning. At school the principal, Fr. Eugene O'Brien, put Kennedy on the public address system, some time in the afternoon when Nixon finally conceded. I and Fr. John McDonald, my religion teacher and staunch Kennedy supporter, were exultant, but not everyone was. I didn't realize it, but the country had just elected the two guys who would get us into Vietnam deep enough to send me there nine years later.

By the time 1972 rolled around, the so-called Reform Democrats in New York had been chasing the working class Regular Democrats out of the party for several years. The Reform Democrats were anti-war at a time when Inwood's Irish Catholic sons were fighting in Vietnam in large numbers. The Reform Democrats were also more concerned with liberal social issues and less with bread-and-butter economic issues. And Inwood was filled with people who cared about those issues: members of the Transport Workers Union, the International Brotherhood of Electrical Workers, the Teamsters, Iron Workers Local 42, the Policemen's Benevolent Association, the Uniformed Firefighters Association, and 32B or 32J of the Service Employees Union International. They worked for Con Ed—the utility company—and for New York Telephone; they were construction workers, cops, truck drivers, letter carriers, firemen, bar tenders, doormen, subway train conductors, and bus drivers.

I even remember drinking in Goode's Bar on Broadway near 204th Street with the security guard who was guarding the Pentagon Papers for the *New York Times*. The Pentagon Papers revealed that both the Johnson and the Nixon administrations had been lying to the American people about the prospects for victory in Vietnam. It was the fall of 1971, and the fellow, an Irish-American who lived in the neighborhood, had been missing from Goode's for most of the spring and some of the summer; he was being put up in a midtown hotel by the *Times*. He was apparently highly trusted although he didn't know the contents of the small locked safe that he was assigned to watch in the hotel room.

He could finally enjoy a shot of Paddy's Irish Whiskey and tell his story in Goode's after the Supreme Court ruled in the *Times'* favor. His job and other solid working-class jobs have now migrated to the suburbs or have been turned into low-paying contract worker jobs. We didn't see that Kennedy's assassination in 1963 had actually been the beginning of the end...

Telling What Happened

When I first put this uniform on,
I said, as I looked in the glass,
"It's one to a million
That any civilian,
My figure and form will surpass." …
I said, when I first put it on,
"It is plain to the veriest dunce
That every beauty
Will feel it her duty
To yield to its glamour at once."[27]

—W.S. Gilbert. From *Patience*,
an operetta by Gilbert and Sullivan

That end culminated with the war in Vietnam to which I followed many other young men from Inwood in the 1960s. Although war lacked the glamor suggested by a Gilbert and Sullivan operetta, I wasn't raised to be ambivalent about military service: it was expected of Irish-American young men in a quiet sort of way in my house, at least. My father told me frequently that anyone waving a flag usually had something to gain by doing so. And the gain was material, not spiritual.

I found myself going to Vietnam as an army intelligence officer, but I did not come home in a box. I know quite a few guys who did. In my experience, not many academics of my generation knew anyone who was killed in Vietnam. Occasionally the odd academic will know of one or two. I can rattle off the names of at least 20 guys who went either to grammar school, high school, or college with me or who played with me as a child, and then I knew guys whom I met in the army who were killed in Vietnam. It's true even that several of the guys I knew on my advisory team who were killed or seriously wounded during my year there had Irish surnames: I recall Kelly, Duffy, and O'Brien, and there were others. Throughout my adult life I have had repeated flashes of consciousness about the guys who are now long dead and never got to be older than 22. Among several others, I remember Andy Garrity—my classmate at Good Shepherd

53

School. The world acts like these people are in the past: I am entangled with them, even with those whom I knew only slightly as was the case with Mike Morrow, Mike McGoldrick, and Tommy Minogue—all of whom kicked my butt when I was a kid in Inwood. I remember McGoldrick pinning me to the ground on the lower field of Inwood Park when I was nine years old. He was a couple of years older and much stronger. It was torture, but fighting was a sport in Inwood.

One definition of being Irish-American was to be a fighter: the definition still holds. Collins, Dempsey, Fallon, McCaffrey, Keane and many others: the roster of recent prominent American military leaders is filled with Irish-Americans. More than 50 percent of the winners of the Congressional Medal of Honor have Irish surnames; eleven winners named Murphy received the award while fighting for the Union during the American Civil War. And then there was World War II Medal of Honor winner Audie Murphy—the very epitome of courageous service coupled with Hollywood recognition. Most recently, Michael Murphy received the award for service in Afghanistan, and a U.S. Navy vessel has been named after him. And my mother's maiden name was Murphy.

When this son of a Murphy came home intact from Vietnam, I tried to act like I had never been away, yet I was in the army for almost two years. I was trying to act like I was as hip as the hippies when I really was not. I wanted to act like I was in tune with all that was going on back in the States as if I hadn't missed a beat although any fair judge of my dancing and musical abilities will tell you that I rarely hit the beat. I went to graduate school and earned a Ph.D. in English with my primary focus on Irish literature. I was a graduate student from August 1972 to August 1978. I rarely mentioned I was a Vietnam vet. When a fellow grad student would find out that I was a vet, there was a way of asking about my experience that implied I was morally defective: "What did you do in Vietnam?" I was guilty as suspected, but I and two fellow Vietnam vet grad students, Peter Katopes and Lucas Carpenter, figured out that the best response was to plead guilty to atrocities. My standard answer became, "I burned babies." Since frequently we could guess that the response fit the question perfectly, we learned to enjoy the shocked response of fellow grad students, who were free of moral taint.

In the years since, I've generally not let people know I am a Vietnam vet—for a mixture of reasons and feelings but mostly because I don't want to deal with the reaction of the person who looks at me with curiosity after finding out that I actually went to Vietnam. I reject the oft-heard claim that vets don't want to talk about the war; the people back home don't want to hear what he might say. I especially do not tell my students about my war for a good pedagogical reason: I don't want them to clam up. The all-too-frequent response of students who happen to find out about my war service is some species of "You were there. You know, and I don't."

So I mostly shut up about the war in my academic life until 2010 when I finally talked about my year in Vietnam to a class of 15 Honors students. The course was entitled "The Wunderkammer of Knowledge"; its goal was "understanding the dynamic balance that exists between programmatic knowledge and emerging (creative) knowledge." A Wunderkammer was a curiosity cabinet, and the concept became popular in Renaissance Europe. The idea was to place disparate objects in close proximity to one another in order to tease out deep, previously undiscovered connections among them. We sought to inspire both faculty and students to "utilize 'being overwhelmed' by knowledge during an incubation phase and to develop the ability to cross disciplines and worldviews creating an active network of enterprise." Each faculty member did a presentation of his or her personal Wunderkammer. I was one of the last to do so, and, by then, I had begun to feel comfortable about talking about the mess that was in my head that I call "Vietnam." Somehow my Wunderkammer deserved a full

New York Mets pitcher Tug McGraw (right) and I posed for this photo in November 1969, after the team had won the World Series and McGraw visited Can Tho on a USO tour. In the background my room on the second floor of the Team House is visible.

German title, so I called it "Eine Krieges Wunderkammer" or "a curiosity cabinet of war." I prepared a PowerPoint with copies of my father's draft notice, my draft card, my son's Irish passport (that I procured for him so that he would have somewhere to go if Uncle Sam ever decided to draft him), and other items like aerial photography of bombed paddies. I also included a photo of myself with New York Met pitcher Tug McGraw who visited as part of a USO tour group. The Mets had surprised everyone by winning the 1969 World Series, and McGraw was the star "closer" on the team although the term "closer" did not come into vogue until later. Saves, or getting the final outs in a close game, did not become an official statistic until 1969. I wonder whether there is some relationship between McNamara's calculus of body counts and the statistical analysis of baseball that has grown ever since the 1960s. (That's a kind of Wunderkammer bit of thinking: I had never considered that the trend in baseball might parallel the trend in war or even in car making. McNamara had been CEO of Ford.)

Nostalgia

I was emboldened by the example of six of my colleagues from various departments who talked about their personal Wunderkammers. So I talked about the war for the first time in a public setting: there were about 20 people in the room. Afterwards I suddenly felt that I was ready to write about the war. I'm not sure why. I did think that I wanted to inspire the students to think about war, and maybe I did. The humility of their reticence to discuss it with a veteran is charming, but it's not appropriate: non-vets must feel free to talk about war. How else will we ever deal with it? And I've begun to think that amnesia is now a national disease. I talk to students all the time who know little about 9/11, except that many of them remember that adults tried hard to shield them from it. They have grown up conscious of that awful day, but they do not talk about it at all. Yet they have the vague idea that our boys and girls have fought for us in Iraq and Afghanistan because of 9/11.

My war has been with me every day since I landed at Travis Air Force Base in California and was then mustered out on October 29, 1970, at Oakland Army Base. The continuing consciousness is not mere memory of incidents, and it is not an obsession or a recurrent nightmare. I realized that night that there was going to be no escape from the war. I stayed with one of my dearest friends on the planet, Rich Lundy, who was living in Oakland. Right after I took my uniform off for the last time, we went out to a club in Berkeley where a band was playing. As the band set up and began to tune its amplifiers, one musician set off a feedback sound that almost put me under the table. I'll never forget the feeling: I thought it was incoming mortars. It was surreal: no one else even flinched. My heart was pounding. I remember thinking that I was no longer like those other people. I was back in "The World," but in some ways I never left Vietnam. Maybe no American has—even if she never wanted to dive under a table because of amplifier feedback.

"The World" appeared to move on after the Vietnam War ended on April 30, 1975, although Americans had lost interest after the last American troops were withdrawn on March 29, 1973. Sometimes it has seemed like many Americans have not and could not move on. Vietnam, for them, is still the fish bone they're choking on. Hardly anyone gets her throat blessed any more on February

3, the feast of St. Blaise, and America needs both St. Blaise and the Heimlich maneuver to dislodge the blockage.

Today some Irish-Americans from the New York area seem to be frozen in a past dominated by the war and the Irish neighborhoods they grew up in during the 1950s and 1960s. Nostalgia derives from the Greek "nostos"—home-coming-and "algos"—pain.

This "home pain" will, a few times a year, drive an old pal to send me a photograph display labeled "The Bronx As It Was" or "Remember When?" The exhibit will show Loew's Paradise on the Grand Concourse or Jahn's Ice Cream Parlor on Kingsbridge Road. A strong feeling exists that the "World" back then was better than the one we have now. It almost seems that these Irish-Americans are stuck right now in some sort of make-believe Vietnam which they find hard to square with "The World."

And the Irish World of Inwood has all but disappeared. But there are still some Irish people and a few Irish bars in Inwood. On December 15, 2002, a *New York Times* reporter described a visit to one of the bars:

> The old crowd still gathers at the Piper's Kilt, one of the few surviving Irish pubs. It serves up Irish nachos (French fries with cheese and bacon) and a fish luncheon special on Fridays. Sitting under a fading photo of the Polo Grounds, one resident of the neighborhood for nearly 40 years introduced himself by name, Ralph M. Rourke, and the Irish county, Leitrim, where his family originated.
>
> "There aren't many Irish left in Inwood, but we have not given up," he said, an Irish lilt creeping in by the end of the sentence.[28]

The reporter uses "surviving" to describe the Piper's Kilt—a word one might use to describe the aftermath of a disaster. And then Rourke's "'not given up'" suggests soldiers unyielding in war.

9/11, to be sure, awakened many of these dormant feelings. Inwood has memorials to those who died on 9/11—more of them than ever were erected to the soldiers and marines killed in Vietnam. 9/11 has intensified efforts—paltry as they are—to reclaim the sacred memory of "our" neighborhood in "our" youth. My grammar school, Good Shepherd School, now has a dedicated fund-raising group that has fought to keep the school open when very few of its students are Irish in background. But John Brennan, the retired CEO of ICT Group–a call center telecommunications company—who grew up in 30 Cooper Street, is working overtime on saving the school.

Memory of the nurturing the school gave us coexists with and complements Irish-American patriotic impulses, yet many Irish-Americans feel alienated from the country they claim to love. They are homesick for the mythical worlds that existed in their youth in their neighborhood and in the vision of Ireland they inherited from their parents. The war permanently fractured Irish

Americans' sense of community, family, and countries (America and Ireland). Other changes were in the air—black power, feminism, gay rights—but the war threatened the Irish-American cosmology in a much deeper way than any other social change.

I am not immune to nostalgia about the world of my youth. In August 2011, on a beautiful sunny day, I took a walk in Inwood Park where my buddies and I had spent many a lazy summer afternoon in the 1960s playing a card game called hearts on a grassy hillside overlooking Spuyten Duyvil where the Harlem River meets the Hudson. The rivers, Inwood Hill Park, and the cliffs of Riverdale seem to frame the Henry Hudson Bridge. The Palisades of New Jersey are visible and framed by the arch of the bridge. I remember thinking that the bridge seemed built to last. A good photograph would freeze it in such a way as to make it appear timeless, yet the bridge had only opened in 1936. Like the bridge itself, I somehow felt that the world would never end, and the world was that nice lazy feeling of good company and getting mad at the cards we were dealt. We didn't gamble: the games were just for fun and one-up-manship. I used to pull out bunches of grass and break it into little pieces: it was a delicious feeling.

But then we got too old to do that: Most of us were dealt cards that sent us to war, and the war seemed to take away the green grass of our park and the pavements of our neighborhood. When we came back, the neighborhood was changing because changes in the immigration laws dried up the supply of Irish immigrants, the old women were older, there were fewer red-cheeked, hard-drinking Irish old men on the streets. And we were all onto the next thing. We didn't really think about what we were doing, although most of us did well in life. We had great kids. But we would be perpetually seduced by nostalgic rec-ollections of Inwood Park on a beautiful summer day.

The war has seemed to kill some part of each of us—even if most of us are still above ground. The cause was such phony nonsense—a mythical North Vietnamese torpedo boat attack in the Gulf of Tonkin, and we're still trying to recover our integrity. I recently read Nick Turse's *Kill Anything That Moves*—an indictment of the murderous assault on the Vietnamese people by U.S. forces: This is as hard to swallow as the Castor Oil that was a standard laxative in my youth. I participated in missions that Turse cites specifically, but I can't deny he has made a very disturbing case for the routineness of American atroc-ities.

My Lai was more the norm than the exception. And, in the wake of reading Turse, I do question the military validity of the operations I went on during my year as an army intelligence advisor to the Vietnamese Popular and Regional Forces. I wasn't a major monster; after all, I never fired my M-16 on those missions—a kind of technical virginity. Claiming innocence on such grounds makes me feel like a "flabby devil," to use Joseph Conrad's phrase in *Heart of Darkness*. Revelations tells us: "So then because thou art lukewarm, and neither cold nor hot, I will spue thee out of my mouth." I and my fellow American advisors were, at the worst or best, lukewarm monsters.

Who's Fightin' Here?

We did not have explicit military roles; our commanders occasionally tried to make us responsible for the conduct of the war, and we could claim that we did very little that our Vietnamese allies did not approve. But the case could also be made that, without American air power, the level of hostilities might have been much lower. Statistics, reliable in this case, show that more than 50 percent of the contact with the VC in 1970 in Phong Dinh Province was American-initiated or instigated. The S-3 (Operations) Advisor, Major Robert Jackson, openly wondered about the effectiveness of the friendly forces in the May 1970 Province Monthly Report: "A more accurate picture of the effectiveness of friendly ground forces can be realized by considering what those totals [of enemy killed] would be without the overwhelming [American] air assets available to the sector forces."[29] We were told continuously that the Ninth Division had withdrawn (after its murderous Operation Speedy Express that Turse describes in excruciating detail), so the war in the Mekong Delta was a Vietnamese war.

Well, maybe not. Bob Burns actually wrote: "For all practical purposes, I have performed the normal duties of a S2 as well as an S2 advisor. This situation exists because of the increasing demand from MACV Command Elements to reproduce the Vietnamese efforts in intelligence reporting and recording."[30] While the Ninth Division had left the Delta in early 1969, American air "assets" and advisors on the ground may have been the catalysts for keeping the war more than simmering when the population was exhausted by endless war. The February 1970 Province Monthly Report states: "Twilight Phantom, KBAR/Mini-Packs, and other available air assets in the Sector have accounted for more than 50 percent of the total enemy casualties during the reporting period. The total enemy casualties for the reporting period were 144 killed, with air assets accounting for 74 of this number."[31] Six months later, the Province Monthly Report for July 1970 states: "During the reporting period a total of 179 enemy casualties were reported as killed by air assets, as compared with only 58 enemy eliminated by friendly troops."[32] (And those casualty figures coupled with estimates of enemy strength that did not fluctuate ought to have led everyone to wonder about the "miracle" of VC replenishment of manpower.)

Despite these claims of VC losses, in May 1970 the VC ambushed the 382 RF Company in broad daylight and "all but decimated" it.

Bob Burns was quite correct in his view of his role as an active purveyor of intelligence information that would make Americans the initiators of combat. He and I regularly sent out intelligence reports to all of our District and Mobile Advisory teams. Most of the contact reported in the daily logs was instigated by U.S. Air Force Forward Air Controllers (FACS), Army L-19 pilots, and helicopter gunships from the 307th Aviation Battalion, notably the Vipers of the 235th Armed Helicopter Company. Or advisors in the back seat of Hueys on K-Bar (airmobile) operations called for air support for troops inserted into hot Landing Zones (L-Zs). The TOC logs for Phong Dinh are filled with the comments, "U.S. is walking today" or "U.S. on ambush tonight." And when the Regional Forces or Popular Forces did not perform according to the U.S. play book, we cajoled, embarrassed, pleaded, and complained about their non-performance, but their slackness was attributed to a certain backwardness, not any indifference to the anti-communist cause. Americans assumed that the Vietnamese did not act in their best interest. We had a lot of chutzpah: Vietnam had seen almost continual war since World War II although the state of war owes its origins to French colonialism, dating back to the nineteenth century. When the Vietnamese want to fight, they are very good at it: just ask the French about the battle of Dien Bien Phu in 1954.

And the Viet Cong were providing ample evidence of the military competence of the Vietnamese. Advisor comments are loaded with reference to corrupt GVN officials, yet no American seemed to acknowledge the obvious: the GVN was not a noble cause that could inspire dedication. Yes, there were some very good and honest officials, but there were far too many crooks. It amazes me that Colonel Edward J. Porter, the Province Senior Advisor from June 10, 1971 to December 8, 1972, could write in his November 15, 1972, "Completion of Tour Report" that "the development of capable, inspired and patriotic leaders in the numbers required ... is one of the most serious failures of the GVN."[33] His report cites continuing problems with corruption, and he writes a full two years after I left Vietnam and only months before the American withdrawal in compliance with the Paris Peace Accords of 1973. Porter's report shows how little we advisors accomplished. The GVN was not ready and never would be ready to defeat the communists, no matter how much we cajoled, manipulated, and worked around our counterparts.

In theory, we couldn't do much all on our own. Although I worked in Vietnamese offices and went on missions always with a Vietnamese officer counterpart, maybe I deluded myself that my war was not a colonial war. We did not exactly tell the Vietnamese what to do, but it is also perfectly obvious that they were doing mostly what we wanted them to do—at least on the surface. We created an army that could not be sustained without immense American resources, so we were not preparing them for a future without us. As a 22-and 23-year-old lieutenant from Inwood, I lacked the sophistication to see, at least initially, that the Vietnamese in Phong Dinh Province were protecting the big firepower of U.S. airplanes, helicopters, and artillery. There were two major air facilities: Can Tho Air Field and Binh Thuy Air Base. The RF and PF companies were pulled in tightly to protect the airplanes and helicopters. But because the companies were guarding these bases, they were not guarding their home villages and hamlets—where the real war was. Yet they had been recruited for the express purpose of providing security for their own homes and villages. The generals sacrificed local security to safeguarding the big belchers of fire. Maybe George Orwell could have enlightened me about the colony's relationship to its master. I never made sense out of what we were trying to accomplish.

It's fashionable in some circles to look at the American War in Vietnam as the defeat of the imperial power and the liberation of Vietnam. In 1969 I did not buy the argument that the U.S. was a colonial power, probably because I saw the U.S. in the twentieth century mostly as the liberator of Europe and the conqueror of an imperial power—Japan—not the oppressor of the Third World: that was the botched job of the British and French. I wasn't ready to buy the left-wing arguments about wars of national liberation. Communism seemed to be fake equality, but I also had no understanding of the geo-politics that made a war in Southeast Asia seem like a matter of urgent national interest to the old men who ran the American government.

A Servant of the Crown

I might have thought differently if I had ever gotten to know my paternal grandfather: he might have explained the colonial politics of South Africa to me. Edward Augustine Hagan (1868–1953) was a career soldier of sorts. It seems odd in the light of my family's dislike of the British, but he reversed his emigration to America and joined the British Army, c. 1898. He apparently met my grandmother in New York although they may have known one another in Ireland. She arrived in New York on May 25, 1891, aboard the *Ethiopia*. She was then 20 years old. They were married on August 25, 1895, in New York at Holy Cross Church in the heart of Hell's Kitchen—a really dangerous and sordid place of violent Irish gangs in the 1890s. Family lore says my grandfather either owned or worked in a livery stable, i.e., he took care of the horses that drew trucks and other conveyances in the 1890s. Life on the other side might have seemed more attractive—even in the British Army. He served during the Boer War (1899–1902) in the 2nd Battalion of the Royal Scots Fusiliers and then later served in the 1st Garrison Battalion of the Royal Scots Regiment in World War I. Family lore has it that he deserted from the British Army at some point, probably during the Boer War, but he was allowed to wash the slate by re-upping for World War I. Apparently the British were so hard pressed for manpower during the First World War that they welcomed deserters back. He re-enlisted in 1915 and stayed for the duration of the war. Since he was born in 1868, he was 47 at the time of his enlistment and at least 50 at the time of leaving the service after the war was over, probably in 1919.

His Boer War records survive. On August 26, 1901, he was awarded the South Africa Medal and Clasps for his service in battles at Cape Colony, Transvaal, Tugela Heights, and the Relief of Ladysmith. If he deserted, he probably did so in a subsequent battle, but less than a year remained in the war: it ended on May 31, 1902. Family lore about his World War I service says that he was one of only five men in his unit to survive the 1915 Battle of Gallipoli. Since his records indicate that he entered the Egyptian Theater of War on October 25, 1915, well after the main actions at Gallipoli were over, it is unlikely that my grandfather was at that battle, but, hell, he was in the vicinity—if Egypt and Cyprus count and if guarding captured Turks on Cyprus suggests some sort of role in the aftermath of Gallipoli. An artifact of his time there sits on my cousin's mantel: a stuffed snake with the words, "Turkish Prisoners Ashibaba Cypress 1916" woven into the snake's back with small beads. It seems like a project from a prisoners' arts and crafts class.

I think we needed this story of my grandfather's survival at Gallipoli to think well of the guy, to forgive his absence, to salve his pain. He died alone and impoverished in Glasgow while four of his five sons sired 17 grandchildren in America, I being the youngest but the only one named after him. We now know from studies of combat infantry during World War II that prolonged combat eventually led even soldiers who had served valiantly to desert eventually. In short, it's now believed that every soldier has his breaking point. Perhaps that explains the periodic rotation of troops through com-

Edward Augustine Hagan (1868–1953).

bat zones. So it's not necessarily any shame if my grandfather did desert.

My grandmother, Helen Avery Hagan, is remembered as a dictatorial shrew so bad that my Aunt May risked the wrath of the neighbors and her husband when she moved out of 90 Terrace View Avenue in Marble Hill when she couldn't brook her mother-in-law's interference—at least for a time. May had the proverbial heart of gold, so Nanny must have been impossible. And maybe too, Edward Hagan couldn't live with her without killing her. And, maybe too, Nanny is the source of the story of Edward's desertion.

In early October 1969, when I was at home on a 30-day leave prior to going to Vietnam, my uncle, Dan Hagan, my father's oldest brother, showed up one evening at my family's three-room apartment. Dan was a notorious drinker and probably one very tough guy. He and my father actually had a fist fight when Dan was in his nineties and my father was about 82. Dan threw the

first punch too. I remember seeing him
bolt shots of Seagram's, followed by
Rheingold Beer chasers, on many
occasions. On most occasions he
seemed well "lit" when he arrived
at our house. He spoke in a
loud voice and cackled with
laughter, but it was hard to
understand his thick North
of Ireland accent: "car" was
pronounced "k-yar" with a
soft "k." I normally would pick
up only about half of what he
was saying, and the drinking
served to thicken his speech.

I cannot remember the
details of any other conversation
with Uncle Dan although I had seen
him about once a year when I was
growing up. But on that night in October,
as usual, he was wearing a
rumpled jacket and a soiled
tie, he needed a shave, and he
was puffing vigorously on his pipe. (The smell of the smoke stayed in the apartment for days after he visited.) He spoke directly to me about going to Vietnam.
Possessed of some notion of a family myth, he was keen to tell me that I came
from a long line of Hagan warriors. I needed to live up to their standards or
face being haunted by their ghosts. It seemed very important to Dan that he
tell me this: I was not to embarrass the family with cowardice. Uncle Dan shared
the neighborhood's ethos even though he didn't live in the neighborhood. At
West Point, seven years earlier, General Douglas MacArthur had issued a similar warning to the assembled cadets in his famous farewell address:

Helen Avery Hagan (1871–1943).

> The long gray line has never failed us. Were you to do so, a million ghosts in olive
> drab, in brown khaki, in blue and gray, would rise from their white crosses, thun-
> dering those magic words: Duty, Honor, Country.[34]

Uncle Dan was not eloquent like MacArthur, but I remember being con-
fused by his words to me. Grandfathers, uncles, cousins, and my father had
served in a variety of military forces: the British Army, the IRA, and the American Army. I was expected to follow them. I had a vision of being haunted by

them all, even as I had profound doubts about my upcoming, undesired service for my country. Uncle Dan seemed to be calling in the chips of my upbringing on the Irish-American streets of Upper Manhattan.

I remember that my cousin Cooey Hagan was on call to go to the Dominican Republic in 1965 with the 101st Airborne. My Aunt May couldn't sleep because she feared he was going into Santo Domingo. A year after I returned from Vietnam, my Aunt Anna told me on the telephone that I had done a wonderful thing in Vietnam. I was calling home from Tennessee, and my father was displaying my war medals to the relatives—proudly, I guess. He got the approval from the relatives that I didn't want. I was nonplussed by her praise, but I was conscious that the post-war praise meant that I had done my duty as Uncle Dan had prescribed.

The IRA and Clan Hagan

Dan had surely been presenting a myth, maybe even the myth promulgated by John Wayne movies. I have little doubt that Dan meant what he said: his words were the only serious conversation we ever had. But my father, Hugh Henry Alphonsus Hagan (November 19, 1907-March 30, 1993), had somewhat inoculated me against heroic myths although he had some sense of following family tradition in naming me. "Edward" was my grandfather's name to which my father added "Alphonsus" as my middle name—apparently in a belated change. My birth certificate actually has me as "Hugh Francis," but those names are crossed out and "Edward Alphonsus" is written in. Uncle Dan had dubbed my father "Fonty" when Dan couldn't pronounce "Alphonsus"—a name given to my father by the priest who baptized him. My father was the first baby baptized by this priest, and tradition held that the priest could add a name to the child's "handle." (The priest was probably a Redemptorist: St. Alphonsus Liguori founded the order in 1732. And my father's parish church in Dungannon, County Tyrone, was a Redemptorist parish.) My father returned the favor by passing "Alphonsus" on to me—a cause of much torture by my fellow students in grade school whenever a teacher would for some reason call out my full name. "Alphonsus" seemed most peculiar in the Inwood of my youth, and any myth of St. Alphonsus as a beneficial patron was lost on me. And St. Alphonsus along with John of the Cross, it turns out, would have been a terrific influence on my youth. He was a staunch opponent of the sterile legalism and strict rigor of the kind of Churchmen who have since reduced the Catholic Church to a system of rules. Pope Francis is trying to undo the damage by stopping the finger pointing.

Fonty Hagan had removed the romance from Irish-American myths about military service that my Uncle Dan apparently thought important. As a child I thought my father, as a World War II soldier, must surely have engaged the Germans in battle. I told him he must have been very brave. He said, very deliberately, "Let me tell you something: the only time I fired a rifle in World War II was on a day that I shot at two crows and missed." He explained that a fellow soldier had told him that he would never be able to shoot a crow. My father took up the dare, but every time he got a bead on a bird, it moved. My father seemed to think that the birds knew something. I always liked my father's mysticism: he was a big fan of divining rods for finding the right location to drill a well. And crows are smart.

In retrospect, I see my father's words as a kindness: he didn't want me to go around with some chip on my epaulets about military service as a necessary way of being a loyal son. Maybe his caution had something to do with how he wound up in the army. Or, it might have had to do with his memories of his own father's service in the Royal Scots Regiment during the First World War when my father was just a whippersnapper (to use a favorite word of his). I have the feeling that my father grew up keenly aware that his father was not home much; I know my grandfather was away when my father was aged six to twelve-years-old (1914–1919). But the absence has a longer history: the 1911 Irish Census shows my father living with his four brothers and his mother in Dungannon, County Tyrone. My grandfather is not listed, and I do know that eventually my grandparents separated permanently. My grandfather died in Glasgow, and my grandmother in New York, where she was living with her five sons. They were northern Irish Catholics, and they all left the north soon after the partition in 1922 that included Tyrone as one of the six counties in Northern Ireland. My father arrived in New York in 1924: he was sixteen years old. Family lore has it that my uncles had been involved in IRA activities and needed to leave. So British Army soldier Edward Hagan's sons engaged in subversive activities at home in Ireland during the time of the Easter Rising of 1916 and afterwards. (Were they mad at their father as well as the British?) There is evidence that my Uncle Paddy was a member of the IRA, and my father told me that my Uncle Dan joined Paddy in burning a train load of British uniforms somewhere close to Dungannon. They were Irish Republicans. My father sold Irish Free State bonds on behalf of Eamon DeValera in New York during the 1920s and 1930s. (DeValera became the head of government in 1932 and Taoiseach or Prime Minister of the Irish Republic in 1937.) I grew up with DeValera's autographed photo in our house; it now hangs in my office. That signed photo and an Irish tricolor were the payment my father got for his labors. He saw DeValera as the champion of the anti-Partition forces in the post–1922 Ireland.

My father did look up my grandfather in Glasgow while on leave in 1945 after the Second World War was over. My grandfather was an iron worker in the Dandyvan Ironworks—a surviving relic of the Industrial Revolution. When my father found my grandfather in a Glasgow pub, my father was dressed in his U.S. Army Class A dress uniform. My grandfather did not recognize him immediately. I heard the story of their meeting several times as I was growing up. It was obviously tinged with pain: it's a fine thing when your own father does not recognize you. My grandfather did break down and weep, but my father would not have it. He told my grandfather that all that "stuff" was in the past. I suspect that the meeting led my father, a couple of years later, to name me "Edward"—an attempt to heal the wounds of separation.

I know my father admired my grandfather's military bearing, and in that admiration, there are notions of masculinity that I was clearly intended to emulate. When my grandfather was home on military leave when my father was a child, he would take my father for long walks—a trait that my father repeated on many a Sunday when I was a kid. We walked all over upper Manhattan and the Bronx. We used to walk some 49 city blocks south to the Polo Grounds when the New York Giants were playing: we could get into the games for free in the seventh inning. Though a Yankee fan, I remember being thrilled by the sight of Willie Mays in center field, and, on one occasion, Leo the Lip Durocher, the Giant manager, being thrown out of a game after standing toe-to-toe with an umpire and arguing a "bad" call—one of 95 such ejections during his managerial career. Seeing Durocher in action made me a fan of his, and I was gratified to discover that he was Jackie Robinson's Brooklyn Dodger manager in the spring of 1947 before Durocher was suspended for a year for gambling misdeeds. But at spring training he told the other Dodgers: "I do not care if the guy is yellow or black, or if he has stripes like a fuckin' zebra. I'm the manager of this team, and I say he plays. What's more, I say he can make us all rich. And if any of you cannot use the money, I will see that you are all traded."[35]

The long walks were a sort of family rite of masculinity: my sister hardly ever accompanied us. My father did not love the military, but like most soldiers he had gone on frequent and pointless long treks. I'm sure he hated those "hikes." Somehow he still tacitly endorsed them. He often used the army as a source of authority, a magisterium, for what was right, especially in matters of manliness and matters of hygiene. He had a Battery commander who believed in administering laxatives on a routine basis to his men. My father would declare about once a month that the whole family needed to take a laxative: I developed the ability to masticate dramatically and pretend to swallow chocolate Ex-Lax. I'd hold it between my cheeks and gums, then spit it into the toilet, and flush it down the drain. I'd profess great regularity the next day having produced the requisite "sweet smells" that my father's Battery commander would crow about after a Battery purging. (And James Joyce was accused of having a "cloacal obsession" by H.G. Wells?) I learned a lesson that my father did not intend: skepticism about military wisdom.

But I could probably have learned a great deal of that skepticism by the way my father was inducted into the military for the Second World War. On July 31, 1943, the Armed Forces Induction Station at Grand Central Palace, 480 Lexington Avenue in Manhattan—home today to an expensive French

TAG NO. ___377___

VC-HMK-WW

31 July 1943

Special Orders)
         :
No.   127)   E X T R A C T

*   *   *   *   *

kg Par. No. 10   PAC Par 16b AR 615-500 dated 1 Sept. 1942, the following enlisted man, inducted into the Army of the United States this date,
is released from active duty this date, transferred to the Enlisted
Reserve Corps and will proceed to the location of Local Board #   70

Local Board Address   4951 Bway Ny34 NY

     HAGAN, HUGH H   32 993 882

       Effective 21 August 1943, the above-named enlisted man of the
Enlisted Reserve Corps is called to active duty and will proceed from
the above-listed Local Board to Reception Center, CAMP UPTON, NEW YORK,
reporting to the Commanding Officer thereat for duty.

      TDN 1-5020 P 431-02 A 0425-24.

      By order of Colonel CHAPPELLE:

                            H. M. KURTZNER,
                            Major, Infantry,
                            Adjutant.

OFFICIAL:

       H. M. Kurtzner

      H. M. KURTZNER,
      Major, Infantry,
      Adjutant.   N O T I C E

      You are now a soldier in the Army of the United States!
Congratulations! You have been transferred to the Enlisted Reserve
Corps for twenty-one days, as indicated by the above copy of your
Special Orders. You are directed to report to the Reception Center
in accordance with these orders. If you have not received a notice
from your Local Board telling you of the hour and place of assembly
within (19) days contact your Local Board immediately. Strict
compliance with these instructions is required.

      You are not entitled to pay and allowances as a member of the
Enlisted Reserve Corps. Any medical attention or hospitalization which
you may require during this period will be at your own expense. Your
Local Board must be kept informed of your address at all times prior to
your being recalled to active duty.

                (over)

Hugh Hagan's 1943 draft notice, p. 1.

restaurant and white shoe law firms—sent a draft notice to my father. He was
told that he was now a member of the United States Army and that he would
have to report for duty at the Induction Station on August 21, 1943. The notice
itself is rather cute. My father is inducted into the Army as of July 31 but then
put on leave until August 21. Although he is now in the Army Reserve, he is

not entitled to pay, allowances [for dependents], or medical care during the ensuing 21 days. Even then, the government was not going to pay for medical care—after it had already put my father in the army.

After warning my father to wear old clothes to the Induction Center and ordering him in capital letters, "DO NOT BRING CAMERAS WITH YOU," he is invited to take out a $10,000 life insurance policy, "for but a few dollars per month." And then the guilt trip and the signal that the government is not going to take care of you: "Your family will expect this of you [taking out the full amount of $10,000] because it is the American way to provide for one's own." Nowhere does the notice explain that an insurance company will be making money on the premiums.

Then the notice gets heavy:

> Keep in mind the fact that you are now a soldier in the Army of the United States and as such, the manner in which you conduct yourself will not only reflect upon the Army, your community and your family, but it will also affect your military career.... Do not use obscene or profane language. Do not partake of intoxicants in any form during your trip or prior to completion of your processing at the Reception Center. Upon your arrival there you will be given classification and aptitude tests to assist in determining your qualifications for training and assignment. The results which you attain will vitally affect your future in the Army. Therefore it is highly important that your mind be clear and alert.

Wow! So don't show up drunk or you'll wind up in the infantry, and don't curse. (Your son will take care of that for you 26 years later when he drops his socks in the morning while getting dressed for training at the Army Infantry School at Fort Benning, Georgia.) So here is the Army telling draftees that the sharper guys are likely to get jobs that require brains. It's not hard to infer that being sharp increases the distance between the draftee and the battlefield.

A Deal We Can Refuse

Twenty-six years later the army treated me similarly. In March 1969 while a scholar in the Infantry Officers Basic Course at Fort Benning, I attended a meeting where a major from Officer Professional Development (OPD) at the Pentagon spoke to all the Military Intelligence (MI) lieutenants about "career" opportunities in intelligence. Put simply, he said that if you want a cushy safe job, he will accommodate you by training you for a career in MI. But to receive that training, the army was requiring a "voluntary indefinite" commitment or agreement to a minimum of three years on active duty with discharge occurring at the pleasure of the army. (I love the army's definition of pleasure: it sounds sado-masochistic.) If you don't take the deal and insist on serving only the two years you signed on for, you can go to the six-week "quickie" course for Tactical Intelligence Staff officers and find yourself on a charter flight to Vietnam. The army was seeking to put its safest jobs in the hands of the most cowardly of its officers, or at least, that's a fair inference. It was offering a career "path" only to the men who wanted to avoid going to war. "Path" is such a cozy word when used with "career." I was more angry than cozy (although I was amused too) when MI/OPD actually showed up in Can Tho on March 23, 1970, to offer career counseling. And I do remember that Colonel Van Hout counseled all of us that it was necessary to give very positive Officer Efficiency Reports if we wanted our subordinates to have long careers. He didn't seem to see that he was close to condoning lying. Careerism is a military toxin: it reduces service to a job, not a higher calling. Service is supposed to be selfless; careerism is all about looking out for Number One.

I left the MI/OPD meeting with John Goggin and Tim Patton. They were cursing and complaining about the Pentagon desk-jockey playing with our skeptical brains. They were already ticketed for Vietnam after the "quickie" course. They had the correct idea: the army was fucking with us. And John Goggin paid for his unwillingness to take the shirker's deal when he was killed in Vietnam in September 1969. Tim served as a Phoenix advisor in Kien Giang Province; it was next door to Phong Dinh. I ran into Tim several times during my year in Phong Dinh. We drank a few cans of Carling Black Label in Can Tho and commiserated about John. Tim went home to Baton Rouge a few months

73

before I was set free. There is something unspeakable about losing a good friend at such a young age, but Tim found these words and posted them on the Vietnam Veterans Memorial Wall in 1999:

> John was hilarious. He could make me laugh. Laughter was the only way we could deal with the insanity. I only knew him a few short months, Fort Benning and Fort Holabird and then Saigon and then Can Tho, and then we went to our separate assignments (teams) in the Mekong Delta. John was just a good man; he was engaged to be married when he returned. He only wanted to have a life to live. Somehow I know I can speak for him, when I say that he didn't know why he was there, what was expected of him. Was he just there to kill people because they were somehow bad or wrong? What bullshit. We were just good lieutenants, following orders. What else could we do? John—after all these years, I still miss your take on life and would somebody please tell me why I'm not emailing this to you? Why you never had a life?[36]

I was to follow John and Tim to Vietnam months later. While they had been slated for their assignments with their initial orders, I had been tantalized with the possibility of a civilian-clothes job in Louisville, Kentucky. The Pentagon major made clear that I wasn't getting to drink mint juleps at the Kentucky Derby unless I went "voluntary indefinite." So as we exited the super-modern, fluorescent-lit, windowless classroom building at the Benning School for Boys, we found solidarity in the curses with which we filled the air, but curiously I remember that a brilliant spring sun was shining. Somehow that was good. Up until that day, the weather in Georgia from January to March had been bitterly cold. I like to think now that the sun raised my sights (a different kind of aiming than that employed on the rifle range) and allowed me to get beyond the bureaucratic hypocrisy of the army's personnel policies. Maybe there was a reason why so many people have worshipped the sun. I like to think that this moment, too, gave me a simultaneous vision of transcendence and immanence. The army was mired in a pragmatic, dark materialism that the sun gave the lie to. I like to think that my father read his draft notice on a blessed sunny day in New York in July 1943 and was somehow comforted about leaving his wife and baby daughter behind for two-and-a-half years.

Sun Worship

The smallest moments: they return, dwell, endure.[37]

—Colum McCann. *Transatlantic*

Before the Lord the whole universe is as a grain from a balance or a drop of morning dew come down upon the earth.

—Wisdom 11:22

I also like to think that one of my earliest childhood memories of the sun was working on my subconscious at that moment. I remember with high-definition vividness a lazy summer day when a childhood friend, Gerald Sheehan, and I were sitting in the alleyway of 10 Cooper Street. It was the afternoon, and the sun was slanting into the enclosed alleyway that was about six feet wide with a ceiling about 15 feet high. The day was hot but not oppressively so; still Gerald and I were probably seeking the coolness of the alleyway. And we were probably talking about baseball (or its New York City street adaptations—punch ball and stick ball) as that was the most common ten-year-old boys' subject in 1957 in the summertime. We might have been talking about playing punch ball (grounders only) with a pink Spalding high-bounce ball (a "Spawl-deen") at the four corners of Cooper Street and 204th Street, where three manhole covers were conveniently laid out so that each served as a base; a sewer grate served as home plate. Or perhaps we were planning to make a stickball bat out of a broom by breaking off the broom end in a convenient sewer. Those conversations might have happened; I can't recall exactly. But I do remember a vivid feeling that the warmth and light of the sun were good and comforting. I remember also thinking that this day was going to stay with me the rest of my life. It has. And there's nothing else terribly noteworthy about that moment of time, other than that it lives.

In college I read Emily Dickinson's poem, "There's a certain slant of light," and the poem still takes me back to that alleyway. Dickinson says "a certain slant of light" gives us "Heavenly hurt"; it leaves no scar "But internal difference/

Where the meanings are." My slant of light in the alleyway made an internal difference, I like to think, and stuck in my memory because of its duality: Gerald and I were enjoying the cool of the alleyway, yet the warmth of the sun's rays was slanting into the opening of the alleyway. Somehow those streams of light and warmth were comforting. But the comfort lay in our observation of the sun's potential, not in being in the full glare and heat of the sunlight. So we were aware, too, that the sun could make life uncomfortable. I think, now, that awareness of the sun's potential for both comfort and discomfort arose out of the awareness of both shade and sunlight—a kind of "heavenly hurt." There's a beneficial duality of vision in that awareness. It is no surprise that I grew up to like paradox—the stuff of literary texts. I was also prepared to stare, years later, at Edward Hopper paintings of sunlight streaming through windows.

I may have had some intuitive sense that the sun was bigger than me. I like to think now that I recognized that the world was bigger than me although I was part of it, that I was enjoying my observation post, but I wasn't able to encompass it all. I like to think this vision of the sun reinforced the injunctions against egocentricity that I received from my parents, my church, and my school. Nevertheless, there may have been some sense of being empowered by the grandness of my vision in such a simple moment of being.

The moment was also peaceful and contemplative: Gerald and I were not running around like crazy as we often did. I was a big fan of the Lone Ranger, and I recall many games of "Cowboys and Indians" with him. We would pursue one another through the hallways and basements of all the buildings on the west side of Cooper Street and even upstairs on to the roofs and across the roofs from one apartment building to the next. We were oblivious to any danger in crossing the roofs. But on this day, we were budding Irish Catholic Buddhists, simply sitting around, talking.

I had some sense, I think now, of something bigger than myself, something so deeply intrinsic, universally pervasive, yet invisible to the eye but not to my developing consciousness of the world. That something was more grand than me although I felt at least a touch grand for perceiving the moment as one to remember. Immanence locates divinity in material reality and is usually contrasted with transcendence. The Druids are reputed to have practiced a kind of religion of immanence, and Catholicism with its use of relics, sacred wells, and other holy places, even the doctrine of transubstantiation, suggests that immanence and transcendence are not mutually exclusive. After all, a communicant eats God. As an altar boy I had strong reverence for the mysterious comfort of incense and candles, their apparent ability to connect the olfactory senses of the faithful with the divine. My ten-year-old thinking was not so sophisticated although I did think about God a great deal. By the standards of people other than Edward Hopper, the view from the alley of 10 Cooper Street would not seem pregnant with possibility for an immanence/transcendence meditation. The view would strike most as quite pedestrian, quite narrow, even grim. But I am reminded now of James Joyce's theory about ordinary objects: they all await the right moment to epiphanize, or shine forth with the radiance of insight into the wholeness of all—a "sudden spiritual transformation" in Joyce's words. We could see some parked cars, and surely an occasional car drove by. And some neighbors walked by too. I've been waiting for that memory to epiphanize since, and subsequent events have led me to see that 1957 moment as an epiphany.

I know now that the situation contained an *in utero* possibility for the development of critical thinking. Gerald and I might have earned the ire of the building's tenants since neither of us lived in 10 Cooper Street, and even kids who lived in the building were not supposed to hang out in the alleyway. I'm not sure why it mattered so very much to some of the tenants to tell us to get lost, but at least a few would tell us to get out of the alleyway and not block it for the tenants, who actually had plenty of room to get past us with their shopping carts loaded with food from the A&P. I like to think now that there was a bit of license in our enjoying a slightly unacceptable place to get out of the heat. And I'm rather certain that the superintendent would have chased us out of the alley if he had happened to come upon us.

On February 23, 1970, I was shot down in a helicopter in the Mekong Delta. The co-pilot was shot through the head, but the rest of us managed to survive the crash landing. All of this does jar the teeth a bit. I didn't sleep well that night, but I remember getting up the next day, dressing, and going to breakfast. The sun was shining. I said to myself, "So that's how it is." The sun did not make me optimistic about the future, but it did seem to communicate a sense that what will be will be. That morning gave me new appreciation of Maurya's words at the end of J.M. Synge's play, *Riders to the Sea*. She has lost all her sons to the sea, yet she is able to say: "No man at all can be living forever and we must be satisfied."

In recent years I've begun to be able to ask how the Viet Cong felt when they woke up on February 24, 1970. Did the sun help them too? After all, I got out of the situation with my body intact. All hell rained down on them. Reports claim that 20 VC were killed. I don't trust the claims. But I do know that it would have been hard for the VC to appreciate the sun. After all they ruled the night. Its darkness protected them—much as the alleyway protected Gerald and me from the heat of the daylight sun.

The sun had saved me at Fort Benning from the allure of the cushy job and the careerism of the Pentagon's Mephistopheles who was offering counterintelligence jobs in Germany as the price of our souls. While I, like Tommy Johnson in the Coen Brothers' *O Brother, Where Art Thou?*, wasn't using my soul, I didn't sell it to the devil in the bitter cold of the Georgia winter. The sun was shining when we escaped the devil's guiles. Maybe the sun smiles too?

I remember my mother thought that the sun was healing. When I was hit by a car when I was about 10 years old and suffered a large black-and-blue bruise to the hip, she took me up the hill into the woods of Inwood Park and had me expose my hip to the sun for about an hour. I don't know about a cure, but I do recollect that I felt like I was being healed by the sun's warm rays. I have to think that my mother learned to trust the sun when she grew up in Cloonkeelane—that townland of almost constant rain (although the clouds go sailing through the sky there; the sun peaks out constantly in between the rain showers). Much has been written about the survival of Irish paganism: I believe it has survived. I remember my mother talking about lighting fires in the fields on St. John's Eve, June 23, and offering a potato to the fields. There was a strong sense of the immanence of the spiritual in her rural upbringing.

So am I really a worshipper of the Sun God? Am I fascinated by Newgrange because of its precise, 5,000-year-old understanding of the sun's movement? Or am I simply deluded? I remember my first visit to Newgrange, just north of Dublin—a 5,000-year-old passage tomb that is situated perfectly so as to allow the sun to enter the passage on the winter solstice. On that day only, it lights up the inner chamber deep inside a mound. The chamber was apparently a kind of crematorium for the deceased. The ancient inhabitants of Ireland understood that the sun was life giving, and in death its beneficence and constancy should be respected.

When I look out my window at a beautiful sunny day, I always feel good. At least one recent scholar has argued that the Celtic cross is rooted in the pre-Christian Sun Cross. A Celtic cross surrounds the crux of a cross with a halo. I'll let the archaeologists argue about this one, but I like the ancient idea that the sun is the source of human beneficence. It's a friend, even. I also like Christian religious iconography that makes use of the halo to suggest that the religious figure depicted is, like the sun, a source of light.

But good friendship is not all blooming roses. Sometimes the sun simply lets us see things as they are. It enables us to see although we do not necessarily like what we see. We can handle seeing things as they are although the way they are often puzzles us. It makes sense that poets can refer to the cold light of day when it's the moonlight that is cold. But the synesthesia is puzzling.

I am haunted by a photograph that appeared in *The New York Times* on June 15, 2003. It shows two boys in Little League baseball uniforms. They look unhappy because rain has canceled their baseball game. The photo makes me remember how anxious I was that rain not spoil my Little League games. I can remember staring out our windows into the backyard, hoping that the rain would stop in time to have a scheduled game. My first thought on game days was to look for sunlight. It sounds silly to be saying this as an adult, but sun on a Saturday morning meant that I would get to play baseball. What else could a boy want? On some level we all remain kids looking for the sun in order to play baseball.

Well, I also had to learn that occasionally the sun does not shine, and I needed to learn to live both in sunlight and in shadow—a blessed duality of perspective.

I did not feel so blessed when I was 21 years old and the major from the Pentagon took us indoors and offered his blandishments. But blessed with the dual perspective of the alleyway at 10 Cooper Street, I could laugh about the manipulation.

World War II and Being Irish

My father was 35 years old when he received his draft notice. No American male today at that age would even conceive that the government would send him such a notice. My father was married with a daughter soon to be a year old. He had already served in the New York National Guard and had worked in a defense plant—the Brooklyn Navy Yard. These personal details did not matter, and my father and my mother did not really ever gripe about them. They accepted my father's call to service as a matter of duty. There certainly was no thought of going home to Ireland, for, since my father was a Catholic from the North, he might have found employment only in the British Army as his father had. My parents were committed Americans by that time anyhow; Ireland was the "old country."

My father did see service in the army as fraught with the same problems that Catholics faced back in the north of Ireland, especially following partition in 1922. On many occasions my father told me stories about the Masonic Order and its pervasive influence in his unit. He claimed that he actually confronted his commanding officer about preference in promotions going to members of Masonic lodges. I have to think that the example of the Orange Order back in Dungannon, County Tyrone, was on my father's mind. My cousin Cooey tells me that my father burned down the hall of the local Orange Lodge in Dungannon, some time before his immigration to America in 1925. So it is possible that his association of the Masons with the Orange Order continued a personal vendetta that was reinforced by the Church in America: Catholics were prohibited from joining the Masons. My father's final rank was Tech–5 or Tech Corporal—a rank the army eliminated in 1948. He obviously earned his two stripes somehow, so I don't know if he was correct about his belief. But he was more vehement about that subject than any other connected with his war service. He claimed that Masonic manipulations led to a delay in his return to the states. Soldiers were sent home from Europe in an order based on time in service; my father claimed his service credits were not computed correctly to account for his time in the New York National Guard. He thought the miscalculation was deliberate so as to send the Masons home sooner.

My father's attitude makes sense in Irish terms: he always spoke respectfully of Protestants and would even say he was a Protestant if he could have a good quarrel in a bar as a result. Fellow Irishmen from counties in the Irish Free State disparaged northerners as "Far Downs"—because Ulster was "down in the north." The Orange Order was a different matter. It was the organization of the Bully Boys. The distinction between Orangemen and Protestants does not make much sense to an outsider, but my father saw a real difference.

Although my father missed the crows when he fired at them and never was under fire, he must still have seen a great deal during his three years in the army. His unit, the 133rd Anti-Aircraft Battalion, saw no action after it landed on Utah Beach on August 23, 1944, two-and-a-half months after D-Day, and then moved to Omaha Beach. Eventually the battalion made its way to Munich, Germany. Along the way the 133rd was charged with the air defense of Cherbourg, which had been liberated by U.S. forces on June 29, 1944—soon after the D-Day landing. The 133rd moved from Omaha Beach to Cherbourg on September 30, 1944. Defending Cherbourg was crucial; it gave the allies a deep water port from which to support the divisions already in the field and to land further ground troops and supplies—directly from the United States and by-passing England. Fortunately for the men of the 133rd, the German Luftwaffe had been defeated, and there wasn't much need for anti-aircraft protection for ground troops or ships in harbor. Since anti-aircraft battalions had lots of trucks, the 133rd was pressed into service to transport men and materiel to the front.

The war on the Western Front ended on May 8, 1945, and thereafter my father's battalion guarded civilian prisoners and American deserters. My father told me about seeing camps full of American deserters who were being held. Signs were posted proclaiming the shame of the men in the camps. They were men who refused to fight for their country. I know my father was amazed at the sight, but he was non-committal about its meaning for him. He was quite somber when he described the situation to me. Such camps get lost in the glow of victory. The Army apparently let most of the deserters go at the end of the war, but I do wonder how many of them were plagued with "bad paper" or dishonorable discharges for the rest of their lives—even though many of them may have performed well under fire for some time.

But my father must have seen the devastating results of war. The battalion history records the satisfaction of its men in "a simple matter of retribution": the "sight [on April 12, 1945] of rubble-littered, smashed buildings and charred ruins as we followed in the wake of our victorious armies."[38] My father had enough service points to come home to be discharged on January 14, 1946; in the interim, the 133rd guarded Civil Interment Enclosures—a wonderful euphemism for prison camps. The 133rd released Fritz Kuhn on April 26, 1946 (after my father had gone home). Kuhn was the controversial, Hitler-appointed leader of the American Bund—a group that had packed Madison Square Garden with 20,000 people on February 20, 1939. I have to think that my father as a New Yorker would have been well aware of who Kuhn was. I'm struck by the fact that my 38-year-old father guarded prisoners as his father had during World War I. I guess the old guys were suited to such duties.

I'm not sure when the Army stopped informing the troops about political events. My father's 133rd AAA Battalion was following Army policy in 1946: "Complying with the Army policy of keeping the troops informed on world matters, regular duty hour orientation sessions were held in all batteries. Along with this was included the Six Hour Orientation Course on Germany and the occupation."[39] I suspect that the orientations were biased, but I can't help but contrast my father's experience with the one-time-only briefing on "world matters" that I received at MACV Headquarters upon landing in Saigon in October 1969. I never heard another word about "world matters" for the following year.

In the vague hope of understanding the Vietnamese better, I did try to learn their language during my year, but, unlike my father, I was mostly unsuccessful at learning the local tongue. He picked up some German while in Germany. After he had had a few jars in his later years, he would start speaking in German. He also spent about six months in France—at Cherbourg, principally, so he also broke into French with a few taken—but less frequently than German. I can't say whether his German or his French was actually coherent, but he could put on a good show lasting as much as a half-hour. He bought a book for me, *German Through Pictures*, while I was still in grammar school. During the summers he made me study German, and, then later, he insisted that I take German, and not French, in high school. He obviously admired individual Germans, and I have to think also that there was a bit of his perverse nature in liking the Germans, our defeated enemies, more than he liked the liberated French—just as he liked Nixon after Watergate but not before. Whatever his motivation for liking the Germans and German, he probably did have a facility for languages that he wanted to develop but never did. That was to be my job. We probably lived in the only apartment house in Inwood that had many German tenants. The landlord, when I was small, was German: Mrs. Fischbach. My parents loved how clean and orderly she kept the building. Many of the tenants, with names such as Randerman, Anderman, Dieckmann, and Wallach, had German accents, so oddly I grew up liking Germans in an Irish neighborhood. My father used to tune into German-language radio programs. I could hear their echo in the alleyway between 24 and 30 Cooper Street as the German families in the building tuned in too. I knew all the words to "*Du, du, liegst mir im Herzen*," and I loved the rousing end to the first stanza, "*Ja, ja, ja, ja, weißt nicht wie gut ich dir bin.*"

Part of my grand plan to evade the war in Vietnam was linked to my father's affinity for German. I had made a decision after my second year of college in the spring of 1966 to join the Army ROTC two-year program. I figured that the war would be over by the time I graduated from college in 1968, and then I'd be sent to Germany and serve six months only on active duty. I even changed my major from English to German; I thought the Army might notice. I could be an MI German linguist. I was very naïve.

My father used the G.I. Bill to learn a trade—printing—after he returned from the war. He went to the New York Mergenthaler Linotype School to become a linotype operator and eventually worked in a print shop for Macfadden/Bartell, a major magazine producer. Macfadden was the publisher of *Sport* magazine, so I devoured every issue for many years. I am still a sports nut today—to the amazement of some of my academic colleagues who are surprised by how much I know about sports. *Sport* precursed *Sports Illustrated* and featured very attractive, large color photos of Mickey Mantle and my other baseball heroes. Ed Fitzgerald was the editor of *Sport*—an Irish-American whom my father liked. In 1961 Fitzgerald ghosted Yogi Berra's autobiography—no doubt a linguistic feat second only to channeling Casey Stengel. Fitzgerald became the executive in chief of the Book-of-the-Month Club and founded the Quality Paperback Book-of-the-Month club. Any sign that the Irish were successful in America would arouse my father's attention. He was an encyclopedia of the Irish ancestries of famous people whom most would not recognize as Irish. Charles de Gaulle was a hero because his grandmother was Irish. Years later when I read *Ulysses*, I understood the authenticity of Joyce's great list of heroes and heroines of Irish antiquity, Patrick W. Shakespeare and Brian Confucius, among them.

Before he went to work at Macfadden, my father seems to have had trouble initially in settling into working class family and work life. I remember a long stretch when I was quite young when he simply wasn't home. Eventually he wound up in Fordham Hospital, having been seriously beaten up in a bar fight, somewhere in the Bronx. I remember that his ribs had been cracked. He settled down after that, stayed at home, and went to work in the print shop until he retired when the company closed the print shop. In 1960 he was a staunch supporter of John Fitzgerald Kennedy for president. Clearly he wanted an Irishman in the White House. My parents went into mourning when Kennedy was assassinated. That was a watershed in Irish-American consciousness. Irish-American households frequently set up little "altars" with a framed picture of Pope John XXIII and JFK—our saints.

So it came to me as a sacrilege when a Southern racist captain told me one night in Vietnam that lots of people were not unhappy to see Kennedy assassinated. And the "not un-" construction was exactly the way he put it: I needed to smarten up and realize that the world was better off without JFK. Only a naïve person would think otherwise. He was very fond of himself as a leader of men. I viewed him as a creep. He had no concept that I was a member of the Irish Catholic tribe, of the tribal meaning of Kennedy's ascension to the presidency, and of the communal mourning when he was assassinated—the bus-trip pilgrimages of Irish organizations to the Arlington gravesite with Mass right at the grave.

One night, about 2 a.m., soon after the conversation about Kennedy with the Southern captain, between stints in the air on a helicopter patrol of the perimeter of Can Tho Army Air Field, I couldn't sleep, so I decided to write home to my parents. I was burned up about the Kennedy slam and wanted to communicate with those who had worshipped Kennedy. But I didn't talk about Kennedy. For the only time while in Vietnam, I actually said what I was doing, although, truth be told, most of what I was doing, including flying the perimeter, was safer than riding the subway at 2 a.m. In the letter I said we're flying around looking for Charlie (as the Viet Cong were called; VC in military radio talk is Victor Charlie, so the troops took to calling the VC by the second word, for short. Sometimes "Charlie" morphed into "Charles," "Uncle Charlie," "Sir Charles," or even "Lord Charles"—later the nickname for Dwight Gooden's curve ball).

About a week later my mother wrote back and told me she didn't like to hear that I was out looking for Charlie. I kicked myself for ever uttering a word. My mother thought I could stop looking for Charlie. While I wondered what she was thinking, I realized that saints don't understand war—God bless them. She seemed to think that war was like a Boy Scout camping trip. She did try to stop me from joining my friends on a camping trip to Lake George when I was eighteen years old. I let her think she had succeeded then: it was easier than fighting with her. I wonder now whether such moments lead veterans to keep their mouths shut about what happened "over there." It's at least part of the reason: no one wants to hear or even imagine the truth. When I watch the extremely graphic and realistic HBO miniseries about the Iraq war, *Generation Kill*, I understand why parents don't want to know what their sons are doing or even saying. And the troops seem to engage willfully in socially prohibited graphic language, just to be sure that they really are being obscene. I cursed very little until I entered the army. I was raised to think that cursing was a sign of irreverence for the person spoken to and to civil society in general. It was in a league with taking the Lord's name in vain—a sign of treating the sacred profanely. Now I think the army was rife with irreverence because of the dirty work we were called to undertake. Our service developed tarnish and lost value.

I'd Rather Fight in Dungannon

To grow up in Inwood was to be aware that it was normal, virtuous, and honorable to serve in the IRA, the Marines or the Army, or even the Republican side in the Spanish Civil War. I remember a guy named McNiff who used to give bartenders in Inwood headaches that no expert in myofascial trigger point therapy could alleviate. He claimed to have fought with the Fascists in support of Franco during the Spanish Civil War. He was a loutish galoot, and he was thrown out of bars all over the neighborhood. Although he was a tough customer, he never spoke callously about war. Going to some sort of war was not unthinkable for a young man from Inwood.

When I was in Vietnam, I kept thinking that I'd like to fight in a "good war" as in Northern Ireland. In Irish pubs in New York I had sung rebel songs like "Sean South of Garryowen." Lines like these had stirred me and made me feel I actually had a fighting Irish soul:

> They scorned the danger they might face
> Their fate that lay in store
> They were fighting for old Ireland to claim their very own
> And the foremost of that gallant band
> Was South from Garryowen

In Vietnam I was inspired by reading Brendan Behan's *Confessions of an Irish Rebel*, which showed up in one of the mysteriously packed boxes of books Team 56 would receive occasionally. I kept thinking that Behan had it right, but I certainly couldn't feel about my service in Vietnam like he did about service to Ireland. Vietnam was making a pacifist out of me, or, at least, a future pacifist. When I found out in 2009 the role that Brendan Duddy, an Irish Nationalist pacifist, had played in bringing peace to the north of Ireland, he became my hero. Duddy was the secret intermediary between the Provisional IRA and British Intelligence for over 20 years and passed the message that led finally to the 1998 Good Friday Agreement. Duddy's remarkable courage has inspired no popular Irish ballad; the ballads of gallant warriors like Sean South never seem to be completely out of vogue. "True Grit" is just stuff for the movies.

The POW Charade

Once only did I really want to go on a mission: we had good intelligence regarding the presence of American POWs in Phong Dinh Province. I could see merit in rescuing fellow soldiers, but our commanders apparently saw no special urgency to launch a rescue mission.

I was shocked by the complacency of virtually everyone in this matter. I certainly followed the SOP for information about American POWs. "Brightlight" was the code word for reports on POW sightings. On August 13, 1970, Phantom Twilight was operating in Phung Hiep District and apparently ran into the VC —not an unusual occurrence since the VC controlled large swaths of the district. The gunships put in their strikes and headed back to the airfield. About an hour later, an ARVN soldier showed up in Phung Hiep district town and claimed that he had escaped from a VC POW camp during the Phantom Twilight strikes. He said there were two Americans—"one Caucasian and one Negro"—in the prison camp with him. The INTSUM—the daily intelligence report—for August 16 gives the exact grid coordinates of the camp.

This information was potentially explosive, I thought, and I dared not screw it up. I went immediately to the SOP. It said that verifiable information of American POWS, anywhere in South Vietnam would require an immediate operation by a brigade of the First Air Cavalry Division to the site of the report.

I spoke with our L-19 pilot almost immediately upon hearing the news and told him the probable location of the camp. He knew the area well, and in the INTSUM for August 18 I wrote: "Shotgun 38 [the L-19 pilot's call sign] reports that over the past 2–3 weeks he has sighted several structures completely surrounded by water which may well be a POW camp at WR 7977. Shotgun 38 has also sighted a similar configuration of structures at WR 8273 and on 18 Aug 70 he sighted 11 sampans and numerous personnel in this vicinity. This second area is in very close proximity to the place of capture of the two detainees [the two women described below]."[40] The INTSUMs went to the commanding general of Delta Military Assistance Command and to J2 in Saigon—the intelligence staff office of Gen. Creighton Abrams, the commanding general for MACV. So everyone, right up to Saigon, knew or should have known about this intel.

The response was stunningly slow. On August 18 a middle-aged American Caucasian in an Izod Lacoste shirt and khaki pants (he looked ready for 18 holes of golf) arrived from Saigon with his polygraph machine in hand along with a mug shot book of missing Americans. The plan was to polygraph the escaped ARVN POW to check on his veracity; it was not unwarranted to check him. ARVN soldiers deserted all the time: concocting a story of captivity might explain being AWOL. But surely this was the slow way to follow up on hot intelligence. I met the polygrapher at Can Tho Air Field, and he immediately asked me for a soundproof room. Only a Saigon warrior could ask such a question. A soundproof room? In the Mekong Delta? Did he think he was on West 57th Street? Well, I told him that was impossible, and he became evasive when I tried to find out if polygraphing was useless. I found a reasonably quiet place for him to test the ARVN soldier. Later the polygrapher said he had not detected any evidence of lying. The INTSUM says the ARVN's "answers were considered truthful."[41] Then the polygrapher got back on the plane for Saigon, and I heard no more from him.

On August 17, a company of ARVN Rangers had walked down the canal toward the location of the suspected POW camp, met with some resistance, and picked up a couple of women and a baby very close to the reported location of the POW camp. At the same time our psychological operations people dropped leaflets offering a reward for information leading to the return of American POWs. Now the Ranger operation was notable: no blocking force was put in place to catch anyone fleeing the advance of the Rangers. So it was the usual operational charade: I walk down the canal line, and so do you, backwards. It's a kind of waltz; no one gets hurt unless you booby-trap the path with 105mm artillery rounds before you "di-di-mao" (or move quickly) down the canal. We eat lunch and go home.

I was told that the two women and the baby were at the TOC, so I asked if I could talk with them. Both were illiterate, and the mother breast fed her baby while I asked her about a POW Camp. She was wearing a blue and white head scarf around her neck that the Vietnamese interpreter regarded as a form of VC insignia. It seems unbelievable, but she "stated that there was a POW camp 500 meters from the place where she was picked up by a helicopter on 17 Aug. Source also stated that there were 2 U.S. POW's in this camp and an estimated total of 20 POWs."[42] Now she might have been telling me that because she figured it was what I wanted to hear, but it is also true that her information dove-tailed with the ARVN's story. The ARVN was given a glimpse of the woman, and he said "that he had seen this girl inside the POW camp while he was detained there. She was in the company of the POW camp chief, and he [the ARVN] felt that she was his daughter."[43] With all of this information, I thought some operational commander would feel the need to check out the area, given the polygraph and interrogation reports. We just dropped leaflets. No one got too concerned. Just a dim light for Brightlight.

I went home in October, and on November 21, 1970, Nixon made headlines by authorizing a raid on a POW camp in North Vietnam—at Son Tay. When I read about the raid, I was furious. The intelligence on the camp was more than 24 hours old. Dale Andrade, a senior historian at the U.S. Army Center of Military History, has studied the Son Tay raid in depth. He concluded that by the time of the raid, "it was known almost without a doubt that the POWs had been moved." He asks the obvious questions: "Why did the raid go on even after it was known almost beyond a shadow of a doubt that the prisoners had been moved? Why did no one tell the task force planners that they had been moved?"[44] There was a serious risk of a wider war with China or the Soviet Union if the U.S. sent troops into the North on a raid. So, I ask, why was there no raid in South Vietnam three months earlier when such a raid could have been launched without the slightest political repercussion?

Cowardice

While I like to think I would have willingly participated in such a mission, I was otherwise ready to go home when I arrived. I read Bernadette Devlin's *The Price of My Soul* when I was in Vietnam and was riled up enough to want to go to my father's Dungannon and cause trouble. Devlin was a student leader at Queens University Belfast—a leading advocate for the civil rights of Catholics; her leadership of the civil rights movement led to her election to the British Parliament where she made headlines with her protests against the blindness of British rule of Northern Ireland. Her indictment of the Northern Irish Orange State and British complicity in systematic discrimination against Catholics aroused my sense of injustice. Only a raid on a POW camp offered any glimmer of worthwhile combat in Vietnam; otherwise I grimaced inwardly and did as I was told.

But even now 45 years later, I still feel uneasy as I write the last paragraph. I wonder whether I simply was too cowardly and slipped too easily into self-justification. There is no way out of that dilemma. All the kind words of loved ones who tell me that I should not be ashamed do not assuage the unease I feel. I went to the war. I was a coward. Tim O'Brien has it right.

I saw little merit in fighting for the anti-communist cause in Vietnam. James William Gibson's *The Perfect War: Technowar in Vietnam* reveals just how corrupt, mechanistic, and futile the whole enterprise was. And "enterprise" is a good word for the theory of limited war Gibson describes. The theory, he states, created "a kind of production system in which the officer corps served as managers, the enlisted men functioned as workers, and the product was enemy deaths or body count. To the war managers, American economic and technological superiority over Vietnamese insurgents and North Vietnamese regular forces was inevitable; any temporary setback could be reversed through escalation."[45] In short, it was hard to work up patriotic fervor for an assembly line mode of fighting. New Hampshire was not under attack. I developed far better reasons for opposing the war after I became an American advisor to the Vietnamese Regional and Popular Forces. On a daily basis I observed the corrupt nature of the Government of Viet Nam and the futile efforts of many good men who tried their best to bring peace, stability, and security to South Vietnam.

The Boy Scouts and High-Mindedness

One report by William Bach, the Senior Advisor in Phong Phu District, presents his most sincere attempt at building a worthwhile future for the boys and girls of Phong Phu—a stronghold of the Hoa Hao—a Vietnamese Buddhist sect fiercely opposed to the Communists. Hoa Hao boys and girls would seem the least likely prospects for outside organization. Hoa Hao religious practice emphasized private family worship and resisted ostentatious public ceremony. The Hoa Hao slogan-"Practicing Buddhism While Farming Your Land"—reflects the inwardness of its focus. Phong Phu's paddies were almost completely under cultivation; I observed tractors in the fields on several occasions—a sure sign that the VC had little influence.

To read Bach's report in the 21st century when the Boy Scouts have moved from accusations of pedophilia by leaders to embrace of gay scout leaders and scouts doubles its implausibility as a project for Hoa Hao children. Bach was trying, with great sincerity, to impart the most noble values of his America to the Vietnamese Hoa Hao children. Those values now seem quaint and dated: it's hard to imagine what effect they had on the children of Phong Phu. Bach writes on April 15, 1970:

> Our cherished hope for a district Boy and Girl Scout organization came to be last Sunday with the first muster of the initial 104 scouts. Suddenly the terrifying reality of having to meaningfully control and guide a large number of kids is upon us. I think that because the prospect is so frightening we have a tendency to over-plan, over-guide and over-regiment. Though I am no advocate of the permissiveness that has turned many of my own country's schools and youth centers into bedlam, I do feel that our scouts must be given a voice even in this formative stage of their organization.[46]

Bach worries about permissiveness in April; by June 15, he has become shrill in a letter to his Vietnamese counterpart:

> In the case of the Scouts, my constant fear is that we are creating an attractive, well-out-fitted, melodious group of song-singers, hand clappers and makers of toothpick decorations. Probably I am impatient, but I long to see the day when

these kids fulfill the promise of that line in their song where they "spill sweat" for their country. At this early stage I do not think they would compromise the idea even if they spilled more sweat for themselves (i.e., helped in the construction of their own center.) You especially, know the feeling of gratification produced by participation in a project that produces material results. How much more significant to the Scouts' sensation of involvement and usefulness [sic] would be a day spent in the mud, developing their own area, than one hundred days more of emasculating toothpicks and songs? Who knows but that one day war historians might say that the battles of Cambodia, Laos etc. were won on the playing fields of Thoi An? Even if they never say anything like that at all, we will, by letting the scouts work and sweat out their own future installation, save them from whatever miserable fate too much singing and hand clapping causes.[47]

So Horatio Alger lived in Thoi An Village in Phong Phu in 1970, and we did find much to laugh hopelessly about. As I read through the Team 56 files from 1969 and 1970, I found countless written statements from fellow advisors about the folly of our endeavors. Jaime Concepcion, a native of the Philippines and a naturalized American citizen, expressed his outrage on December 20, 1969, in the most extreme terms. Confronted by the fact that a village chief was allowing Cambodian refugees to starve by denying them the rations and resettlement money promised to them, Concepcion seems to have lost respect for due process. He wrote: "Grafting officials taking undue advantage of repatriates for their own nefarious ends should be lined to the wall and removed permanently." Concepcion had particular reason to be particularly concerned about the treatment of persons with ambiguous status. He was the New Life Development Advisor, i.e., he advised the Vietnamese on the re-settlement of refugees. He went on: "GVN Province is aware of the weak and incompetent officials. Petty, conniving, exploiting village officials who would take undue advantage of the helplessness of refugees (repatriates) should be made example of not only as a deterrent to other would-be abusers but as necessary castrations for this type of bureaucratic cancer."[48] No one else was so definitive about the remedy, but virtually everyone spoke of graft, corruption, and cowardly behavior.

Writing almost a year later on September 4, 1970, about the same situation, Captain Douglass R. Hemphill expressed similar ire and suggested that the problem was not confined to just one village:

> It is readily apparent to anyone with even a remote understanding of the Vietnamese economy that subsistence is impossible on the quantity of rations these people have been given. I find it hard to believe that the village chief has been issued no more than this ration to feed these refugees. I also doubt that either the Province Chief or the District Chief are [un]aware of this situation. And if this problem exists in one village, it is more than likely that it exists elsewhere. Not only is the inhumanity of the refugees' plight deplorable; it also provides the

VC/VCI an extremely fertile ground for proselyting [sic] activities. After eight months I am not naïve enough to be shocked at corruption among GVN officials. But with the emphasis currently being placed on the refugee problem, this is one situation which should be able to be resolved.

I ought to add that my Phung Hoang [Phoenix] team, whose members are certainly neither stranger to corruption nor bleeding heart types, became more angry than I have ever seen them when they saw the treatment the refugees were receiving at the hands of the village chief.[49]

By the time Hemphill was writing, I had read many similar reports. I arrived in Vietnam skeptical about the war's merit, but even committed career soldiers were writing about their frustrations with GVN corruption. So while I remember having countless theoretical arguments about the war in Uee's Bar in Inwood, I realized that I now had the goods to make a convincing case for American withdrawal. But those pre-war arguments in Uee's were circular and endless. Uee's had become my pals' hang out after its owner, Hugh McSherry, decided to renovate Hughie's—a dank old men's bar—and make it a younger guys' hangout. Somehow raw timbers with jagged edges, butcher block tables with cane-backed chairs, a dart board, saw dust on the floor, and textured wall paint required an updated kitsch spelling of "Hughie's," long before text messages started butchering spelling. My pals and I consumed gallons of beer in the new fancy, stemmed glasses and talked to all hours of the night. I thought the *craic* would go on forever.

But it didn't, and on October 16, 1969, Rich Lundy walked me home from Uee's. I got on a plane for California the next morning in order to catch my plane to Vietnam from Travis Air Force Base. I knew that my foolhardy decision to join ROTC to beat the draft had landed me in Vietnam. I hadn't really considered that I had actually volunteered to serve in the United States Army. I had thought about finding a way not to go to a war I didn't believe in, but there was no one to counsel me but my close friends—and they were of mixed mind about my very limited options. I didn't know what I would do in Canada as a deserter. My family would be horrified and would think me crazy. No Irishman from Inwood, then the largest Irish neighborhood in New York City, ever did that. My parents would not have understood: I'd have brought shame on the family. My best friends would support me, but they were not about to go to Canada with me. And, anyhow, I was an officer, not a draft resistor. That would put me in line for real punishment as a deserter—a wholly different category than that of a man who simply never showed up for induction and had never taken the oath.

I couldn't relate to the anti-war protestors and to the hippies: they were middle-and upper-class kids, spoiled rotten by their parents, opposed to the war because it interfered with their living of their personal, selfish lives. Jerry Rubin, the leader of the Yippies and orchestrator of the 1968 Chicago riots, became a multi-millionaire in the 1980s—an early investor in Apple Computers. It galled me that people like Rubin regarded themselves as intellectually superior: their superiority was convenient. I think now that they have won: contemporary America seems more filled with self-satisfied, selfish, self-righteous creeps who want to make war from 50,000 feet or via Cruise missiles while maintaining a guise of fake philanthropy.

I went to an anti-war demonstration in San Francisco in October 1968, three months before I reported for active duty on January 19, 1969. The demonstrators were waiting outside the hotel where Hubert Humphrey, the Democratic candidate for president and Johnson's vice president, was expected. A half-crazed guy was uttering every foul word he could think of as we all waited for Humphrey. The guy was obviously a sad case. He was demented, but he was being encouraged by yuppie hippies who professed to enjoy his display. Having doused themselves in hippie perfume—patchouli oil—they seemed more intent on outraging middle-class propriety than on ending the war in Vietnam. The patchouli covered the smell of marijuana smoke on their pseudo-Navajo and rummage sale clothing with an unpleasant earthy odor, sure to annoy people who conventionally took showers or baths to wash off odors. I realized the demonstrators' goal was to promote public outrage against themselves—ultimately a narcissistic act.

When I went to ROTC summer camp in the summer of 1967, Edward Ridley Finch Cox, a Princeton student, was a member of my platoon. He later married Nixon's daughter, and not only did he never go to Vietnam, he got headlines when he served six months on active duty. I remember being ticked about the publicity he received. When it was safe to do so, he served with the 11th Special Forces Group—no doubt sampling the best of German beers. Yet in 1967, he had a reputation as a forward-thinking kind of guy, and he was really a decent sort. I remember the adoring rapture of a fellow Princeton cadet: "He's so liberal." To the Princetonian mind, it was utterly amazing that a young man of Cox's background should be so advanced in his thinking. In Inwood we drank our beer and grumbled about duty. So much for the hippies and the Princetonians.

RFK in Absentia

I graduated from Fordham College on June 8, 1968. Bobby Kennedy was supposed to be the commencement speaker, but he was killed in Los Angeles on June 6, two days before he was supposed to speak. I remember sitting in Uee's Bar with Brendan Brophy watching the news of the California presidential primary on television. We witnessed the scene in the Ambassador Hotel in Los Angeles, right after Bobby had won the California Democratic primary on an anti-war platform. Rosey Grier, a retired New York Giant football player, was Bobby's bodyguard. I remember that he wrestled the gun from the assassin's hand. I just stared at the television. Somewhere in my consciousness, I knew then that my chances (and Brendan's, too) of going to Vietnam had just increased.

I had supported Bobby, mostly because he was against the war, and, unlike Senator Eugene McCarthy, Bobby had a real chance of winning the general election in November. Along with graduation, I was commissioned a second lieutenant with assignment to the Military Intelligence branch as were a number of my fellow ROTC graduates. I didn't know it then, but the army was increasing the number of MI lieutenants because it was gearing up for the Phoenix Program—a program of shaky moral dimensions: it targeted Viet Cong political leaders for killing or capture, a violation of the part of the Geneva Conventions that guaranteed safety for civilians.

I was strongly influenced by my two closest friends—Denis "Hayseed" Hynes and Rich "Mellow Man" Lundy. They were skeptical of the war—but also of most forms of authority, pseudo-belief, and political posturing. Collectively we later called ourselves "The Maybe Brothers" to suggest ambivalence as our general state of mind. Hayseed joined the Peace Corps and went to what was then called Dahomey (now Benin)—a move that didn't exactly make him draft exempt, but it did slow down his draft board. Mellow Man eventually applied for conscientious objector status, and I was pleased to write a letter testifying to his sincerity. I don't actually know what happened to his application as he found other ways of dodging the draft: he taught at a Catholic school in Harlem for a couple of years. And then he received a high number in the lottery draft that was held for the first time in December 1969, a couple of months after I arrived in Vietnam.

As a boy, I wondered how I would act in a tight spot. I wondered whether I would have the guts to face up to a physical challenge like a war when I grew up. My neighborhood encouraged young boys to prove their physical prowess in constant street fights with other boys. I was also trained rigorously in facing moral challenges, defined as they were by the Baltimore Catechism. We were told, for example, "If the government commands citizens to do something opposed to the law of God, their duty is to refuse to obey, for they must obey God rather than men."[50] But Cardinal Spellman was the military vicar, so it was unlikely that the government would ever oppose the law of God. I am not being entirely fair: I can remember being taught in Catholic grade school that adult moral decisions would sometimes be difficult, that seeing the right choice to make would not always be easy. I didn't quite imagine the difficulty of those choices.

Fighting was sport in my neighborhood. Competitions to determine the toughest kid on the block in each age group never ceased. In the 1950s the younger guys knew who the tough older guys were: they carried packs of Lucky Strikes up the sleeve of their plain-white Tee-shirts or they carried loose cigarettes behind their ears; they turned their collars up in winter ("rocks" we called them); they combed their hair duck-tail style—with waves on the side so as to look like James Dean; they wore thick black garrison belts with their dungarees; they called not-so-tough guys "faggots," probably with little understanding of the homosexual meaning of the term. (Loose girls were called "whoers," not "hoars.")

A favorite sport of the older guys was to round up and torture the younger guys. They played a game called "Concentration Camp": they would get all the younger guys into a courtyard and interrogate us. They made us concentrate all right: there was no way to answer the questions correctly: when asked what my name was, I'd say "Edward Hagan," only to be told that I was "Hagan, Edward." This would produce some form of physical torture like yanking hard on an arm so as to dislocate it from the shoulder socket briefly. I remember one day I was tied to a lamppost with my friend Billy, and a teenage "rock" was lighting matches and burning us. My father came along unexpectedly and took a swing at the teenager. I wasn't really pleased by my father's intervention: I knew I'd pay for it the next time I saw the older guy, and I did. He gave me a few punches in the stomach, just to let me know who was boss. I didn't tell my father about the retribution.

Some of the guys who played the role of Nazi persecutors in our childhood game of Concentration Camp would grow up to become police officers or serve in the military. It was common to see a young man transform from being a "rock" to being a rookie New York City police officer, clad in gray and carrying a night stick, a gun, and a gym bag to work. Or a young man would return home on leave after basic training in the Army and would wear his uniform every-where—to church, the park, the pub. Such guys were suddenly "with it"; they had answers to the physical courage questions: we all thought it certain that they would act well under fire. I can imagine what my fellow professors would think today about kids playing a street game called "Concentration Camp." Although we didn't realize it, we were growing up in the long shadow of the Second World War: our games derived from what our parents discussed. Nazis were just the bad guys who could be emulated in a kids' game. I played with toy soldiers, collected trading cards about World War II, and even knew before I was ten years old that a bazooka referred to a recoilless antitank rocket launcher as well as to a kind of chewing gum. Even though it was possible to see Jewish people on the benches in Inwood Park with tattooed numbers on their arms, courtesy of real Nazi Concentration Camps, the horror did not compute with us.

"Concentration Camp" and other games like "War" made me skeptical of my own fortitude if I ever really had to contend with such situations, yet I did not back down from fights and usually held my own with the guys my age. Such fighting was usually triggered by some cause, and I used to think that I only fought when it was necessary to defend myself or to put a stop to some shenanigans by some "punk." (I'm glad that none of the punks are around to dispute my claim.)

Armed with such sophisticated principles, I was not itching for a fight with Viet Cong punks, especially since I didn't really care much about a civil war on the other side of the planet or a skirmish in the Cold War. Other than saying prayers after Mass for the conversion of Russia, I had little ideological backing for my participation in the fighting in Southeast Asia. But I still had to measure up to neighborhood standards for toughness.

I don't know exactly what effect my family's military past had on me, but my family expected that I might have to serve in the military, and there was not much that could be done about that. Alternatives were not on offer.

My Sainted Mother

I remember seeing my father's Class A army jacket in the closet almost every day. I shared a closet with him in the three-room apartment in which my Mom and Dad lived with my sister and me. My sister was four and a half years older. She was born on October 15, 1942, and I was born on May 2, 1947. She was the pre-war baby; I the post-war baby. When my parents married in 1941, my father was 34 years old and my mother 32. So when I was born in 1947, my mother was 37, nearing the end of her child-producing years. My parents' marriage was no doubt delayed by the Depression and by their immigration from Ireland. It was common for young people to wait until they were economically capable of supporting a family before they married.

My mother, then Winifred Murphy, worked as a live-in maid during the 1930s for the Kernans—a rich family that lived in a townhouse on the Upper East Side of Manhattan. Francis Kernan was an investment banker and philanthropist. He was a founder of Lincoln Center and a trustee of the New York Racing Association. His wife, Maud Tilton Kernan, managed the household and oversaw charitable trusts that were still distributing sizable sums in 2002, when $2.5 million were distributed to worthy causes. Mrs. Kernan was the classic rich person with a conscience—a vanishing breed now, I think. I hated that she taught my mother to answer the telephone with an aristocratic (dare I say, British) accent. The 1940 census lists my mother as the cook in the household. The relationship continued well into their 80s. My mother resumed her work for Mrs. Kernan some time in the 1970s after years of receiving cookies each year at Christmas from the Kernans.

My father worked in the Brooklyn Navy Yard at the time of his marriage to my mother in St. Ignatius Loyola Church in the Upper East Side of Manhattan; St. Ignatius was the Jesuit parish of the ultra-rich Catholics. They married there because my mother lived in the neighborhood, working for the Kernans.

Although my mother worked for the Kernans, she and I didn't come from the landed gentry, and I had a well-developed sense of inferiority. Consequently, I've been working to develop arrogance for 68 years. By birth and upbringing, I was insecure. While being Irish is a source of pride, it builds in the irony that being Irish means I also carry a bag with a big belt of inferiority around it, like the big belt that fortified the suitcase my mother carried with her when she arrived in New York aboard the *Adriatic* on September 23, 1928, from Cloon-keelane, a townland near Enniscrone in County Sligo, Ireland. (I still have the belt: my mother's brother, John, bought it for her in Ballina—the nearest large town.) My father carried these qualities with him also from Dungannon, County Tyrone, Ireland. He landed in New York on October 27, 1925, aboard the *Tuscania*; he was sixteen years old. My parents brought with them great love of Ireland and a strong sense that rising very far in the world was probably not to be their lot. They also felt that they could never go back to Ireland, so we had to make do in America. My mother made only one trip back to Ireland; in late August 1936—in the aftermath of the untimely deaths in 1935 and 1936 of three of her siblings—Michael, John, and Agnes, she visited her family for a week. My father returned only in late 1945 while on leave from the U.S. Army in Germany.

My mother declared her intention to become a citizen on December 17, 1929—a little over a year after her arrival and two months after the stock market crash of late October 1929. Her "first papers" declare: "It is my bona fide intention to renounce forever all allegiance and fidelity to any foreign prince, potentate, state, or sovereignty, and particularly to George V, by the grace of God, of Great Britain, Ireland, and the British Dominions beyond the seas, King, Defender of the Faith, Emperor of India." The George V part is stamped on the form—the stamp a sign that many people from Britain and Ireland were swearing off the old country, but the fullness of description of the King is amusing now. "The British Dominions beyond the seas" sounds satirical. But I'm sure my mother was delighted to dispense with the Crown. My father had filed his first papers earlier that month—on December 4, 1929. Both also swore: "I am not an anarchist; I am not a polygamist, nor a believer in the practice of polygamy."[51] It seems odd that anarchism and polygamy are the two specific banned practices—almost as if those two represented some sort of present danger. Anarchism makes me think of the Sacco and Vanzetti executions in 1927 and the fears of anarchism that it mined, and polygamy makes me think of the Mormons who gave up polygamy at the end of the nineteenth century. So maybe the formal, anti-anarchist and anti-polygamist oath-taking suggests an American tendency to fixate on particular topical threats. I think of the communist scare that sent me to Vietnam and the more current Islamophobia.

But my mother and father were well-disposed to swearing off anarchism and polygamy along with the British royalty. The British, it seemed to me always, were responsible for our exile—fortuitous as it was. The British were history that I was not to forget even as I became a loyal American.

I was cautioned against wearing patriotism like a badge of superiority. That near-hysterical claim to American superiority seems to be all the rage now, but, over the years, I have discovered many advantages to not inflating my worth on any basis. An "inferiority complex" has gotten an undue bad reputation, brought on by shrinks, golfers, South Carolina retirees, and the American promise of happiness.

I have derived much fortuitous pain from my inferiority. When people salute some accomplishment or other of my life, I am mindful of the closing words of Malcolm Wilson, a fellow alumnus of Fordham Prep and the commencement speaker at my graduation in 1964. He quoted "the words of St. Francis:'Take care to be as good as people think you are.'"[52] Wilson was then Nelson Rockefeller's Lieutenant Governor of New York State, and Wilson later went on to become governor when Rockefeller was appointed vice-president after Gerald Ford ascended to the presidency in the wake of Richard Milhous Nixon's resignation. In any event I never forgot those words: how many people can remember a speaker at a high school graduation making a statement that lasts a lifetime? The words resonated because they remind us that we're all really "not so hot."

I guess folks will be divided on whether I have been careful enough about being good. I know that I've earned the disgust of certain administrators at Western Connecticut State University for fighting for truth, beauty, and the union contract for the last 36 years. (Note: just for the record: I'm rather proud of that disgust, so it lacks merit, pride being one of the seven deadly sins.)

I'm also keenly aware of my ignorance. The intellectual life of the academic should be spent in pursuit of truth. But the pursuit seems always to produce nebulous results. I have a standard question for my daughter: "Have you figured out the meaning of life?" Each time I ask, she tells me she's working on it. That's a great answer although I keep wishing that there were some short cut. One summer when my dear friend and colleague John Briggs was going on his annual pilgrimage to France, I told him: "When you come back in three weeks, I want you to tell me the meaning of life." John replied, "I already told you that, but you didn't listen."

He's probably right: there's quite enough of meaning on tap at local bars and in New York City cabs although I haven't frequented bars since I married Denise Lepicier at age 28 and I have never had the ready cash to ride in cabs when in New York. I do strongly believe that any meaning available with a pint of Guinness would remind me to be humble.

But writing a memoir requires enough arrogance to think my story is worth someone's reading. And we seem to have grown more arrogant, to the point of being narcissistic, in recent years. So what does it say about me that I am writing a memoir about my year and ten days (October 19, 1969–October 29, 1970) in Vietnam? And why write it in 2015 when I am 68 years old? I was 22 when I arrived in Vietnam and 23 when I left. What took 45 years? Maybe I never left Vietnam. Or is it that the recent rise in narcissism has overtaken me? I'm worried.

Jim Carroll,
Kareem Abdul Jabbar
and the Other Guys

… if you were ever on a helicopter that had been hit by ground fire your deep, perpetual, chopper anxiety was guaranteed.[53]—Michael Herr, *Dispatches*

Making a fuss out of myself violates a very strong taboo of my youth. So what were the taboos of my Irish upbringing? Well, there was a question—"What will the neighbors think?"—and a warning—"You're getting too big for your britches." As I write, both are on my mind. How much of the dirty laundry can I air? And who gave me the right to think that my life is important enough to merit anyone's interest?

Can I talk about the people I knew in my youth and mention them by name—especially if I want to make critical remarks about them? Why am I bothered by all this? I might have to reveal stuff about myself that I've been hiding from the neighbors for years. It has taken 45 years to summon up the ego, the fortitude, the chutzpah, the impudence, the self-centeredness, the guts, the cowardice, the gall to write a memoir. Life has taught me ambivalence; I am embodying its lessons in writing about its sometimes blissful confusions. I am now of a certain age—old enough to have lost the sense of time past and passing. I've become entangled with all kinds of people, and I have had much luck to have had great friends and a great family life.

As a teenager I was intensely shy, capable of blushing easily, and afraid to stand out, except in the socially approved ways. Eyeball-to-eyeball contact with a pretty girl would turn my cheeks and even my ears a bright crimson and paste my tongue to the roof of my mouth. Blushing, upon reflection, is actually evidence of sexual desire, thwarted though it may be. The blusher fails to hide what he actually wants. I was not successful in overcoming my shyness—actually ever. Academic success came early on although I had mixed feelings about being successful in the

101

classroom. This feeling persisted into adulthood when I felt I should have been a fireman or cop, or a construction worker, or a bartender. As a child I preferred to hit home runs or jump shots. I wasn't bad at sports, but I wasn't blessed with great natural talent either. I played baseball constantly up until the age of 12. Then I became possessed by basketball and wanted to play for the Knicks, but I couldn't make my high school basketball team. (The team *was* very good.)

I did play basketball with the poet/punk rocker Jim Carroll on the courts of Inwood: his prowess as a basketball player was exaggerated when he became the darling of the hip-oisie. And I've always thought his autobiographical *The Basketball Diaries* was overrated. Carroll traded on being from the neighborhood and always seemed to be acting superior to it. He was a couple of years younger than I was, but we played ball together frequently in Inwood Park for several summers. May God rest his soul: he came back to Inwood to die in 2009. I also played Little League baseball with Lew Alcindor (who later became Kareem Abdul Jabbar), but I never played basketball with him. But both Carroll and Lewie (as we called him in Inwood) went on to different kinds of basketball fame.

While Carroll and Jabbar became famous, the guys I remember most poignantly came home in boxes. Like most guys who went to Vietnam, I took a chartered flight home on a commercial airliner. I wanted to act like Carroll and Jabbar, who built lives for themselves but did not go to the war. I wanted to act like nothing had happened, but it had.

For a few years after I came home, I kept going down in a helicopter in Vietnam as I had done on February 23, 1970. I'd be in my turquoise, four-door 1969 Datsun, driving somewhere, and then I'd feel like I was losing control. I could break out in a sweat. At times I'd wake up in the night as the helicopter rode to the ground once more. I learned later this was Post Traumatic Stress Disorder. After a while the daymares and the nightmares stopped for the most part, and occasionally I'd recall the helicopter shoot down without a great deal of stress. Then on December 27, 2005, I was involved in a major auto accident. My aorta was ruptured. I had 22 broken bones. A cardiothoracic surgeon named Dr. Michael Frymus worked on me for eleven hours and gave me a Dacron aorta. It has been working ever since although my mind found it hard to comprehend Dr. Frymus' death less than a year later on December 4, 2006, of a heart attack. There's something uncanny about a heart surgeon dying of a heart attack. Dr. Frymus, aged 51, appeared to be a physically strong man, a former ice hockey player, and an Air Force veteran. His death reminded me that I have watched people die, out of sync with the way the world is supposed to be, since a young boy, Robert Giuttari, was murdered on December 23, 1960, while delivering a Christmas tree to the apartment house across the street from 24 Cooper Street where I grew up. One night in the hospital in January 2006, I went down in the helicopter again.

The VC Shoot Too

When I sat down on the back seat of the Huey, the helicopter had completed its start-up whine, the rotors were already spinning; their "wop-wop-wop" made conversation very difficult. We were ready to take off from Can Tho Army Air Fiield. A captain, the pilot, was in the front seat along with a warrant officer co-pilot. I put on my headset and hooked up to the intercom and said hello to the captain. His "How ya doin'?" sounded north of Paramus and south of Scarsdale, so I asked him where he was from although I knew immediately that he was a New Yorker. He replied, "Manhattan." So I said, "Where in Manhattan?" He said, "Upper Manhattan." I said, "Where in Upper Manhattan?" He finally said it, "Inwood."

Then I said, "Where in Inwood?" Now he said, "Arden Street." So I said, "Well, I'm from Cooper Street."

Michael O'Donnell was Irish, and we moved to the next order of business: ascertaining which bars we knew in common. We did not need to discuss parishes: both of us knew immediately we were from different parishes. His was Our Lady Queen of Martyrs (known as "Kween o' Martas")—while I lived in the regal domain of Good Shepherd ("Good Shep-id") parish, run by the Paulist Fathers and therefore "special." So we were discussing Garry Owen's Bar (located on the corner of Dyckman Street and Vermilyea Avenue) when Viet Cong guerrillas hit the helicopter with about 71 rounds of .51 caliber machine gun fire on February 23, 1970.

O'Donnell apparently has no memory of our conversation or of the Americans, other than the chopper's crew, on the UH-1 helicopter when it went down. At some point, he posted a report of the mission on the internet; Warrant Officer 1 Peter Thurston, the co-pilot, was killed. O'Donnell's report is obviously flawed: he says only one bullet hit the chopper—the one that killed Thurston. If so, it is unlikely that the helicopter would have gone down. I saw the helicopter the next day after a Chinook towed it back to Can Tho Air Field: the crew chief, Spec 4 Edward Sanderson, told me that it had 71 .51 caliber holes in it. I didn't count, but I saw lots of quarter-sized holes all across the helicopter's body. The VC in that area undoubtedly had had a .51 caliber machine gun. (Those Communists were smart: they added a millimeter to the

103

American .50 cal machine gun and to the 81mm mortar. They could use our ammo, but we couldn't use theirs.) Lieutenant Mark Mills was the Firefly duty officer that night; Firefly was a mission to protect Can Tho Air Field by patrolling the area close to the Air Field with a large search light mounted on a Huey to look for possible attackers. Mills reported that the Firefly lightship was sent to the site of the downed helicopter—about 30 kilometers distant from the Air Field—to protect it until the next day when a Chinook would pick it up. His report states that the Firefly ship took four hits and received ".50 cal fire."[54] The lightship limped back to the Phung Hiep District town.

The goal of the Phantom Twilight mission was to keep the VC away from Can Tho Air Field, with its long lines of revetment-protected helicopters and L-19 spotter planes. The mission SOP called for us (a Vietnamese officer and an advisor—a junior officer like me who controlled permission to shoot) to observe the Area of Operations from 1500 feet while two helicopter gunships fired rockets and their mini-guns at suspected VC targets. We flew this mission at twilight when the VC might be planning to move closer to the air field for mortar attacks.

Lieutenant Mike Murria took a bullet in the leg and was medevaced to Japan after being in country about five days. I had known Mike at Fort Sheridan, Illinois, at 5th Army Headquarters, my duty station before getting orders to Vietnam. Mike had looked me up when he got to Delta Military Assistance Command (DMAC) headquarters in Can Tho; he was slated for assignment to a District Advisory Team as a Phoenix Program advisor. Since I had to go out flying in the late afternoon, I asked Mike if he wanted to join us. In the aftermath I realized that it was decidedly stupid to invite tourists along on a combat mission although I had it in my head that Mike would get some sense of what the Mekong Delta looked like from 1500 feet. But tourists sometimes get a little too close to the sights, and flying at 100 feet might not be as suicidal as going over Niagara Falls without a barrel, but it is close. A slow-moving Huey makes for an easy target for a guerrilla in a well-fortified bunker.

Since Mike wasn't supposed to be on the Huey, his luggage remained in our Team House for about a month until I convinced our S-4 (supply) lieutenant to take responsibility for it and send it to Japan. Captain Steven Black, who was a notorious practical joker, loved this bit: Mike had become the second lieutenant in *Catch–22* whose personal gear was left in Yossarian's tent.[55] Heller's second lieutenant had reported to the operations tent instead of the orderly room and was killed two hours later over Orvieto. Like that lieutenant, Mike was a transient en route to a unit but not yet assigned, so he belonged to no one. So Mike's stuff would still be in Vietnam if I hadn't begged for a personal favor from the S-4, Dave Heinrich, who was a good guy.

As a very dumb lieutenant, I thought Mike was in little danger. I learned that day that the VC were willing and able to shoot back although I had seen tracers miss the helicopter before. They were hardly defenseless: they had a .51 caliber machine gun. Mike got the million-dollar wound: bad enough to be medevaced to Japan but not serious enough to incapacitate him for life. He got credit for a full tour of duty after five days in Vietnam. Years later, I understood Sen. John Kerry's shortened Vietnam tour. Everyone knew that three Purple Hearts was a ticket home on a Freedom Bird, as the big passenger airliners with the comely stewardesses who took us to and from war were called. Those dishonorable bastards who swift-boated Kerry during the 2004 presidential campaign have a warm place in hell waiting for them.

I do remember the instantaneous eruption of blood all across the windshield of the helicopter. And then O'Donnell miraculously put the helicopter into auto-rotation and brought it down to the soft rice paddy below and saved the rest of us from dying. After we hit the ground, there was an eerie silence for a few minutes. We must have been out of range of the VC in their bunkers, and the choppers coming to our rescue were minutes away. We were in a desolate place that should have been flush with rice ready for harvest. The war had made it more like a fetid swamp, but the smell of the rice paddies was not overpowering. Later that night when I got back to the Advisory Team 56 Team House, I realized that my boots were coated with thick coagulated blood. I've never forgotten that smell.

We were flying at about 100 feet when we were hit, having descended so that the door gunners with their M-60 machine guns could open up on the VC who were hidden in bunkers on the ground. At such a low altitude, I realized that we had interrupted the VC in the midst of harvesting rice from irregularly-shaped patches of rice paddy, not readily visible from 1500 feet. I saw all kinds of bowls and harvesting equipment on the ground. I was in the process (between quips about Inwood's bars) of calling for an airstrike when we were shot down. (I now realize how such a strike would have been quite useless, even counterproductive: the VC were well-protected in their bunkers built along the canal banks. I was following the brainless American SOP of blowing holes in rice paddies with 500-pound bombs and then thinking we were putting a hurt on the VC.) Clearly there was a detachment of VC of some size, perhaps a platoon (30–40 men) but at least a squad (8–12 men), on the ground. Inwood seemed a long way off—back in "the World" as GIs would say.

We had been diverted to this area by Steve Black, our L-19 Bird Dog pilot, who had found the VC on the ground. His principal mission in Phong Dinh Province was aerial reconnaissance, but he was also adept at using the eight rockets on his wings to kill many VC all on his own. If memory serves me correctly, he reported killing about 100 VC while operating in Phong Dinh for a year. There was an acronym for this—KBA or Killed By Air—that distinguished the claim from KIA or Killed In Action. The distinction recognizes that killing by air is harder to verify than killing on the ground by infantry soldiers who might actually check out the dead bodies. (It helps to remember that this was McNamara's war—the war of body counts—so there were novel ways of counting bodies.)

We were operating in an area of open rice paddies, just south of Phung Hiep District Town. The area was decidedly controlled by the VC. It was easy to look at the ground in the Mekong Delta and decide who was winning in any particular area. Where the rice paddies were farmed in a methodical, rectilinear fashion, the South Vietnamese government was in control (during the daytime, at least). Where the paddies were either not farmed or were farmed in irregular patches, we concluded that the Central Office for South Vietnam or COSVN was in charge. President Nixon made the acronym well-known when he launched a raid into Cambodia a few months later, on April 30, 1970—exactly five years to the day before the Communists captured Saigon and ended the war. In May of 1970, Kent State and Jackson State erupted back home. We called the Cambodian invasion the Great Heist, since the 21st ARVN Division came back on the motor bikes they confiscated when they "attacked" in the Seven Mountains area. The VC had good intelligence and were long gone, leaving behind muddy and old weapons caches. I don't know where the motorbikes came from although it's a good guess that the victims of the thefts were not inclined to support the GVN.

A month after the Cambodian invasion started, Nixon rounded up eleven senators, congressmen, and governors—all hawks but one—to report on the Cambodian extravaganza. When the President's Committee came to Can Tho on June 6, 1970, I wrote to my Congressman, William Fitts Ryan, on June 12th to tell him about how the members of the committee had failed to connect the invasion with suppressing the activities of local guerrillas. The committee pressed a former VC leader to admit that he had received his training, arms, and munitions from Cambodia; members even tried to trace his birth to Cambodia—to no avail: he was born and trained in a local village. I told Ryan, "Our fine senators and congressmen on the committee don't seem to realize the verity that an insurgency movement can only exist with the support or at least the acquiescence of the indigenous populace." Henry Kamm, writing in the *New York Times* on June 7, reported that "Maj. Gen. Hal D. McCown, commanding general of the Delta Military Assistance Command ... repeatedly expressed a conviction that the Cambodian operations have turned the tide in the allies' favor." Tides, of course, go out ... and come in.

Eating Jelly Donuts

When we crashed, I panicked and told PFC Bob Apfel, the door gunner, that I didn't know what to do. He just stared at me. Our only choice was obvious: set up the M-60 and be ready to shoot if the VC attacked us. Otherwise, all we could do is hope that another chopper would come to our rescue sooner rather than later. It was getting dark, and, fortunately, we weren't on the ground long. Steve Black continued to orbit overhead in his L-19 despite a critical fuel shortage: he won the Distinguished Flying Cross for this incident. He risked his life to rescue us. When his crew chief turned his plane on the next day, the engine sputtered and conked out before he could re-fuel it. A Medevac helicopter, Dustoff 80, landed shortly thereafter, and two more gunships arrived to pound the area nearby that Black told them was the likely location of the VC. I remember how amazing it was to be on the ground when rockets were going off only about 25 meters from our location. The brain corpuscles are re-arranged; the stomach tightens; the heart beats like Bedlam. I can't imagine being on the ground in a bunker when the B-52s let loose, but lots of VC knew exactly what that felt like. We ran to the chopper, carrying Murria and Thurston. When the chopper took off, I remember a moment of panic as the pilots, Chief Warrant Officer 2 Richard George and Warrant Officer 1 Harry Steele, flew just above the treetops—a maneuver, I later realized, designed to make ground fire difficult. Then suddenly the chopper went up, and we flew to the 29th Evacuation Hospital at Binh Thuy Air Base.

At Binh Thuy I discovered that my fatigue pants were ripped from my butt right down my left leg. There was a six-inch cut on my left knee—a superficial wound. A Protestant chaplain visited us in the emergency room. Mike Murria was lying on a stretcher with a bullet in his leg. I had seen the guys from the morgue take Peter Thurston away. The chaplain approached me cautiously and asked if I wanted to talk about God. I wanted to slug him. He seemed to be blessing what had just happened. He wisely left me to my thoughts, saying, "Incidents like this usually make guys want to talk about God." A year later I recalled his behavior when the radio station in Brookings, South Dakota, would broadcast news of a fire alarm sounding. The special report was sponsored by the local insurance company. The Chaplain was selling insurance for losses; we needed prevention of losses.

Medical personnel bandaged the cut, and someone took my name, rank, serial number, and unit. A few weeks later I found out that I was awarded the Purple Heart for this cut. It has served me well over the years: I got extra points on the letter carrier's exam when, for a time after I returned, I didn't know what to do and certainly didn't want to sell insurance. So I worked as a letter carrier in a number of post offices in Manhattan and read the messages ("Having a great time. Wish you were here.") on post cards at 2 a.m. when I was bored out of my mind while sorting endless piles of mail and conversation with co-workers was impossible because of the continual groaning of conveyor belts.

Steve Black has remained in my consciousness. He went home a few months before I did. As he was leaving, he told me that he wanted to stay in touch because he wanted his kids to know me. There was something really sensitive about that goodbye although we both knew that further contact was unlikely. But life has a way of keeping us entangled: Steve Black turned up in 1993 as the attorney for Katherine Anne Power, a '60s radical who had been on the lam since eluding capture following a bank robbery in which a Boston police officer, Walter Schroeder, Sr., was killed. I was watching the *Today Show* on NBC as I was knotting my tie on September 16, 1993, and recognized with shock that Steve Black was staring out at me. Black, it seems, had befriended Power because he was plagued by memories of and guilt about his involvement in the killing of so many VC in 1969–70 in Phong Dinh Province. Black and Power had engaged in a mock trial of Black for his war crimes. Power served as Black's defense attorney and argued that Black was following orders. Black was found innocent by the standards of the time of the war but guilty by the standards of the 1990s. (I hadn't noticed our moral progress—especially when we started a war with Iraq in 2003.) Black subsequently succeeded in negotiating Power's surrender to the authorities in 1993 when I saw him on the *Today Show*. I ran to the telephone and called Bob Burns in Brookings, South Dakota, to tell him to tune in.

Somehow Black's staged mock trial and his dramatic appearance on television—his fifteen minutes of fame in the Power case—make me worry about a possible need for public contrition—almost as if Americans need those television moments even to feel as if they are doing some remotely real kind of action. The reality TV fad springs to mind—a kind of fake, safe devouring of danger—a public appetite that never seems satiated.

Americans also gorge themselves on extra helpings of television police procedurals like *CSI* and *Law and Order*. More so than other such shows, *Law and Order*'s popularity from 1990 to 2010 lay in its formulaic plot development; each episode follows a predictable movement of events: most often the show ends with a court room verdict with the focus usually on Sam Waterston, who plays Jack McCoy, the assistant District Attorney. Our pleasure arises, amid often quirky crimes, from the recognition of the familiar, on which the show depends. The show entertains us for an hour, but we are not enlightened because we simply affirm what we thought we knew before we watched the show. We like our favorite chocolate pudding, and *Law and Order* dishes it up in homogenized, tummy-filling quantities.

At war we seemed to be trying to be actors in a very contrived television drama. All units changed the call signs on our radio net once a month; now it strikes me as the *dramatis personae* in the playbill for the television show in which we were appearing. I have to think that the dramaturge who made up the call signs was a joker. I remember particularly that one month I was "Darby Gallows One-Five-Alpha." I guess the call sign was intended to make me into some kind of agent of doom. I felt more like "Scaredy Cat One-Five-Alpha," but I guess that handle would not have been very becoming for the Assistant S-2 Advisor. I was also "Peptic Riser One-five-alpha" in another month; "Bourbon Bucket One-Two-Alpha" during a third month. The first sounds like an upset stomach ready to regurgitate; the second sounds almost like a call sign for an alcoholic. I guess there was no literary realism in call sign creativity although "Darby Gallows" would work well in a segment of *Generation Kill*. "Darby Gallows" mixes British horse racing with hanging, so I felt we needed an editor in the call sign shop.

If we needed an editor, we didn't lack set designers. Helicopter crews used to paint their olive drab helicopters with various fierce images and words. These could be as ghoulish as the "Darby Gallows" call sign. Cobra gunship crews seemed to be fond of painting the nose of their choppers with barracuda teeth, and I guess the 20mm mini-guns mounted on the front end of the chopper could chew up targets like a barracuda could tear up its prey with its teeth. The mini-guns could fire 750 rounds of 7.62 mm NATO ammo per minute. So I wonder whether the cobra should not have been named the barracuda, especially since the VC fought much like the mongoose. As I was leaving, a new captain was assigned as the S-2 advisor. I was skeptical about the joy he took in painting "S-2" and lightning bolts on the new headset we used on the helicopters.

So maybe our war strategy was a crude attempt to create a well-made play with a pre-determined pattern for events. Fortunately, life and war lack such clear cut narrative arcs; we'd eventually bore ourselves silly. Still we keep trying to force our ordinary experiences into such molds: we're fooling ourselves by the illusion of control. Recognition of the familiar offers a comfort similar to eating powdered jelly donuts.

The Smell of Pink Plexiglass

When I went down in the helicopter on February 23, 1970, the incident was the worst moment of my year in Vietnam, but it has never felt like any kind of denouement. Over the years since, an occasional whiff of propane or of wet rags has smelled vaguely like the congealed thick blood that coated my boots, and I do flashback to the moment I heard the sound of bullets snapping through the helicopter's Plexiglas cockpit. I also recall the instant eruption of blood that turned the Plexiglass an odd tint of pink. My nose still twitches when I remember the noisome smell of the decayed vegetation along the canal in that VC-controlled area. But the memories do not convey any ability to offer a glimmer of insight into current realities. I have no words of wisdom garnered from a close encounter with a .51 caliber machine gun. The memories are, nevertheless, so strong that I have no sense of their pastness. Nothing had prepared me for the shock of being within arm's distance of a man being shot through the head. And, *deo gratias*, I did not repeat the experience although I did see other dead and wounded up close in Vietnam. The one-time experience lasts a lifetime: it never ends.

The next day the old Vietnamese woman who shined our boots cleaned mine up for me. She was visibly upset when she saw me the next afternoon. She knew that something bad had happened. She spoke with great intensity and anxiety. My ten words of Vietnamese did not enable me to understand what she was saying specifically although she was talking about my boots and gesticulating toward them. I have wondered what she did when she went home that night. Did she tell her husband or other family members? Was she repulsed by having to clean up the boots? Should I have washed them off? (It never occurred to me that I should have, and I should have. She did not need to see the thick, coagulated blood, much less clean it off the boots.)

The sun had come up that next morning; the world did not stop. And Advisory Team 56 seemed not to notice what had happened on the previous evening. Team 56 lacked the intense brotherhood of the infantry platoon Sebastian Junger has described in great detail in *War*, an account of his year (2008–9) in the Korengal Valley with an army platoon during the Afghanistan war. Junger shows the intimate depth of caring of these latter day soldiers for one another:

they could tell by the smell of a buddy's urine whether he was hydrating properly. Drinking enough water was not just a personal matter: the consequence for the whole group of a guy who might pass out from heat stroke was unacceptable. Junger came to cherish a world in which even the smallest detail had consequence. He discovered how little we think about (or have reverence for) others in so-called normal civilian life. Amidst very dangerous conditions, Junger sees value in the soldiers' politically and strategically pointless service and concludes: "...I sometimes caught myself feeling bad that there wasn't an endeavor of equivalent magnitude in my own life."[56]

On Team 56 we had almost civilian relationships with one another. We cared for one another, but only with the generalized compassion of a not-so-close neighbor or a college roommate who shares a story of death or accident or illness. There could be no Team 56 St. Crispin's Day speech for "We few, we happy few, we band of brothers...." When I went down in the helicopter, I was surprised but moved by Steve Black's willingness to die for me and the other guys trapped on the ground in close proximity to the VC.

But when I got back to the Team House, no one actually knew what had happened. Such was our war and maybe every man's war: it's hard to generalize about the war because everyone is focused on the narrow business at his hand. It's hard to have an overall perspective or the holistic view that I'm attempting to give in this memoir. Bob Burns was away, so I didn't have him to talk to. My roommate, Ben Nelson, was very solicitous; he asked the mess sergeant to make me a turkey sandwich because I had missed dinner, and then we talked at great length. Still I don't think anyone inhaled the smell of my blood-soaked boots—even vicariously. Major Troy Milbank, a District Senior Advisor, told me on the weekend after the helicopter shoot-down that I really showed him something when I went right back out the next day, but I had asked for a day off. Bob Burns confirms that he took on the flying of Phantom Twilight for a while until my brain settled down. He was away for a week, so there was no one to replace me for the next few days. I had to go back up on February 24, 25, and 26. I remember Major Troy Yarbrough, in the most kindly words, telling me in the late afternoon of February 24 that they're calling from the airfield. Yarbrough was a great guy, who drank with the junior officers every night. He seemed to be in early middle-age with an unmilitary paunch and a propensity to need a shave by 5:00 p.m. every day. I knew he didn't want to send me, but he didn't have to complete the thought. I just grabbed my rifle, my bandolier, and headset and went. There were no other captains or lieutenants around, so I had to go.

My Vietnamese counterpart, Vo Thanh Do, also didn't want to go. He was a terrific guy, a philosophy major at Saigon University, a most subtle and gentle man. On the way back from the airfield in the jeep after the shoot-down, he had said, "I guess we need to make haste slowly." He knew it was a cliché, and he knew also that there was a time when a cliché actually had meaning. He went back out with me the next day too. I wonder if a Vietnamese major told him he was a tough guy too. After the war he spent seven years in a re-education camp— probably because he was an honest man.

When I think about how profoundly the helicopter crash affected my later life, I wonder about how the other guys on the helicopter coped with it. Since Mike O'Donnell apparently does not remember the details, I wonder if it was even a blip on his radar. Maybe he had other more horrific experiences as a pilot. (How much worse can it get than having your co-pilot shot through the head?)

There were moments in subsequent years, usually while driving or upon waking from a bad dream in the middle of the night, when I rode the helicopter down once again. I guess I worry that I should not admit to a history of flash-backs. I worry, too, that I'm really a coward who has not handled a bad scene with sufficient aplomb. Do other men feel the way I do? Is the unwillingness to talk about bad situations a residue of some macho ethic? I thought I was beyond all that, but maybe I'm not. Maybe the other guys are not too. And does that mean that they, too, have been haunted by that sickening feeling of helplessness as the helicopter plummeted to earth, right after we heard the snaps of the bullets hitting the Plexiglas and the fuselage of the Huey?

I remember driving on an Interstate somewhere in the Midwest in the summer of 1971. I was in the right hand lane, and I was feeling that awful stress of the chopper going down. At that very moment of recollection, a car passed me in the left hand lane. A young guy leaned out of the back window of the car, stuck out a broom handle, mimicked a rifle, and made as if he were shooting me. It was timed perfectly. I wasn't looking at the car but saw the broom handle come out at the last instant. I recoiled from his "shot." The young guys roared with laughter as they sped off down the road. They had "gotten me." It was like a scene from John Ford's *Wagon Train*.

As I drove on, I laughed at myself, and the strange result was that I was somewhat cured of my daymares after that. At least their frequency greatly diminished. My pal from Brookings, South Dakota, Jay Jackson, says he remembers that I had told him that I felt paralyzed behind the wheel of my blue Datsun. Feeling out of control while operating a car can bring on white knuckles and vivid memories. I wasn't the pilot of the chopper, but I am the pilot of my car. So the feeling of helplessness comes when I think I cannot control the car.

And then there was the harrowing night in Danbury Hospital in January 2006 following the December auto accident. The flashback came while I was dosed with pain killers, and it came at 2:00 a.m. Although I was really in the Intensive Care Unit, I slipped into the chopper before I even realized what was going on, and then the auto accident meshed with the helicopter shoot-down. I have no flashbacks about the auto accident and can deal with it dispassionately. I drive through the intersection where it happened every day when I go to work. There's no hint of trauma associated with the location for me although I do think about the crash a fair number of times per month when I go through the intersection. But I can't characterize that specific memory as traumatic. The terror of December 27, 2005, has melded with the terror of February 23, 1970.

Courage? No Choice

My voice quavered on the radio after we took off that next evening—February 24, 1970, and I called in the grid coordinates cleared for shooting by the gunships. Major Milbank had heard my voice on the radio, so he knew it was me. I tightened my seat belt extra tight. Somehow I thought I might slide out of the chopper on one of its orbits around the area in which the gunships were firing.

I developed "cred" for going out the next day. I was a tough guy. Huh? I did learn thereafter to use the black first lieutenant's bar on my collar to tell the warrant officer pilots that mission rules said we were to circle at 1,500 feet. Shooting an M-60 machine gun at 100 feet is needlessly risky—at least in the wide open rice paddies of the Mekong Delta. VC dug into bunkers along the canal banks could take their time and wait to get our lumbering helicopter in their sights. Meanwhile at most we were shooting at unseen targets. Shooting at hootches along the canals seemed like little more than a lark for the door gunners. The machine guns jammed too damn often anyhow. I often wondered about the obvious rust on the M-60s on the barrels. Too often the door gunners would get off three or four rounds, and the M-60 would jam.

One day when we had descended to shoot at a canal bank, a pig ran out of a hootch. The door gunner was ticked at me when I said let's go home and let the VC pig live. I like to think the pig was a refugee from George Orwell's *Animal Farm*, and my sparing his life proved that he was "more equal than other pigs."

And then there was the day that the American guards on the Can Tho Air Field discovered what they thought was a VC booby trap inside the concertina wire on the perimeter just off the runway. Concertina wire is a particularly pernicious kind of barbed or razor wire that, combined with strung barbed wire, should have presented great difficulty for any intruder. The area outside the runway was cleared for about 100 meters and strung with the concertina wire. We received an anxious call from the air field security people. They found an artist to draw a picture of the "booby trap" and asked that we show it to the Vietnamese S-2 people so as to identify what kind of device it was. Well, when we showed it to the Vietnamese, they burst into laughter. Vo Thanh

Do explained to me that the "booby trap" was actually a rat trap, designed to capture a live rat for dinner. So I guess the "VC infiltrators" had decided that the best hunting grounds for rats was just off the perimeter, inside the wire, in full view of the American guards stationed in bunkers and no doubt catching a lot of sleep every night. Clearly the locals didn't think much of American security since they obviously were planning to come back periodically to check the trap. I'm not sure how many rats were captured, but any American who might have been inclined to disparage the Vietnamese RF and PF soldiers would have done well to think about our own laxness.

I now have some idea of what old-timer soldiers mean by "this chicken shit outfit." They have a certain contempt for the play-acting that goes on when life and death are not at stake—and this could be true in Can Tho, the capitol city of the Mekong Delta (and much more so in Saigon). Americans could create a feeling that we were insulated from the war when we were at the air field or in the Team House. We felt entitled to watch a movie like *Patton* or *M*A*S*H* every night and drink Schlitz beer sold at 10 cents per can. The old timers know better; they prefer real war to the fake war. They're always asking, "How can I get out of this chicken-shit outfit?" There is something really contemptible about watching movies and drinking beer while all around us the Vietnamese were suffering from our elephantine, clumsy, careless destruction of their country. Ironically, Colonel Conger had made it a goal in 1968 to create a team house for the Province advisors and to separate us from Team 96, which was the IV Corps advisory team in Can Tho. Conger, a 6'1" ruddy-faced, crew-cut, soft-spoken, business-like leader, did not engage in much small talk even on social occasions. He did feel the need to build unit cohesiveness, but he wasn't running an infantry company. We developed the camaraderie that might be found on a not-so-serious, weekend sports team.

The Calendar and Sex

So, like Vladimir and Estragon in Samuel Beckett's *Waiting for Godot*, I spent my year in Vietnam in a chicken outfit—waiting endlessly for something to happen. I only wanted to get back on the plane and go home. I entered a war already in progress for years if I can use "progress" to describe running in place. The war had no positive or negative momentum for me or anyone else: it was all about the waiting. Winning was never a goal. GIs talked incessantly about how "short" they were, i.e., how close they were to their DEROS (Date Eligible for Return from OverSeas). Everyone had a different DEROS, so everyone's war was waited out in isolation. When I finally left on October 27, 1970, no one else from Team 56 left with me. I finally was so short that I was gone— the great disappearing act of time served in Vietnam.

In his military history interview in late March 1969 Captain Gary Hoebeke, who was then the adjutant or administrative officer of Team 56, complained at great length about the military inefficiency of the one-year tour. The length of the tour and the lack of unit integrity has been the subject of much post–Vietnam criticism of the American military. In line infantry units morale problems resulted from the resentment of the "short" grunts for the "newbies" or "cherries." The seasoned grunts thought the newbies would get them killed just as they were about to get a ticket on a Freedom Bird. Unit cohesiveness was almost impossible when grunts were cycled through units like parts on the Ford Motor Company assembly line that McNamara once oversaw. Hoebeke stated that this system was a particularly bad way to run an advisory team. An advisor spends a year building up a relationship with his Vietnamese counterparts, who know that he's going to leave after a year. The date stamp on each advisor undermines the relationship. You can imagine the Vietnamese counterpart's thinking: "Why mind the advice of a guy who's going home in six months or three months or two weeks? I'm never short." Hoebeke suggested a minimum two-year tour for an advisor, or, at least, a rotation that would bring a career officer back to the same unit after six months in the States.[57] Even when career officers were on second or third one-year tours of Vietnam, they were not sent back to the units they served with on previous tours. There is something hideously wrong about the mechanistic thinking that underlay this

116

rotation of bodies through the military machine. It's actually easy to see why the advisory effort could not work because there is no respect for human nature or individuality in the system.

Mostly we waited for the calendar to move—day-by-day, week-by-week. There was some distinction between the weekends and the weekdays: we used to be off on most Saturday afternoons and all day on Sunday, unless our turn on the duty roster for regular missions or duties denied us late sleep on Sunday morning. So, occasionally, on a Saturday or a Sunday, I served as the duty officer in the TOC or I went out flying as the "backseat advisor" on missions labeled Firefly, Phantom III, or Phantom Twilight. Otherwise I drank beer and joked with my fellow junior officers—lieutenants and captains. We were locked in an eternal present. DEROS seemed impossible—even when it was a month away.

So life was odd: there were no women to associate with, so the "normal," boy-chases-girl narrative of young, single guys did not structure our days. Sure, we saw plenty of very attractive Vietnamese women in Can Tho, but we did not associate with them. And the junior officers I associated with, to my knowledge, did not frequent the downtown brothels. There was one captain who was a dandy; he fancied himself a great lover although my guess is that he was paying for sex. I remember hearing a story about his swimming naked with a Vietnamese woman in the pool at Palm Springs—the posh compound for CORDS employees, mostly American civilians. Palm Springs looked like it could have been located in Palm Springs, California. As I recollect, it was a walled compound with a guard station in front and separate small bungalow type buildings with the pool in the center. A contemporary real estate agent would describe it as "a gated community with a 24-hour concierge." Apparently the captain was cavorting in the pool with the woman and didn't expect any of the VIPs to show up. They did, but the captain was not abashed: he and the woman simply dressed, giggling all the while, and left before the shocked VIPs could react.

Palm Springs was also one of the locations of the many trysts of John Paul Vann—the central figure in the American War in Vietnam according to Neil Sheehan's *A Bright Shining Lie*. Sheehan makes the case that the biography of Vann is also the quintessential history of the war. Vann was a master of deception, but for a long time he was the most clear-sighted critic of the American strategy in the war. Vann saw the foolhardiness of General William C. Westmoreland's big battle showdown strategy. Vann, among others, advocated the counterinsurgency small-unit strategy that some think General David Petraeus invented in Mosul, Iraq, in 2004. During 1969–1970 Vann was the number two American in the Mekong Delta. Rumors abounded about his behavior. I heard that there were wild parties at Palm Springs. I also was aware that Vann was given to flying around in his Light Observation Helicopter (LOH) in the late afternoon. Rumor had it that he was also given to firing off M-79 grenades without asking for permission to shoot and without making a report of his activities. I did see him once when I was out with Phantom Twilight: he was flying at low altitude over contested paddies at dusk and just hopping along— it seemed.

I briefed him about the intelligence situation in Phong Dinh on at least two occasions. On the second he was in company with Sir Robert Thompson—a British guerrilla war expert who listened carefully to my briefing and then asked an intelligent question. I can't remember the question exactly, but I was struck that in a year in Vietnam I had just been asked the most intelligent question by a guy who had never been to Phong Dinh before. I do remember that he was asking about what motivated the VC. I had the feeling that Vann wanted to interrupt my answer to Thompson, but I suspect that he liked what I was saying—whatever it might have been.

It's hard to think about Vann and about the dandy captain on Team 56 since they are both dead now, but the issue of sexual promiscuity does bother me now and did then too. It was disgusting to use Vietnamese women for one's pleasure and then dump them when it came time to go home. I remember another captain—a graduate of a Jesuit college, by the way—who apparently maintained a relationship with a Vietnamese woman for most of his year, and then one day he went home without telling her. She showed up at the Team House with her mother, irate about being duped into thinking he would marry her and take her back to the land of the Big PX [Post Exchange]. (I wonder if the Big Box stores like Costco and Home Depot owe their origins to the concept of the Big PX.) And then there was the bigamist sergeant who had a Vietnamese family and an American family back home. War makes it possible for the soldier in the Big Army to take advantage of women in ways that would be more difficult back home.

I write now with a decidedly pro-feminist view of the world. I hardly thought about the subject prior to 1968. But it's important to note that the military that was firing shells willy-nilly into Phong Dinh Province was fueled by PXs in which the best-selling magazine was *Playboy*. I can remember thinking that my Irish Catholic background, despite its prudishness, had also taught me that sexual drives can and must be controlled, that sexual abstinence is not impossible.

I remember clearly how eye-opening it was to read Sheehan's book soon after it appeared in 1988. His use of John Paul Vann as the part that explains the whole seemed then and still seems to be a wholly reliable guide to the Vietnam War. The sexual promiscuity of Vann speaks to self-indulgence escalated to a perverted view of the world. I used to see Vann fairly regularly in 1969–70 as he frequently ate in our mess hall. But he was ubiquitous: he would pop up in all kinds of unexpected places. I might see him at CORDS headquarters, which I had to visit for one reason or another on occasion or I might see him in a Land Rover. He had an intense look in his eyes and did not smile when he returned my greetings. He was a man in a hurry.

I had no idea that his hurry was dominated by his desire to have sex at a rate that I've since associated with Wilt Chamberlain, who is said to have slept with 20,000 women. Sheehan traces Vann's sex life thoroughly: even on the day he died, he apparently had already had sex three times with three different women. Sheehan presents Vann as a transitional figure, but one who ultimately sold out to the power elites of the World War II generation. Sheehan reveals how the proclivities of the big power womanizers had distorted national priorities. And I think he made a great case: the trouble is that we seem to have learned little from Sheehan's work. Despite all the apparent advances of women in our society, we still managed to lionize the womanizer General Petraeus, and we put a womanizer in the White House. And there is no permanent stigma to being revealed as a womanizer. It almost adds an aura of sexiness that is hard to fathom.

Vietnam was certainly ravished by American power, and we seem to be clueless about how powerful we actually are. When we sneeze, it matters in Borneo. Misogyny is at the root of the troubles in *The Deer Hunter*; Neil Sheehan was right to foreground it in his depiction of the most pivotal American figure in the Vietnam War. It was literally "Vann's war." And Vann was a statutory rapist in the United States and an abuser of all of the women in his life. That personal life cannot be separated from the whole life. That's just a postmodern lie of fragmentation: the private Vann and the public Vann cannot be separated. Sheehan shows persuasively that Vann became an advocate of counter-insurgency when his personal life wrecked his military career. Being a maverick sexually was akin to being a military maverick. And, then, once he recovered his stature sufficiently to become the most important American in Vietnam, Vann resumed his career in the "big battle" mode. Guys who use women feel powerful even though it is women who know that they are not the studs that they like to pretend to be.

I got sick of talking to guys all the time. There was not one woman on Advisory Team 56. Something was unnatural and wrong about our lives. This occasional revulsion was not about sex: I simply wanted to talk to a woman, have an intellectual discussion with her about, oh, let's say, the war in Vietnam. I was definitely not suited for William C. Westmoreland's army, even though he had departed the scene by the time I arrived in country.

The calendar did move, and eventually guys went home and disappeared into America. The war seemed not to move at all. The VC staged high points once a month, i.e., they attacked several outposts on the same night, often a moonless night, just to let everyone know that they were still out there. Outposts were small fortified, permanent "forts," usually located on key intersections of canals. The RF and PF troops inside the outposts were supposed to patrol the areas in the vicinity of their locations. Most of the time they simply walked down the canal and then walked back, avoiding contact with the VC. These operations were foolish: the VC knew the routine and booby-trapped the canal banks. Major Philip Kim in his March 1969 military history interview explained the foolishness. The RF troops were "taking casualties from mines and booby traps" without ever seeing the VC. The patrols were "demoralizing" the troops. There were "very few casualties from sniper fire."[58] The VC could fight the war without ever having to attack their opposition frontally.

Yet the number of armed friendlies was ten times larger than the most generous estimates of VC manpower. I remember that we calculated that we could line up all the allegedly friendly forces in the province and stomp all the VC to death, but nothing so logical was ever devised. Instead virtually identical months followed one another. Oh, yes, we created narratives of progress toward pacification, but we knew that we were marking time, slouching in place.

Careerism

We junior officers watched the behavior of the field grade officers—majors, lieutenant colonels, and colonels—with some bemusement: we realized that they wanted to make rank as they had made the army into a career, which is a narrative of sorts. Such a narrative could not culminate with an end to the war: how else would they make rank? There was a conflict in narratives in all this: the World War II concepts of victory—the occupation of Berlin or the signing of the surrender on the battleship Missouri—were the templates for the victory narrative. The career narrative actually fit with the American War in Vietnam: the war sort of petered out, and the West Point ring-knockers and other pretenders made rank.

Occasionally there would be ominous chatter about a RIF, or Reduction In Forces, if the war ever wound down. I remember a major (not a member of the West Point Protective Association) telling me that there was a special tab on his 201 (Personnel) file: he said he was told at the Pentagon that he was to be retained if ever there was a RIF. He was clearly proud to have the antidote to RIFfing. I just absorbed the major's teleological view—more small talk in the eternal year in Vietnam. It was hard to imagine a year—or "short, unaccompanied tour" as the Army termed it—in suspended animation as a "career component." The word "tour" suggests the language of tourism, and I guess we were getting to see a strange and beautiful part of the world that we were also cratering with 500-pound bombs. Or as Private Joker says near the end of Stanley Kubrick's *Full Metal Jacket*: 'I wanted to see exotic Vietnam ... the crown jewel of Southeast Asia. I wanted to meet interesting and stimulating people of an ancient culture ... and kill them. I wanted to be the first kid on my block to get a confirmed kill!"[59]

Careerism was not just an officers' fixation: career NCOs were also on the lookout for points for promotion. The army grants points toward promotion for decorations for valor and for service, so a motivated NCO is keen to collect as many decorations as possible: they count toward promotion. Such a system lends itself to corruption because it puts a monetary value on valor. Or, the mere appearance of valor. (There were rumors of scandalous buying and selling of awards.) While I personally didn't give a damn about military decorations, the interest of the career NCOs in garnering as many ribbons as possible was very high. I went home without wearing any ribbons, and I could have had three rows of ribbons. (I am not above listing my decorations on my curriculum vitae when it suits my purposes.) While the helicopter crash was harrowing, I certainly deserved an award for stupidity—especially for bringing Mike Murria with us as a combat tourist. The citation for the Vietnamese Cross of Gallantry that I received following the helicopter crash is spun from the fabric of the inflated claims needed to process the paperwork:

> 1LT Edward A. Hagan distinguished himself in the operation conducted by Phong Dinh Sector 13 kilometers Southwest of Phung Hiep Subsector, Phong Dinh Province, RVN, on 23 February 1970. Although the enemy power was strong, he patiently coordinated with the operational force in the attack at the enemy positions and the killing of 20 Viet Cong on the spot. Many other Viet Cong were wounded and carried away by their comrades. Important equipment and documents were captured.[60]

Almost none of the statement is true. To start with, describing the operation as an action of Phong Dinh Sector suggests that the friendly Vietnamese were heavily involved in the action. The action was initiated by Steve Black who spotted the VC on the ground and diverted Phantom Twilight with its Cobra gunships to the area. Only one Vietnamese soldier, my counterpart in the back-seat of the Command and Control helicopter, was involved in the action. There were no friendly ground troops in the area, so it would have been impossible to claim 20 VC KIA, much less to pick up equipment and documents. Yet the citation also states that I was an "Outstanding officer with rich experience in combat who has always shown the highest devotion to the service." At the time I had been in country four months. "Rich experience in combat"? I don't think so.

But the Vietnamese had learned from the Americans how to write citations so as to insure that the award would be granted. The Vietnamese read us quite correctly: they knew that Americans wanted to go home with ribbons on their chests, and they knew that they had to make the report sound like the American involvement in combat was part of a Vietnamese action. So the lies make perfect sense: They were necessary so as to give me the award. The Vietnamese also wanted to give me an Honor medal when I was going home, but I politely declined and the matter was dropped. This is a cheap claim to a good conscience.

Ben Nelson, one of my roommates at the Team House, was a Notre Dame-trained architect, who actually drew up architectural drawings for marketplace structures in a few villages. Two of them were built—a remarkable feat since such projects often ran afoul of corrupt practices: Building materials would simply go missing. Ben was about 5'10", thin, with reddish hair and glasses; he was given to shrewd but low-key comments. Mostly he was involved in "good works" projects, so it is kind of amazing that such projects faced such difficulties. But there was a culture of deception in all our advisory activities that was consistent with honoring me for stuff I hadn't actually done (although I had surely been in a position to die, but that's no reason to cite me for gallantry). I can remember Ben offering appropriate sardonic remarks about my tom-fool "bravery."

Much has been written since about the avalanche of ribbons awarded since the Korean War. Colonel David Hackworth, in particular, has written much about this inflation of awards, most notably his query into the display of "V" for valor devices on some of Chief of Naval Operations Jeremy Boorda's decorations. Boorda did not come under enemy fire as required for wearing the "V" device. Hackworth's inquiries seem to have led Boorda to commit suicide on May 16, 1996. Hackworth made a career out of writing about how bureaucratic niceties had led to "perfumed princes" in the Pentagon who wouldn't know the sound of a bullet but could make life hell for real warriors.

This thinking has its parallels in civilian life: in the world of education people making decisions about curriculum are often far removed from the classroom and sometimes make two or three times as much money as classroom teachers. The world also treats college vice-presidents, school superintendents, and educational think-tank gurus as worthy of emulation. In my academic life since Vietnam I've noticed that administrators think professors want to grow up to be deans. Well, majors in the army assumed that lieutenants wanted to grow up to be majors too, if not, at least, like Private Joker, to get confirmed kills. We didn't share the majors' or Joker's ambitions: in this regard there wasn't much difference between us and draftees. We wanted to get out of the army as soon as possible. We had no goals for our service, except continued respiration, cheap beer, and a ticket home. While in Vietnam, I actually received a notice for jury duty in New York: I wrote to the New York County Clerk, Norman Goodman ("Dear Normie," I began), and said I was willing to serve but I needed a plane ticket and a note for my commanding officer. Norman, a neighbor in Inwood, never replied.

Goalless War

In April 1970, Colonel Van Hout became the Province Senior Advisor. The word was that a Province Senior Advisor assignment was a ticket to becoming a Brigadier General, and all West Pointers apparently had stars in their eyes. Very romantic, eh? Van Hout arrived, full of a bustle that seemed to lack a goal. He was the perfect guy to lead us in our goalless war. Van Hout exuded pointless exuberance that seemed to suggest that we needed to get going although as advisors we couldn't make much go that our Vietnamese counterparts didn't buy.

We kept repeating that we were making progress without any real evidence for it; like Estragon in Beckett's *Waiting for Godot*, we muttered "Nothing to be done" and then spent our year trying to do just that. And we were good at doing nothing: we could kill a lot of people but we couldn't win, so we tuned into the "ballgames" or canal-clearing operations every morning and evening, and then a year would be up for each of us, and one-by-one each of us went home alone, never again to see almost 100 percent of the guys we had spent a year with. And when we got home, hardly anyone noticed that we'd been away for a year, so maybe we had been in a Beckett play. Iraq and Afghanistan war veterans have been getting an empty "thank you" accompanied by studied ignorance by their fellow Americans of what they did in Iraq and Afghanistan. We got the ignorance without the "thank you." We've progressed from indifference to insincerity.

And Two Years Later...

"Ballgames" was the word used each morning by the night duty officer at his briefing when he announced the schedule of operations or "walks in the sun" for the day. Airmobile operations were called "K-bars"—named, it seems, after a popular U.S. Marine Corps knife. The officer also re-counted the incidents in the province the previous night. Usually there were a few reports of contact with the VC, a few people were KIA, a few were medevaced; then it was time to get some coffee and find out how the Yanks did last night. Baseball was a good metaphor for the American war in Vietnam: because there is no clock in baseball, a game can go on forever if the score is tied. And surely there was a deadlock in Phong Dinh Province in 1969–70. We could expect the ball scores reported at each morning and evening briefing to remain just about the same. The evening briefing included the daily intelligence briefing, and either Bob Burns or I would deliver the briefing. We could have used virtually the same briefing in October 1970 as we used in October 1969. The VC were sighted (or more accurately: were reported to have been sighted) in the same locations, with the same unit names and strengths, after a year of ballgames, gunship strikes, artillery barrages, and ground-shaking, paddy-puncturing, pre-planned and immediate air strikes.

I edited the Province Monthly report for ten months; each month's report listed the friendly and the enemy casualties. From December 1, 1969, to September 30, 1970, we reported that 1,432 VC had been killed—an average of 143 per month. VC unit strengths in the province were estimated, generously, at a total strength of about 2,000 men. The number of reported kills never seems to have diminished the estimated strengths of these units. And no one but Bob Burns seems to have asked the obvious question: how are the VC maintaining unit strength? Do they have a good pension plan? Do they offer R 'n' R in Moscow? Borscht with Brezhnev? Bob Burns did this analysis as he was leaving on July 25, 1970: to my knowledge he inspired no further curiosity.

The Intelligence Summary (INTSUM) for January 27 and 28, 1973, reported the same VC units, but they were involved in 58 contacts with RF, PF, and PSDF forces in two nights, so maybe the VC were winning as we pulled out.[61] They overran an outpost, fired at Firefly, posted VC flags, launched two, very hefty 122mm rockets at Can Tho City, and even forced villagers to march on a PF outpost. We had called 12 incidents on the night of November 6 & 7, 1969, a "high point" for the month. The Province Monthly Report for May 1970 suggests that our body counts were not an indication of success. The Report says: "...the friendly and enemy KIA totals were more closely comparable than they have been in many months, a considerable achievement for the VC when the overwhelming assets that are available to the friendly forces are considered."[62] Maybe there was a narrative arc to the war; it just wasn't the one that the Saigon storytellers were fabricating. Or American operations were so counterproductive that most of the country simply wanted us to go home and stop the killing, no matter who won.

Thuan Nhon and Phong Thuan Districts, along with Phung Hiep, had been VC strongholds in 1969–70, and both districts were led by corrupt officials whom the advisors openly criticized. Two years later, and many air strikes, artillery rounds, lazy ambushes, walks in the sun, noontime siestas, and lots of advisory effort later, the VC were still able to operate quite freely. On December 27, 1972, six VC were able to propagandize the people in Thuan Nhon, only 1,500 meters from the District Town.[63] The VC reportedly delivered a death sentence for one civilian: The VC Phoenix Program was working even when the Phong Dinh GVN program was languishing. The VC also distributed a leaflet in Phong Thuan on December 8, 1972. It sounds triumphal and reads:

> To: The Officers and Soldiers in the Saigon Army
> Peace will come to one people.
> The American defeatists are withdrawing to the United States. All of you should create victories to save the nation. Leave the enemy's rank to return to the people and your family. Do not follow operation orders. Do not endanger the people and do not kill the patriots.
> Do not let Americans and Thieu use your bones and your blood to prolong the war.
> [If] All of you do not hold the enemy's weapons, peace will come immediately.[64]

It would take a little more than another two years for the GVN to collapse, and it is hard to claim that the leaflet was just propaganda since the evidence was strong that the GVN had not succeeded in winning the people's allegiance or at least an allegiance that would inspire the people to resist the VC. The B-52 strikes just prior to the American pull-out in 1973 speak to the desperation of the GVN's position even in the model province of the Mekong Delta—Phong Dinh. In 1969–70 the result that would come on April 30, 1975, seemed remote but not impossible.

Central Intelligence

In the meantime we continued with our very elaborate charades. About every two weeks or so, usually after the morning briefing, two CIA agents, Lance Hopkins and Starr King, would stop by the S-2 office. They were "touching base with us." Hopkins was rather blasé; King was more business-like. Both wore civilian clothes because no one would suspect that two Caucasians carrying attaché cases and visiting the S-2 Advisors' office would be CIA agents. And those names: well, maybe they were actually Christened "Lance" and "Starr," but Bob Burns and I were skeptical.

I do remember that one day one of their agents had wound up in the local clink after some fracas in which he was—without a doubt—unfairly arrested. Hopkins, if I remember correctly, asked Bob to intercede with the Vietnamese S-2 to get their man out of jail. After all, we couldn't have all that brilliant super-spook work grind to a halt just because someone had drunk a little too much Ba-Muoi-Ba or Beer 33, the local Vietnamese brew. Bob must have done "the right thing" as New York cops are given to say about slightly illegal but correct actions. The agent was sprung quickly, and his status as an agent was not compromised. Ho-ho-ho.

We did suspect that there were many occasions on which ordinary criminal matters were papered over as VC incident reports. In his military history interview on March 27, 1969, Williams Saunders, then the advisor to the National Police in Phong Dinh, confirms this suspicion. Saunders had spent 15 years in the Newport Beach, California, Police Department before he joined Team 56 in Phong Dinh in 1967. Saunders was a soft-spoken but obviously shrewd guy. To illustrate his opinion that non-political criminal matters were frequently re-classified as VC attacks or sabotage by both the Vietnamese and the Americans, he told a story that he heard from a fellow police advisor from Newport Beach, who was assigned to a province in II Corps:

> They had a grenade thrown into a bar. 13 GIs in the bar got wounded, plus some other people. He [Saunders' friend] had been called on; new in country, he had been there about two weeks. He went down to the bar, did some talking, took an interpreter down there; talked to the Vietnamese, talked to what Americans he could that weren't taken off [medevaced]. And he found out that there was a

fight in the bar between an ARVN soldier and his girlfriend ... or a girl, we'll put it that way. He wanted to take her home to bed, and she said, "No. I'm going home with this G.I." If he took her home, it was either love or it was practically nothing. The G.I. was going to give her fifteen hundred piasters. She went home with him. He [the ARVN] got mad, went outside, got a grenade, and threw it in the bar.

OK, this man [Saunders' friend] filed his report that way. It went to Saigon. About the next day, or the day after that, there was some two-star general in Saigon, read the report: "What the hell are 13 G.I.s doing in a warehouse?"

About that time some little WAC [Women's Army Corps] says, "General, you better read it again."

"A whorehouse! What the hell are they doin' in there?"

So they sent a CID team up to re-investigate this because this all tumbled back down, you know. Friend of mine caught hell for sending a message out there— which was the truth. They spent two weeks investigating it, declared it a VC incident, and awarded 13 Purple Hearts.

That actually happened in II Corps.[65]

Saunders' story is instructive, whether or not the incident actually happened or happened as he reported it to the military historian. It illustrates Saunders' belief that criminality was easily transmuted into VC terrorism. Saunders hams up the report of the general's reaction. Since he has no direct knowledge of the general's reaction, he or his buddy invented a disconnected, foggy-headed general in Saigon. (How much tennis was the general playing?) And then we get the awards of the Purple Hearts when the matter was little more than a bar fight gone badly. Saunders obviously enjoyed the notion that the general was a buffoon.

Buttoned Up and
the Catholic Cabal

For the first few months of his tenure, Colonel Van Hout closed the top button of his fatigues despite the heat of Vietnam: an indication to us that there was a new regime in town. In retrospect, this button behavior sounds like some half-bright idea out of a management training course. Or perhaps he had participated in a West Point student-exchange program with Sandhurst, and the Brits had told him about how they had ruled the world with all their buttons buttoned. (Being Irish helps to imagine this possibility as very realistic.) Van Hout struck us as a buffoon. In April 1970, he succeeded Colonel Conger, who was a straightforward kind of leader—soft-spoken and not flamboyant in any way, Van Hout didn't need the button routine to make us realize that he was more than a bit absurd. We certainly never figured out what his goals were although we all believed that he wanted a star.

So we figured Van Hout's narrative was a template for his own personal advancement since he was drawing attention to himself as a consciously different kind of guy, perhaps even a bit narcissistic. After a while, most of us simply regarded him as ineffectual. He was not given to harassing us; as far as the S-2 shop went, he seemed uninterested. We briefed him every evening but received no directives or feedback from him. That was fine by most of the junior officers since we didn't want to do anything but go home.

But there was an incident on October 5, 1970, about three weeks before I went home that left me with a lasting distaste for Van Hout. We had a fund in the S-2 office for the payment of the Vietnamese intelligence agent nets. Each month Bob Burns would go to IV Corps headquarters and pick up a huge wad of Vietnamese piasters, or dong, as they were called in Vietnamese. I took over this duty in August 1970 when Bob had gone home, and Bob's replacement had not yet taken over the fund. We would give most of the money to the Vietnamese S-2 who would sign for it, and then, a month later, would produce receipts, allegedly signed by the agents. Bob and I had no illusions that the money was actually being spent on agents, but the system was in place before either of us had gotten there, and we did not rock the sampan. We occasionally

129

fumed about the expenditure of taxpayers' money to enrich the S-2. And the S-2 submitted the receipts each month so the fiction was intact.

At 3:15 on the afternoon of October 5, 1970, I walked into the Vietnamese S-2 office to ask for the receipts for September. It was time for me to go to IV Corps to pick up the Collection and Classification of Information (C&CI) Fund for October. I had not yet received the previous month's receipts, so I told the Vietnamese NCO in charge of the fund's disbursement staff that I needed the receipts. But as I spoke to the sergeant, I noticed that he was standing over the desk of a member of the staff who was mass-producing the receipts. No agent was signing the receipts. About ten minutes after I had observed the receipt manufacturing, a Vietnamese staff member handed me the receipts that he and his compatriots had just prepared.

I was incensed by all this, and maybe I was looking for a final climactic scene, worthy of a *Daily News* headline: BRASH YOUNG LIEUTENANT ENDS CORRUPTION IN PHONG DINH PROVINCE. VIETNAMESE PEAS-ANTS HAIL BRAVE NEW WORLD!" Maybe I was hoping for a day of reck-oning for our Vietnamese puppets who were not our gallant allies but our all-too-keen students of our business practices: clearly they knew that I had observed the creation of the fake receipts and must have thought that I accepted them as business as usual. There appeared to be no recognition that creating false receipts was taboo. Actually, there was a serious flaw in the whole proce-dure: what real agent would actually sign a receipt acknowledging payment for betraying his comrades-in-arms? The Vietnamese understood how corruption works: it's just there, everyone knows it, and we all live with it. Ho-hum. When Tim Timrud, the civilian PSYOPS or Psychological Operations Advisor on Team 56, was asked about graft and corruption by the military historians, his answer was priceless: "Well, first of all to be absolutely honest, we live with it." I like the definition of absolute honesty. Timrud also said regarding psycholog-ical operations, "...I don't like to use the word 'manipulate,' but certainly to indi-cate to the people some form of rationalization why they should continue with the present government and the future that it holds."[66] I'm sure Timrud meant to say that the goal of PSYOPS was to offer the people a rationale or a basis for support for the government. His sentence tries too hard, and he probably didn't understand that Merriam-Webster offers a definition of "rationalize" that might have troubled him: "to provide plausible but untrue reasons for conduct."

I've only recently begun to understand the irony of all this: I was getting worked up over fake intelligence, fake intelligence nets, fake receipts, fake accounting.... Reading Robert Musil's *The Man Without Qualities* has re-oriented my grip on reality. "Part II: Pseudoreality Prevails" offers a useful expla-nation: "No one who speaks of the greatest and most important thing in the world means anything that really exists."[67] You might think that news of enemy locations would be important in a war, but it's not necessary that such news actually reflect reality, especially if you really don't want to close with and destroy the enemy—the stated goal of the U.S. Army Infantry. (Colonel David Hackworth pointed out that "closing with the enemy" was a strategy for European land wars and exactly the "worst thing you could do in Vietnam."[68]) We all lived with the pseudoreality quite comfortably until at least 1975, and, guess what, the 2015 Vietnamese seem to be now embracing that world view as they encourage tourism, especially to exotic places like the Cu Chi tunnels. Tourists can re-live the war by firing M-16s or AK-47s and eating rice in the tunnels: it's sort of like riding a gondola on the Grand Canal in the Venetian Hotel in Las Vegas as opposed to Venice, Italy. But maybe the Vietnamese are still smarter than we think: apparently Western tourists flock to the Cu Chi tunnels for a "genuine war experience." Maybe too the Vietnamese have been watching how successful American reality TV shows have been at manufacturing fake perils.

In any event we ran the S-2 Advisor's shop in accord with the prevailing *status quo dum bello*: Sebastian Junger calls the occasional eruption of such thinking in today's Afghanistan a Vietnam moment: we had a year full of such moments. Junger says, "A Vietnam moment was one in which you weren't so much getting misled as getting asked to participate in a kind of collective wishful thinking."[69] Uncle Sam asked for complete acceptance of our mission while yet acknowledging that nothing was working just right. We mostly grumbled and sighed.

I wrote up my gotcha moment and sent it through the chain-of-command to Colonel Van Hout. I offered several possible courses of action and recommended that the C&CI Fund be distributed at district level—a very strong rebuke for the Province S-2, Captain Minh. (Actually he was supposed to be "whacking it up," as the NYPD cops say, or splitting it with the intelligence officers at District level; he probably wasn't.) A couple of weeks later, Van Hout finally discussed the matter with me. And then, he told me I was a naïve young man; he practically patted me on the head. The last thing he needed in his outfit was a guy who wanted to blow the whistle on corruption. (It was fortunate for both him and me that I was "short," and he knew it.) He asked me what I had expected. I told him that rumor had it that the S-2 ran the whore houses downtown, and that he had bought the whore houses with our money. (William Saunders, the National Police Advisor, said in his military history interview that "most of the whorehouses are owned by ARVN officers."[70]) Van Hout laughed and made it clear that nothing was going to be done.

I signed the C&CI fund over to the new S-2 advisor and went home in October 1970. There would be no final Sam Waterston plea to the jury that moves it to vote to convict. This scandal was my second close encounter with Vietnamese corruption. The first was the case of Dai-uy Liem, the S-2 of Thuan Nhon District, who dropped a Vietnamese dong on Major Bon, his District Chief, on February 28, 1970—just five days after my horrific helicopter crash. The report begins: "All village chiefs must pay Major Bon 30,000$VN, 2 bags of rice (200 lbs. per bag) and two jars of nuoc mam [fermented fish sauce] per month for the security of their jobs." It goes on to reveal that Major Bon was running illegal casinos and a complete shake-down of all businesses, was not feeding the RF forces, was accepting bribes from draft dodgers, and, in league with the National Police, was taking bribes from captured VC to secure their release. I'm really struck now by the complicity of Catholic authorities with Major Bon. The report, written by Bob Burns, says: "When a negative report is submitted by an American advisor concerning Major Bon's conduct, Major Bon sends his wife to see a Catholic priest in Tan Hiep District, An Giang Province. The priest then writes a letter to BG [Brigadier General] Hanh, IV Corps Headquarters, who takes care of the complaint. Major Bon visits General Hanh in Can Tho on an almost daily basis."[71]

Well, Wow! Here is the link between the Catholic Church and the corrupt GVN. I should have been aware of this because, as a senior at Fordham Prep, on October 11, 1963, I was ushered into the Fordham University gymnasium to listen to a talk by Madame Ngô Đình Nhu, the famous "dragon lady" of the Diệm regime. Madame Nhu was a Catholic as was Diem. Her husband, Ngô Đình Nhu, was Diệm's chief advisor, and many thought Ngô exercised the real power. It was very odd that Prep school students were sent to this speech; some think that Cardinal Spellman had placed a call, requesting our attendance. I didn't realize it at the time, but Madame Nhu had been greeted with sharp criticism and, as she said, "very poor manners" at Harvard.[72] Students at Princeton had also been inhospitable; Columbia would follow suit two days after the polite Fordham reception. The Diệm government had taken steps to suppress Buddhist dissent. When asked at Fordham about the government's treatment of Buddhists, she deflected, "'Why do you not pay the same attention to internal strife in Hungary and Tibet as to that in Viet Nam?'"[73] So why was the gym packed with Fordham Prep students? Unlike Fordham college students who could be less reliable, the Prep students could easily be required to treat Madame Nhu with the respect that she wasn't getting at the Ivy League schools, and perhaps Cardinal Spellman was going to make damn sure that Catholics treated her better. So I was part of the great Catholic Southeast Asian plot long before I knew it.

In Phong Dinh Catholic influence was evident in Major Bon's connection with Brigadier General Hanh, but it was also apparent, for better reasons, in the apparent fighting spirit of a single Catholic priest who was the pastor of a congregation of about 1,200 right in the middle of a VC-controlled part of Phong Thuan District. I'll never forget the oddity of seeing a miniature Gothic church planted in the midst of the flat paddies of Phong Dinh as I flew in one day on a helicopter. Father Phan Trong Kim's church, built in 1909, was pock-marked with bullet and B-40 holes; the nose on the statue of the Virgin Mary at the front of the church was shot off; our advisor told me that the people showed up for Mass in droves virtually every day. I remember seeing Fr. Kim in the TOC one day in August 1970. He was picking up an M2 Browning .50 caliber machine gun. He slept in a bunker dug into the rectory building adjacent to the church. He was terrified that the VC would shoot him some day when he was elevating the host at Mass. But he was undaunted. His policy was defensive; he did not pursue the VC aggressively. He wanted to reach some sort of accommodation with them. (It's noteworthy that he was seeking another private peace treaty like those in affect in other places in the province, like Thuan Trung.) In March 1969, he told the military history interviewers that he had not seen the bishop from Can Tho since 1967.[74] As a result he had a backlog on Confirmations although he continued to run classes for the adolescents in his parish. The advisors offered to pick up the bishop in Can Tho on a helicopter whenever the children were ready. I don't know if this ever happened although obviously Fr. Kim did get to the TOC in Can Tho somehow.

Fr. Kim sounds like a priest Pope Francis would like; the bishop does not.

Local Truces and the
Killing of John Goggin

The bishop's behavior disgusted me then, but he was just another leader I could not respect. I, like most Americans, went home and tried to bury the war deep in my subconscious, and, as the years have gone by, I am no longer quite sure that I was ever really there. I never succeeded in cutting the war out of my brain, but I certainly succeeded in paying little attention to the "progress" of the war in Phong Dinh. I did not find out until 2012 that the enemy's units were being reported in January 1973 as still operating in the same areas of the province with similar unit strengths, that is, if any of the agent reports at any time were even slightly accurate. But who knows? I wonder if, after the war was over, the VC revealed that their Chau Thanh A unit was simply a phantom.

I feel compelled to use quotation marks when I refer to the "war" and other pseudorealities—as though I have to indicate that the terms I use may not possess real reference to empirical truth. In our postmodern world it is now common to accept the impossibility of truth: it's actually a hangover from the American War in Vietnam. Soldiers commonly felt they were in some very odd place, but I spent an entire year thinking that "intelligence" gathering might just be a hoax, punctuated by the odd tracer whizzing past a helicopter. Tim Timrud, the PSYOPS advisor, helped the Vietnamese Information Service (VIS) to create propaganda designed mostly to get the Viet Cong to give up and rally to the GVN. Timrud was a USIA (U.S. Information Agency) officer, a former news guy who decided that the news needed a push every so often—a precursor, perhaps, of the "fair and balanced" m.o. of current-day Fox News. His counterpart was the Province VIS Chief. When interviewed in 1969, Timrud said, "The main difficulty that I have found with my counterpart is that he believes that information is to be taken literally rather than PSYOPS, and so I have the opportunity of trying to PSYOP him into a PSYOPS program."[75]

So Timrud told the military history team; it's a pearl of PSYOPery (fit for the Grand Old Opry). The Team 56 TOC logs in the National Archives reveal other loose truths. The logs recorded the "war" in Phong Dinh Sector—the military word—or Province—the civilian word. They are an hour-by-hour record, mostly of radio traffic that reported contact with and sightings of the VC, medevac operations of the wounded and dead, and more benign matters like recording the locations of visitors. The logs are probably accurate records of what was said on the radio waves, but whether they reflect reality is another matter. The KBA/KIA distinction illustrates just how shaky casualty claims could be, especially when Officer Efficiency Reports were based, in part, on the volume of such claims. "KBA" is only a potential truth. (How postmodern is that!) Since there were no American ground units, just advisors, in Phong Dinh Sector, rating an American advisor on the number of kills by Vietnamese troops seems ridiculous. Yet the "war" of the "body count" went on with its fuzzy math. Maybe "W" concocted the term while not on duty with his National Guard unit.

Concocting plausible enemy unit sighting reports was not a difficult job. Anyone who looked at the ground from 1500 feet could write reports with reasonable verisimilitude. So in 1969–70 if anyone had asked me where the VC were, I could put him on a chopper and have him look at erratically farmed rice paddies that the VC controlled within 10 minutes of take-off from Can Tho Army Air Field. He could speed-write a realistic novel.

Now what's amazing about all this is that the sighting reports generated by agents were treated as if they were dead accurate, but they had little value. The Vietnamese S-2 office churned out about six or seven sightings every afternoon about 4 p.m.—just the right number for the American briefing at 5 p.m. The 5 o'clock follies in Saigon were the laughing stock of the press corps. We had our own version that we put on five nights a week. No briefings were apparently needed on the weekend because, after all, it was the weekend, and Charlie ought to take a break, have a few beers, and chill out. And Charles generally was cooperative. The war was a bore, and I have to believe that enemy units like the Tay Do I Battalion that had been operating since World War II felt it ought to take the weekends off too. Colonel David Hackworth, the most decorated American of the post–World War II era, tells the story of his counterpart Colonel Hanh's view of the war: "...the war under Hanh was a nine-to-five, five-days-a-week, business-as-usual kind of affair..." When Hackworth pressed Hanh to attack the VC on the weekends, Hanh replied, "But Colonel Hackworth ..., my men have been fighting for twenty-four years. They need to rest on the weekends. It is different for you advisers. You only stay for one year."[76]

Hanh had a point even though Hackworth couldn't be happy with Hanh's complacency. Americans were constantly pushing the war: we had a real interest in reaching an end, undefined as the end might have been. The Vietnamese knew they had to live with one another when we had gone home. The truth in this regard in Phong Dinh Province was startling: every month the number of VC killed was caused disproportionately by Americans.

Captain James Pederson in his military history interview in the spring of 1969 expressed his disgruntlement with the Vietnamese zeal for the war. He attributed part of the problem to a rigid top-down management style, but he found the problem to be most disturbing during the afternoon siesta when it became impossible to get any kind of reaction to reported VC movements until 3 p.m. when everyone finally went back to work.[77] Major James M. Kraft, the Air Force Liaison Officer attached to Team 56 in March 1969, complained similarly: "There are four hours each day when the Vietnamese are not working. We cannot find our counterparts."[78] The VC surely knew that they were safe to move between noon and 2 p.m. although Pederson states that nothing could happen until 3 p.m. I do recollect that one day we went out on good intelligence at 12:30 p.m. and caught the VC out in the open. The gunships blasted away, sank sampans, set off secondary explosions, and probably killed some of the VC who might have been planning a siesta-time picnic. While that operation was very effective, no one suggested that we repeat it. And, interestingly, the intelligence had come in directly to the S-2 advisor's office, so the action was entirely American-instigated. A call to the airfield had produced instant gunships on station.

I always had the feeling that there were understandings among the Vietnamese. The friendlies and the VC seemed to understand the "war" as a dance that would probably end some day, so why get too carried away about bringing that day along faster? There was ample evidence of informal accommodations between the Vietnamese friendlies and the VC. Less than a month after I left, Colonel Van Hout wrote a letter on November 16, 1970, to the Province Chief and complained: "I noticed that for the month of October the sightings of enemy units and the areas of friendly operations seldom coincided. Although the Province is divided into areas of responsibility for each unit, in actuality the VC have easily avoided contact during the day by remaining in hideouts, and at night the VC are free to move almost anywhere except into some of the hamlets where alert PSDF [People's Self Defense Force] are on duty. The principle [sic] reason for this is that the RF and the PF units are literally confined to an area only a few meters in diameter around their outposts."[79]

Howard Potter is far more explicit about what he observed in 1965–66: "...by tacit agreement each side would leave the other alone." He goes on: "... the district town and the strings of outposts that surround it have remained relatively free from the harassment of local guerrillas. Likewise the GVN district chiefs have shown little inclination to probe the NLF-controlled area to seek out and destroy the guerrillas known to be based there. In fact the last two district chiefs admitted they had agreed to a local truce with the NLF [National Liberation Front]."[80] Reading this assessment for the first time in 2011, I suddenly re-thought the death on September 11, 1969, of Lieutenant John Goggin—a classmate at Fordham as well as at the Infantry and Intelligence Schools. John was a Phoenix advisor in Thuan Trung District—easily the most "pacified" district of the seven districts in Phong Dinh. About half the population of Thuan Trung was Hoa Hao—a Buddhist sect with a very strong antipathy toward the Viet Cong. In April 1947 the Viet Minh (the predecessor of the National Liberation Front) had assassinated the Hoa Hao founder and then publicly executed his two sons in Can Tho. The Hoa Hao did not forget this, and, consequently, Goggin should have had one of the safest assignments in Phong Dinh. There were few incidents in Thuan Trung during my year, and Co Do, the District town where Goggin was living, was very secure. The Hoa Hao were the living proof that the VC could be defeated if the people in a locale wanted to defeat them.

It dawned on me when reading Potter's account of his tour of duty in Phong Dinh that there might be some possibility that there was a specific reason Goggin had been killed. I was told when I arrived that Goggin and Captain David Haller were getting into a boat when a VC guerrilla dropped a hand grenade into the boat and killed both Americans. Colonel Conger thought it important to specify in the TOC log that Goggin and Haller were killed "by shrapnel, not bullet wounds."[81] And Colonel Conger rarely dictated specific TOC log entries. Then the Province Monthly Report for September 1969 says the two were killed while in a boat convoy—a suggestion that they were not on an offensive ground operation. Conger was clearly trying to point to the curious nature of the deaths.[82] When I heard the explanation about the grenade when I arrived in October 1969, I figured then, as did every American I spoke with, that Goggin and Haller had simply had bad luck. In 2011 I thought about Goggin's job assignment—advisor to the Phoenix program in Thuan Trung. For the first time the possibility that Goggin had been targeted hit me: Phoenix was an assassination program. Potter says: "At the district and village levels only tacit arrangements between the officials of both regimes explains [sic] the low level of violence directed at the officials themselves. Assassinations have become relatively rare occurrences on both sides."[83] I have no proof that Goggin's death was an assassination, but the description I was given and Conger's carefully chosen words suggest that it may have been. Goggin's activities were directed against NLF officials. He and Haller were not killed in a firefight: their VC nemesis was close enough to drop the grenade in the boat—possibly an indication that the action was wholly unexpected.

If the Phoenix Program, imposed by higher headquarters, was disturbing local informal agreements, then Goggin's death might have been as deliberate an assassination as any undertaken by the friendly "hit squads," known as the

PRUs or Provincial Reconnaissance Units. Potter was writing about the status quo in 1964–65, and although there were early attempts to "neutralize" the Viet Cong Infrastructure, its political leaders, Phoenix was adopted as the name of the program in 1967, and the mass assignment of MI lieutenant advisors to every district in South Vietnam was only reaching full operation in 1969 when Goggin was assigned. (He may have been the first MI lieutenant on the Thuan Trung district team.)

In any event no one, except Colonel Conger, seems even to have been slightly suspicious about the manner in which Goggin and Haller were killed. But then we hadn't read Potter either. I was on leave when Goggin was killed, and I went to his wake and to his funeral Mass at St. Raymond's Church in the Bronx. John, a sharp-looking, 5'9," thin man with dirty blonde hair and a perpetual look of mirth on his angular features, was engaged although I did not know his fiancé. He was a great guy—a quintessential sarcastic Irish-American New Yorker. He would talk out of the side of his mouth and deliver the most exquisite pin pricks to the balloons of the fatuous people who were trying to enlighten us about military procedures and tactics.

My favorite Goggin story grows out of a briefing we received at Fort Benning on Viet Cong tactics and capabilities. We were told, among other sage lessons learned, not to wear deodorant because the VC could smell it in the jungle—a claim that might justly be thought a bit inflated. A better reason for not using deodorant in Vietnam is that the wetness of the climate can lead to underarm rashes. I know: I quit using the stuff about a month after I arrived. You might notice that I wasn't worried about the VC's preternatural olfactory abilities.

About a day later the whole company was sent out on a night compass course on a moonless night in thick, jungle-like Georgia woods. It was also a bloody cold night. We were told to find our way from one point to another, traversing rough terrain while carrying our M-14 rifles, web gear, and compasses. We were to maintain silence because the VC could hear as well as smell. Well, the night's activities did not go well. We crashed through the underbrush, fell down frequently, and, finally, started cursing, regardless of the severe warnings we had received. Ultimately we knew that this was a training exercise, a bit of play-acting. And, the soldiers' logic prevailed: "They're sending us to Vietnam. What are they going to do?" Finally Frank Dursi, another guy from Fordham, said, "Fuck this," and lit up a cigarette. Out of the night, a loud Bronx voice sounded, "Dursi, put out the fucking cigarette. The VC'll smell it." Maybe ya hadda be there, but this was pure Goggin cynicism. Everyone heard the remark and full-scale laughter and talking erupted. The compass course ended, mercifully, soon thereafter. The cadre who were running the course seemed to grasp that their exercise had not been well-conceived.

I corresponded with Goggin after he went to Vietnam, so I knew he was a member of Advisory Team 56. When I arrived in Can Tho, a few weeks after attending his funeral Mass, I thought, "Oh, my God! I'm his replacement." I was assigned to the Province, not the District, Team, but everyone knew who Goggin was. It was eerie to be flying over the spot where he was killed about three weeks after the funeral. John has never left my consciousness since then.

Faking Ourselves

If it is true that Goggin was targeted, then questions should have been raised about the top-down implementation of the Phoenix Program. One size does not fit all—especially in combat. But the concept of the war was already in place when we arrived, and we were given duties in line with grand designs. The system of intelligence collection was in place: its relationship to realities did not matter. But there were moments when the absurdity of our efforts became obvious. As GIs would say in the French-Vietnamese slang of the red light districts, we were "beaucoup dien cai dau" or "boo-koo dinky dow," i.e., "crazy in the head."

Bob Burns tells the best story about "intelligence" collection in Phong Dinh. To tell it, I have to explain the American 525 MI (Military "Intelligence") Group, which allegedly "operated" all over Vietnam and had a detachment that "operated" in Phong Dinh. We used to receive "agent" reports from the 525 almost every weekday afternoon. (I don't know what the 525 did on weekends.) Usually a Spec Four would show up and simply hand the reports to me since Bob Burns had made the 525 my "management problem." It's certainly true that he gave the reports very cursory attention, and I, too, looked at them very briefly and then put them in my "In" box, only occasionally giving the information to the Vietnamese. We hardly ever included a 525 sighting report in the evening briefing. We handled 525 "intelligence" like this for an entire year, without any kind of real consequence.

About once a week, a captain from the 525 would stop by and "shoot the shit" with me about life in general, and only occasionally about the "war." Burns would busy himself at the desk and leave the diplomacy to me. (It's worth noting that Burns had a fondness for my lack of tact: I was young and willing to call out assholes.) I never actually told the captain that his reporting was nonsense, and about once a month I'd fill out the evaluation form for each report. I'd do so by looking up the TOC log for the date of each report and, when it was plausible, I'd say that the VC were contacted in the general vicinity of the agent report. This method kept the paper flowing to my "Out" box, and I learned the great virtue of not upsetting the dragon fruit cart by telling the truth: any contact with the VC was merely incidental and not caused by reaction to the 525's

140

agent reports. After all, we hardly ever told the Vietnamese what the 525 was reporting. And I did hear that the 525 passed out decorations for the worthiness of its intelligence gathering; I enjoyed my part in the 525's success—as the fiction writer of the evaluation reports.

So here we have it: the Vietnamese were probably also giving us fictitious agent reports every evening: they understood that the American army was a kind of cargo cult, i.e., we shuffled papers and made it seem as if results were caused by the shuffling. Cargo cults were common in the Pacific, especially after World War II, when native populations mimicked the behavior of the Americans and Japanese in the hope of causing manufactured goods to arrive mystically at their islands. In some cases airfields with control towers were built in the hope of getting deities to bestow materiel upon the devout. The Vietnamese had observed the Americans closely and had figured out what they needed to do in order to keep the Americans happy and their materiel coming. The problem is that it's hard to know who was gulled more by the behavior. The American bureaucracy was quite happy with fictitious reports. The Vietnamese were too. At least to some extent, they acted like the Viet Cong were a fictitious threat. And we all know what happened in 1975 when the whole Government of Viet Nam charade collapsed in about three months.

There were two key moments in our relationship with the 525 while Bob Burns and I were there. The first must have occurred when I was away. Somehow the 525 got one of its fictions to the Commanding General of our umbrella organization, Delta Military Assistance Command. Apparently the 525 reported that the Viet Cong were massing for an attack about ten kilometers from Can Tho City. The general must have contacted Colonel Van Hout and asked what he was doing about the impending attack on the city in which the general himself resided and went to parties at John Paul Vann's compound. (Those parties, "it was reliably reported," would have made Hugh Hefner blush. I had heard the rumors about sexual escapades in Vann's CORDS Compound—a bit of decadence with a bravado to it. Vann always presented himself as "in charge"— a cock of the walk.) Well, real shit is too viscous to flow downhill, but the proverbial bullshit did slide downhill, and Van Hout chewed Bob Burns out. It's important to note this: the reality of the report didn't matter. What mattered was that Van Hout was blind-sided, and even if his S-2 didn't deem the report worthy of his attention, his S-2 should have anticipated that the Commanding General would be making Colonel Van Hout look bad, and we all knew that colonels don't become generals when they're proven not to be "on top of things."

Well, Bob went out to the air field and called in a few markers. He got a Huey and a light fire team (two Cobra gunships) to go to the site of the Viet Cong massing. (Think about the cost of launching three helicopters with full crews, and note that Bob didn't ask the Vietnamese to confirm or deny the report.) Well, when they got there, nary a soul was to be found. So Bob had the Huey land right on the site, the precise grid coordinates, of the "massing Viet Cong." He could have had a picnic. Needless to say, Bob went back to the colonel and told him about the bogus "intel" and then laced into the captain from the 525. He told him to stop alarming the general with the 525's bullshit reports.

Well, a few months later, the same captain visited us and spoke to me. He told me that he needed permission to shoot in our sector on the next day. He started by telling me that the 525 and the U.S. Navy were planning air strikes the next day and wanted to be sure that permission would be promptly granted when they asked for it. I knew that I was being asked to sell some "super spook" bullshit to the Vietnamese, and they would have questions. After some probing, the 525 captain revealed that one of his agents was going to sell fish to the Viet Cong and then paddle down the canal a short distance and plant a homing device along the canal bank. (The fish sale story was probably bogus: the VC could fish for themselves. I often saw their nets extended across canals on criss-crossed poles.) The homing device would mark the exact location of the Viet Cong, and then the Navy planes would drop their 500 pound bombs on them. (These bombs put big holes in the rice paddies and didn't hit many VC, but the local farmers of Phong Dinh Province had to have been angered when their paddies were blown up. Most air strikes in Phong Dinh in 1970 were probably a fake war tactic: any fool could see that the bombs didn't work tactically. Americans love air power. Infantry troops win wars, but then there are casualties.)

Now in 1970 the U.S. was technically out of the offensive operations business in the Mekong Delta. The U.S. Ninth Division had been withdrawn in 1969 (after Operation Speedy Express had killed, Nick Turse alleges,[84] thousands of innocent civilians), and there were just advisers and aviation people left. And I have to think that the 525, on some level, knew that it was an irrelevant unit. And I do wonder whether this operation was brewed because Bob Burns had exposed the 525's futility previously. It's certainly true that the idea of the mission was to continue an American War in the Mekong Delta after the Ninth Division had departed.

In any event I spent the afternoon haggling with the Vietnamese about permission to shoot. There were reluctant and kept pressing me for details, but I wasn't supposed to give details. This was bloody absurd, so finally I just told them what the 525 was doing. I remembered the overly fastidious secrecy attending my aerial photography mission for Oplan Missouri and dispensed with the fake super-spookery of MI types. With cautious bemusement, it seemed, the Vietnamese agreed to the permission.

Well the next day came and went and nothing happened. I almost forgot about the matter as I was busy with other stuff. So the day after, the 525 captain showed up, and Burns was very attentive. The captain explained that the homing device had never left the city of Can Tho. Burns guffawed and told the captain to give one of those devices to each of the 525's "agents." The captain left. We continued to receive our daily reports, and the "war" crept on "its petty pace from day to day"—a tale told by an idiot.

The M-16:
Success in the Laboratory

One piece of idiocy that has been researched is the so-called miracle of the Mattel toy called the M-16. While it is true that lab tests will certify the M-16's superior accuracy, the AK-47, the Communist and insurgents' weapon of choice throughout the world, is more likely to function under conditions of actual fighting. The AK-47 allows chambered rounds to blow out dust and other debris that might otherwise cause the weapon to jam. The M-16 has tighter tolerances (which probably account for its greater accuracy), but the AK-47 operates more like a machine gun, i.e., it operates by creating fields of fire or kill zones. Such capabilities are more conducive to fighting in close quarters when fire power and reliability are more important. In a way the story of the M-16 tells the whole story: the template for the weapon that the troops would carry in Vietnam was not adaptable to the realities of the Southeast Asian battlefield.

So I was issued an M-16 when I arrived in country after I had carried an M-14 in training and had fired the M-16 once for about an hour—six months previously. So I carried it with me when I went out flying—most of the time—although occasionally I went unarmed: it was easy to get lax about one's own personal security. One day I decided to clean it along with the .45 caliber pistol that somehow came into my personal "arsenal." (It was amazing how weapons could be found lying around with no particular person signed for them.) Unfortunately there was a round chambered in the .45 that I was unaware of, and, when I unwittingly pressed the trigger, it shot the operating rod handle off my M-16. I shook for a while after I did that dumb one, and the S-2 sergeant—the World War II veteran—particularly enjoyed what the lieutenant had done.

But now I had a problem: Dave Heinrich, the supply officer, told me that I needed a story in order to get the M-16 repaired. Note: a story in Vietnam is by definition a lie. So we finally decided that the operating rod handle had been shot off when the helicopter went down. Apparently I could have been held liable for destroying government property if the supply officer had to tell the truth. I love bureaucracy in the middle of a war. There are no accidents when it comes to filling out forms. As a result of my stupidity, I carried an M1 carbine for about 4 months. It was sawed off: I might have been better off with it. Fortunately, I never had to find out. I procured the M1 in the same manner as the .45: it was just lying around in the Team House, complete with a bandolier of about eight magazines.

Nevertheless, it was true that there were real Viet Cong in Phong Dinh Province even if they called it Can Tho Province—the traditional name with traditional boundaries that were swept aside probably so as to create more corrupt fiefdoms for the GVN to oversee. An astute 1969 analysis of Phong Dinh entitled "Contemporary Geopolitics, Phong Dinh," which I read for the first time in 2013, states: "Phong Dinh is entirely an arbitrary designation on a map with no historical justification or provincial tradition."[85] Since none of my contemporaries on Team 56 read this excellent overview of Phong Dinh, we probably were incapable of seeing just how we might oppose the VC effectively. For one, we were prisoners of our own culture and constitutionally unable to see how counterproductive our activities were.

No Lights in the Fog

Stuff happened in Vietnam unlike any scene in the movies running in our heads before we got there. The stuff reinforced the soldiers' feeling that Vietnam was not on the planet as, in soldiers' parlance, "The World" was the States. (That "World" was often defined by its movies.) So the out-takes from the surreal film that the soldiers found themselves acting in do not fit with *Von Ryan's Express* (1965) or *The Dirty Dozen* (1967), although the kind of combat I saw seemed as unreal as the celluloid varieties available in stateside movie theaters. *Von Ryan's Express* ends with the heroic death of Frank Sinatra, and *The Dirty Dozen* finally brings down the Cleveland Browns' Jim Brown. Both movies end with mission accomplished: the trainload of prisoners escapes into Switzerland, and the Nazis suffer greatly from the raid of the Dirty Dozen. War movie plots clear up the fog of battle rather neatly; maybe they also fog our thinking.

My fog was never burned off by the hot Southeast Asian sun. Within a few weeks (November 17, 1969, to be exact) of my arrival in Phong Dinh Province, I had seen tracers miss, by a wide margin, the helicopter in which I was flying, and I had calmly reported to the TOC that we were receiving ground fire. I had even reported the grid coordinates of the likely Viet Cong location, yet I did not quite believe that the tracers were actually intended to kill us. The bullets were long gone before I had a chance to panic, and I had fully expected to panic at the first shot.

Receiving ground fire became rather routine—if that is possible. The TOC logs are filled with reports by my fellow advisors and me of such incidents. Can Tho Air Field and Binh Thuy Air Base were mortared a number of times during my year. On May 8, 1970, I was at the air field when the mortars started dropping at 12:38 a.m. I was flying Firefly that night, and we had landed to re-fuel. I heard nothing because of the sound of the rotor blades. The pilot told me that the tower had called him, and we had to go back up immediately. I have to think that the VC waited for us to land before they fired off their mortars. We didn't find them that night; the searchlights on the Firefly lightship conked out at 3:46 a.m. My note in the log says: "Light was improperly installed & nearly fell out of the chopper." But that wasn't the only problem: "Y-cord was defective and was not replaced. I used door gunner's after much hassling."[86] Flying without communication between the backseat and the front seat was "dinky dow": the chopper couldn't shoot without permission from the backseat, i.e., the advisor and his Vietnamese counterpart. We were really ready for Charlie, weren't we? The VC fired nine 82mm mortar rounds, wounded 11 U.S. servicemen, five seriously enough to require medevac to the hospital at Binh Thuy. Three fixed-wing aircraft and two ¾-ton trucks were damaged. And I didn't hear or see any of it, even though the parked aircraft were not far from where we were re-fueling alongside the runway constructed of PSP, Pierced Steel Planks.

Two days later on May 12, 1970, we had to suspend the Phantom Twilight mission because we did not have an FM radio for communication with the friendlies on the ground. The crew chief had turned up missing when we were supposed to go out. Finally he showed up at 5:00 p.m. but then, once again, I had no Y-cord and had to use the door gunner's cord. We suspended the mission even though we had sighted two sampans sporting the VC flag and a banner in a location not far from the air field. Clearly the helicopter people were having equipment problems because there was no lightship available for Firefly that night. On May 14 Captain Doug Hemphill reported "only 2 lights working" on the lightship. He went on: "The effect is like shining a flashlight out the window of a car moving at 30 mph, except not as bright."[87] Despite all these malfunctions, I was stupid enough to take the S-2 clerk, Larry Quasius, up with me one night so that he could see the war up close. I don't know how many lights worked that night, but who was more "dinky-dow"? Him or me?

Food Poisoning on
Firefly and Senator Javits

While movies like *Green Zone* that feature Matt Damon lead us to expect the extraordinary in combat, everyday reality in my war zone was the stuff of common, ordinary, believable life and made it difficult to grasp that the VC actually wanted to kill us. I routinely ate powdered eggs for breakfast, checked out the scores of the Knick games in *Stars & Stripes*, drank too much Schlitz beer, burped occasionally, dreamed about Mom's Irish bread, enjoyed the afternoon siesta (when the war stopped for two hours), and learned, much to the amusement of my S-2 compatriots, how to drive a World War II-vintage jeep too small for my 6'3" height. My war was odd, quite unlike the war of the infantryman. Most of the time I was not in danger at all, and I watched movies like *Patton* and *M*A*S*H* and read books that arrived in USO care packages. (I remember reading Susan Sontag's *Against Interpretation* in Vietnam; her argument for an "erotics of art" was packaged in a box with somewhat lurid, slightly lascivious potboiler best sellers. Now I think that the guy who packed the books was a postmodern joker.)

Although the army seemed to be trying to convince us that it was possible to imagine that Vietnam was not all that different from life in The World, I was in serious danger occasionally. While I had credentials as a REMF (Rear Echelon Mother F), I experienced intense moments of combat as I was frequently involved in aerial combat activities. I bungled into such moments; other junior officers with similar duties seemed to encounter Charlie less than I did. And flying is strange stuff: on a few visits to Saigon, I remember seeing many Air Force pilots in grey flight suits, casually eating dinner in downtown restaurants. They could eat steaks, jump into their aircraft, and face deadly enemy fire shortly after being served by white-coated waiters in an apparently civilized atmosphere. I know from talking to pilots of fighter aircraft that the pucker factor could be quite high when Charles launched SAM missiles at them.

I had been in Vietnam only about three months when I suffered from food poisoning one night while on duty for Firefly. Stomach cramps gnawed at my belly and twisted me into contortions in search of relief from the pain. I could not say what mess hall meal caused the attack, but I had not eaten Vietnamese food—a common suspect among my fellow advisors to the Vietnamese friend-lies. (Stories abounded among advisors about eating greasy rat—unwittingly.) Food poisoning doesn't seem like a medical problem that a soldier ought to have. It belongs to the world of greasy spoon restaurants back in "The World" or to visits to Mexican border towns like Juarez with subsequent cases of Mon-tezuma's revenge. Now why I should consider Juarez to be part of The World while Vietnam was not reveals the strangeness of the feeling about being in Vietnam.

Food poisoning is a very direct, painful bodily malady; it makes the sufferer bend into a Dutch pretzel to assuage the pain. I got it twice in Vietnam—once when I was on the way home. I remember lying in bed in the transient barracks near Tan Son Nhut Air Base. I was unattached at that point since I had signed out of Advisory Team 56 and was officially a transient. I do remember thinking about that night on Firefly while I groaned in terrible pain. I had to figure out how to get medical aid as a transient, since I no longer belonged to anyone. I remember visiting a dispensary at Tan Son Nhut Air Base where I was treated by doctors with maximum dispatch and indifference. I half-expected them to coat my toe and finger nails with Gentian Violet ala the SOP of the medics in *Catch–22*. (I had used *Catch–22* as a sort of practical handbook for handling the absurdity of "life" in Uncle Sam's Army.) Whatever they gave me worked in a few hours. I could return to The World without suffering on the plane con-tinuously for 14 hours.

Sharp physical pain reminds us that, come what may, we are all dead even-tually. Combat seems to isolate us from "normal" biology, but we're living, breath-ing, sweating, urinating, defecating, horny bastards, no matter where we are or what else is going on. All that stuff reminds us of mortality right at the moment that a different kind of *memento mori* is going on. Actually we feel more alive when the choppers rev up and take off, so being sick on the chopper seems like a reminder that we're still in The World, even when we thought of Vietnam as a sort of dream.

Soldiers are trained to be precise in their movements: their training starts with learning how to execute a Column Right movement in close order drill, and then they learn to execute various other kinds of battlefield maneuvers in sync with their fellow soldiers. The training aims to create a well-coordinated machine. Food poisoning gums up the clicking heels.

I ate dinner early on January 19, 1970, and then went out for the all-night Firefly mission. The duty officer with Vietnamese counterpart would join the crew of a Huey to patrol the perimeter of Can Tho Army Air Field, principally, and, occasionally, the nearby Binh Thuy Air Force Base. The advisor and his counterpart were needed in order to gain permission to shoot at likely targets. We would fly at about 50 to 100 feet and search the ground with a gigantic cluster of searchlights mounted on the side of the chopper. The mission aimed at interdicting VC traffic and preventing infiltrators from sneaking onto the air field to blow up the long rows of parked helicopters and small, L-19 fixed-wing aircraft. Most of the time this was a routine mission: not much happened except that the Firefly officer and his Vietnamese counterpart lost sleep. (I do remember spending a leisurely night on the day before New Year's circling Can Tho and listening to rock music on AFVN (Armed Forces Viet Nam Radio) while we enjoyed the holiday cease fire.) We would fly for about four hours on a normal night, mostly making lazy circles around the airfield with occasional forays as far away as ten kilometers from the airfield. The helicopter was also outfitted with a large tub of flares that could be dropped in support of Vietnamese Popular and Regional Forces in outposts that might be under attack. Usually this involved going up to about 2,000 feet and dropping the flares out of the helicopter. A flare was capable of taking away the cover of night from the VC guerrillas operating in our area. Their attacks were usually mere harassment and might actually have been diversions so as to draw attention away from their movements elsewhere.

On this particular night I began to have stomach cramps before we went up at 9:30 p.m. on our first flight of the night. We wandered about three kilometers from the airfield with our searchlight on. We were about 100 feet up when we came upon a complex of spider holes (small one-person bunkers arranged in a square) designed as firing positions for VC guerrillas. This complex was rather amazing: the VC had built it within mortar range of the airfield, and no one had reported it although surely it was visible to anyone who paid attention. Yet my report to the TOC suggests that we happened on a substantial VC base of operations. The TOC log records that I reported having "sighted 15 heavy cement bunkers, 2 radio positions, 1 meeting hall, 30 spider holes, and 10 camouflaged Lean-Tos."[88]

We circled the complex for at least an hour while my Vietnamese counterpart tried in vain to secure permission to shoot. The best construction I can put on the slowness of the response was that the TOC was having a hard time believing that the VC had a complex so close to the airfield. Other constructions might have been more apt. We advisors never had any real idea what motivated friendly Vietnamese decision-making. Cowardice on their part was often alleged, but that line of thinking went along, just as often, with referring contemptuously to our allies as "gooks." I'm sure that some Vietnamese were as capable of cowardice as I was. The worst that I suspected was that the Vietnamese didn't want to kill one another and hesitated to do so. And maybe that's not a "worst," but a "best." And, curiously, the same people were fighting on the other side, and no one accused the Viet Cong of cowardice.

At one point a door gunner spotted a Russian SKS rifle on the ground, but permission to shoot was still not forthcoming although the TOC log says we were finally given permission to shoot about 11:45 p.m. I suspect that log entry was a cover for what we were already doing. I recollect that we started shooting when we returned fire from the VC. The VC probably became fed up waiting for our bureaucracy to give permission to shoot, and they started shooting at us. I like to imagine that those VC guerrillas didn't like their own hierarchy either, and, Central Office for South Viet Nam (COSVN) be damned, they weren't going to pass up the chance to shoot at some dumb Americans circling an SKS in a low-flying, slow-moving helicopter.

When the VC started shooting, the rules of engagement allowed us to fire. The door gunner opened up, and, if memory serves me correctly, helicopter gunships rolled in on the VC, but I don't know if our guys killed any VC although the TOC log says three VC were Killed By Air (KBA). I have a vague memory of watching a couple of guys in white shirts disappear into the spider holes when we first came upon the complex. Certainly the SKS lying on the ground was evidence of a scramble to get into the holes when our chopper approached. It was nice to know too that their guys were given to screwing up as much as we were. We didn't exactly sneak up on them, flying as we did with bright searchlights on. The door gunner did manage to shoot up the SKS.

The next day I told Colonel Conger that we had destroyed an SKS. That report in the TOC log puzzled him: how did we know? I told him we had fired many rounds from an M-60 machine gun at the rifle. This is a story of the whole war: the Colonel was concerned to get then former Secretary of Defense McNamara's statistics right—a win-the-war-by-calculus strategy. Shooting an SKS was the most reliable casualty report we could offer. We had a confirmed kill: one Russian SKS KBA. This concern for statistical accuracy mirrors what the Russian novelist Fyodor Dostoevsky shows in *Notes from the Underground*: human experience cannot be reduced to an arithmetical calculation. The world is not a two-plus-two proposition. It would be a much better idea to read Dostoevsky than to fight a war to re-learn this lesson. But he seems wholly out of style in our contemporary world where a 22-year-old woman auctions off her virginity for $3.4 million on eBay.

When we were running out of fuel, we returned to the airfield to re-fuel. The warrant officer pilot checked his helicopter to see if the VC had actually hit us. They were often lousy shots, but this time the pilot found a bullet hole in the housing just below the main rotor and about a half-inch from the main fuel line. The TOC log says I reported receiving ground fire "5 or 6 times, no one injured—chopper took 1 hit."[89] The pilot seemed pretty enthused—delighted, even—to tell us how close we were to blowing up. But my stomach seemed to be blowing up, so I didn't much care about close encounters with SKS rifles and AK-47s.

The cramps worsened as the fun-filled night of derring-do progressed. I can remember doubling up on the helicopter floor while looking out the door at the ground with the SKS in full view. The food poisoning made the VC in the spider holes seem irrelevant. I did go out the next morning in a chopper with the Vietnamese brass and their advisors to show them what we had found. But no one seemed very concerned about the matter. Certainly no plan was hatched to have ground troops search the bunker complex or even destroy it. On three successive nights about a month later, on March 20, 21, and 22, Firefly engaged the enemy at almost the same location. The bunker complex was still there, two months later in May 1970, when the air field was mortared; the Province Monthly Report says the VC "demonstrated the ability … to launch an attack from a supposedly secure area and remain undetected."[90] I learned only that you have to watch what you eat.

(Left to right) Colonel Lester M. Conger, John Paul Vann (in the white shirt in the background), Senator Jacob Javits and a Javits aide (at the edge of the photo). Vietnamese children are in the background. Javits' entourage was visiting a local village south of Can Tho on January 23, 1970.

(Left to right) Me, Senator Jacob Javits, and H.W. "Tim" Timrud, the Psyops Advisor on January 23, 1970. (A typical Vietnamese "hootch" is visible on the right side of the photo.)

A few days after the Firefly encounter, on January 23, 1970, Sen. Jacob Javits, a Republican anti-war senator from New York, visited, and we showed off a pacified village about a kilometer away from the VC spider holes, a showcase of the success of the "pacification effort." Since I was from New York, I was selected to accompany Javits on his visit to our province—a fact-finding expedition to check on the progress of the pacification effort. I was really pleased with myself when I was able to take a Javits' aide aside and tell him that he and the senator were getting a bullshit story. Javits was with two aides; I'm pretty sure I spoke with Albert A. ("Peter") Lakeland, Jr., who became one of the architects of the 1973 War Powers Act that limited presidential flexibility in the use of military force. I like to think that what I did next helped Lakeland to see the need to be skeptical of military adventures. I whipped out my map and showed him where he was and where we had had the Firefly contact with the VC a few nights previous. He thanked me profusely and seemed to take my message to heart. His boss went back home and argued for leaving Vietnam sooner, rather than later. Javits told the Senate Foreign Relations Committee on February 4: "It was clear to me that the GVN, as well as some U.S. military commanders, are thinking of a much more gradual U.S. combat disengagement, over a much longer time-frame, than I believe should be acceptable to the American people and the United States Congress."[91]

I left out the ignominious part about the food poisoning when I spoke to Lakeland. It was a sunny day, but Javits was accompanied by John Paul Vann and Ambassador William E. Colby (later Director of the CIA) who had the war fog machine going full blast. Javits visited Long Tuyen Village in Chau Thanh District and was briefed by the Chau Thanh District Chief. Fortunately an old Vietnamese woman opened Javits' eyes, and Vann made a preposterous comment for Lakeland's benefit. I'm glad I had shared my war movie with Lakeland.

After the District Chief's briefing, Javits delivered an American–style stump speech to the villagers who had been rounded up to show just how pacified they were. After he finished, an old, betel-nut-chewing woman was being restrained from asking Javits a question, but he insisted she be heard. She asked him for six sheets of metal roofing for her house—her entitlement for moving into a "secure hamlet." A good guess: her six sheets had been stolen by her village chief and sold on the black market. She created a hubbub, and promises were made to her. I never knew whether she got her roof, but she did have guts.

The dog-and-pony show continued with a boat ride down a canal. Lakeland, a few others, and I got into a boat together along with John Paul Vann and traveled down a canal to Rach Nhum Out Post and from there to Thoi An Out Post, finishing at the Giai Xuan Village Office. We traveled for about a mile just to show how safe we were. Vann was then the number two American in the Mekong Delta; by 1973 he had become the number one American in Vietnam. He spotted a kid on the canal bank with a harelip and asked his assistant, for the edification of Javits' aide, how that could be, since we had "fixed" all harelips in Vietnam. A hell of a war movie. Pretty foggy, I'd say.

Futility

I had lived most of my young life in a fog, so I was well-prepared for Vietnam. One spring day on my way home from high school, an attractive neighborhood girl my age, a blonde with an attractive figure, reached out and touched me. She said something silly, obviously trying to get my attention. I turned red in the face and brushed right past her and never again spoke to her although I did understand her flirtatious intent even when I was fifteen. (That was quite clairvoyant—for me, at least.) And then I never dated a girl from Inwood: there was something too difficult about it. I had to be shy with Inwood girls because I figured that the local biddies would talk about us, and that simply would be too hard to take. I was not unusual in this regard: most of my friends found it much easier to date outside the neighborhood. I have to think that there was some sort of death wish in all this for the neighborhood. The Vietnam War and the 1960s were tearing us apart, and we all made silent plans to make our lives elsewhere and to live those lives in eternal mourning for the lost neighborhood.

Most Irish guys I knew as a young man were capable of blushing for a variety of reasons although the most common reason was a feeling of self-consciousness brought on by seeing a member of the female species. I was particularly given to blushing as any hint of sex was troubling. So why did I blush? Well, confusion was part of the reason at least. It was easy to embarrass me, and I guess blushing reveals a truth that the blusher is trying to hide although knowing exactly what that truth is may not be easy to decipher. But the observer knows a blush when she sees one.

I didn't know how to approach a female who attracted me or whom I wanted to attract. So I'd become aware that I might be tipping my hand and blushing would undo me. So blushing was partly involuntary and partly voluntary. I couldn't control it although I wanted to. I recollect having developed some skill at controlling my impulse and my pulse. But I was never sure that I really ever controlled myself.

I suspect that trouble with blushing was not just a problem for Irish guys, but very light skin made the flow of the blood to the face and neck more evident than it was for guys whose DNA had produced different skin pigmentation.

And isn't it true that Italian guys are born lovers and unlikely to blush? Or so Woody Allen has led us to believe…

But that experience of being out of control but not entirely reminds me of one of Wallace Stevens' thirteen ways of looking at a blackbird: "The blackbird whirled in the autumn winds." Did the blackbird do the whirling? Did the wind whirl the blackbird? How much of the whirling was due to the blackbird's volition? How much to the autumn winds? Is the statement really active voice? If so, then the blackbird is doing the whirling? But the statement implies a passive voice re-statement (that would ruin the line by removing the ambiguity about the propulsion): "The blackbird was whirled by the autumn winds." And autumn winds are a harbinger of winter and death. Autumn winds blow the leaves off the trees and make them seem dead. When I blushed, I was in the position of the blackbird, in and out of control at the same time.

When my wife mentions to people whom I don't know that I went to Vietnam, I either blush or get close to doing so. I've told her to stop telling people we don't know well that I am a Vietnam veteran. People react to that bit of information in a way that makes me self-conscious and leads to blushing. I don't like the feeling although I can't explain why I feel self-conscious about being a Vietnam veteran. Maybe I feel I'm going to be expected to say something profound about the war, and I'm at a loss for profundity about Vietnam. So maybe you may understand why this book is not linear.

Blushing and 105mm Rounds for Sale

And maybe all of America was blushing with embarrassment and felt the need to cover up its embarrassment with a war in Vietnam. After all, it hardly seems credible that a small Third World country could tie a superpower down for almost two decades in a battle without a final victory in sight. After World War II America found itself in position as the dominant superpower and, like an overgrown young lad embarrassing himself in public, we imagined our vulnerability to be much greater than it actually was. When I hear that the current defense budget is larger than the budgets of the next 20 countries combined, I wonder what the hell we're frightened of. What are we scared of?

Vietnam still causes American indigestion in a way that no other war has. We still cannot digest the food it offers for thought.[92] We still gag on it. And we still blush when we have to admit we lost. (Blushing and indigestion are somehow related.) I often think that the need of Americans to shout, "We're Number One," at the Olympics is an attempt to re-capture the illusion of self-control.

And surely our control of Phong Dinh Province was mostly an illusion although I was unaware of the overall picture. I didn't know, for example, until 2011 about Howard Potter's assessment that the VC were mostly in control in 1964–1965; that an overall assessment dated 1966 suggested that the VC controlled all the major canals—and canals were vital to the commerce of the Mekong Delta. Colonel Conger stated that the Xa No Canal, one of the major north-south thoroughfares in the province, had been controlled by the VC for 18 years.[93] I can remember thinking, before I went to Vietnam, that VC claims about how much of the country they controlled were just propaganda. I grew up believing that no one would freely choose communism. I learned to believe that many Vietnamese did prefer communism to the GVN and foreign domination; now I know that very serious leaders like Colonel Conger and Major Potter also believed the VC. Conger was pleased to claim that in 1969 that control had been broken. The truth is that the GVN never actually contested the VC control of the canals until the focus of the war shifted to the pacification strategy in place during my year in Vietnam. Yet it is also true that the Province

Monthly Report for July 1970 states that: "...the major canals in that district [Phong Thuan] are trafficable for the most part by the VC during both day and night because the only significant deterrent to the VC is in the form of U.S. air assets."[94] "Contesting" is not the same as "controlling."

But pacifying Phong Dinh was daunting, for Conger also reported that, when he arrived on February 6, 1968, nine VC battalions were operating just outside the City of Can Tho; and, then, most amazingly I found out that the INTSUMs in 1972 and 1973 reported the same VC units operating as did in 1969–70 with the same estimated manpower. Who could have thought that we were winning although that was the thesis of William Colby's *Lost Victory: A Firsthand Account of America's Sixteen-Year Involvement in Vietnam*? Colby actually believed that pacification was working; the stable enemy unit strengths and the desperation of B-52 strikes in 1972–73 suggest the contrary. Colby's title implies that we won the war in Vietnam but lost it at home. He visited Phong Dinh frequently: I used to see him in our mess hall with John Paul Vann about once a month. We were the model province, but hardly anyone was paying close attention to what the captains and lieutenants were saying about our "progress." Written reports in the National Archives show deep skepticism among the advisors. And we weren't the commie pinko hippie creeps who panhandled on the streets of San Francisco.

As my year moved along, I developed some competency in figuring out where the VC were and what they were likely to do. I was no genius for having done so. I trusted aerial reconnaissance reports and captured documents. I developed strong doubts about the reliability of agent reports: they could be correct in a general sense because the truth is we knew quite well where the VC were. They announced their presence when we got in range of their rifles, and they always contested our presence whenever we entered their sanctuaries. We all knew that the chances of contact with the VC were high in the Twin Canals area and in the Iron Triangle—names that someone had given these locations long before our arrival. And in 1972 one of the B-52 strikes was made on the Twin Canals. I did not ignore agent reports foolishly. I'm struck by the fact that I sent a coded message out to Phong Dien and Phong Phu Districts on January 26, 1970, to tell our team members there that we had an agent report that the VC had acquired 80 new 105mm artillery rounds through its penetration organization. On the same day RF troops tripped five booby-trapped 105mm rounds.[95] The report suggests that the VC had access to friendly supply channels. It would not be ridiculous to guess that someone made a few extra piasters by supplying the VC.

I wrote the following paragraph in the monthly counterpart letter to Captain Minh on August 15, 1970:

Artillery. As I have mentioned to you in the past, I strongly suspect complicity of the artillery units in the province with the VC. The number of rounds reported as being fired does not match the number of "booms" counted by our advisors in the field. However, the stock is minus the number of rounds that are reported as having been fired. Shotgun [L-19 pilot] has also met with refusals by artillery units to adjust fire as he indicates. I would suggest an investigation by the Security Section and/or the MSS. In view of present enemy intentions to infiltrate the GVN and work as legal cadres, I feel this sort of activity should be carefully watched.[96]

Analysis of the artillery logs in the TOC suggests that the paperwork was being dummied, and we were the dummies who couldn't read it. Yet booby-trapped 105mm rounds accounted for a high percentage of friendly casualties. In March 1970, 57 friendly soldiers were killed, most by booby traps, the Province Monthly Report states. I don't recollect a single Field Artillery officer on Team 56 for the entire year that I was there. We were missing a key piece of expertise. I am not sure how I reached the conclusions expressed in the counterpart letter, but I was not a sophisticated analyst of artillery. I must have been putting into writing what I had gleaned from Team 56 advisors in the field.

My letter obviously had little impact. Three years later on January 17, 1973, Warren E. Parker, the last Province Senior Advisor and a civilian, could still complain: "It is unfortunate, but like much of the other U.S. provided material and supplies that are mis-used, poorly maintained, and abandoned or sold, the Vietnamese soldier and his superior will continue to display little concern for his weapon when the United States government continues to effect unlimited supply support."[97] Well, we did find out in 1975 what happened when the U.S. supplies ran out.

How I Learned the
Thousand Yard Stare

When I broke into an immediate sweat upon landing in Saigon in October
1969, I remember feeling disoriented and not in control at all. And I had not
yet encountered the impossibility of monitoring Vietnamese supply channels.
Was I sweating from the heat or the anxiety? And I was filled with anxiety about
what was going to happen as well as remorse about now being in a war that I
found no compelling reason to fight. The larger question, "Why Are We in Vietnam?" was subsumed by the personal "Why Am I in Vietnam?" The answer to
the first question put me in the passive voice, "We were required to fight communism." The answer to the second question was an active voice construction
hard to swallow, "I volunteered for the U.S. Army." Tim O'Brien's narrator says
it best in *The Things They Carried,* "I was a coward. I went to the war." Why? He
says, "I couldn't endure the mockery, or the disgrace, or the patriotic ridicule."[99]

Does the preceding paragraph sound misplaced? Doesn't it sound like it
belongs at the beginning of my story? You might think so. I appear to have just
landed in Saigon. Dear reader, you must join me in re-thinking what you expect
of a story. You want a narrative with beginning, middle, and end. I'm trying to
show you that my narrative doesn't have such a linear movement. I want you
to see how much I, like you, was committed to a traditional narrative of rising
action, falling action, and denouement. That's a fairy tale. So, please pay attention to the realism of discontinuity.

Now back to the program you were watching: I couldn't endure the mockery, disgrace or patriotic ridicule either so I went to the Military Assistance
Command Vietnam (MACV) compound in Saigon to await assignment to a
field unit. I, along with other new guys, was outfitted quickly in brand-new,
very green jungle fatigues. A new guy always looked more green than a guy who
had been around a while. (Repeated washings turned the green to a grey color.)

I stayed for a few days in the transient barracks where the new guys mingled with the guys who were going home after a year in country. It was easy to pick out the seasoned guys from the newbies, simply by looking at their fatigues, but it was also true that the seasoned guys seemed to have some variety of the 1,000-yard stare. A guy with the 1,000-yard stare looks off into the distance and appears to have his mind on some other somber business. He's not fully "there." I felt these guys knew something that we new guys didn't know; a year later I seemed to know it too, but what was it that I knew? The new guys looked innocent to me too—then. But on arrival, it was hard to look the old guys in the eye: the stare was unnerving.

Non-veterans often self-censor their remarks about war when they talk to veterans: "You were there. You know. I wasn't there." Veterans too sometimes lay claim to special knowledge. I once heard a scholar refer to this knowledge as "Soldiers' Gnosticism." Somehow hearing the snap of AK-47 rounds or the thud of incoming 82mm mortars is supposed to convey some knowledge that mere talk about those sounds cannot convey. But really, what is learned? That getting shot at is scary? Huh? Do I need to touch the stove to know it's hot?

Knowing that the stove was hot did not preserve me from bewilderment when I met all those guys sporting the 1,000 yard stare. So when I finally reached my unit in Vietnam, Advisory Team 56, I was in a daze. I certainly could not admit to anyone how I felt. I remember that Captain Bob Burns, my boss, said I should go out with him on a Phantom Three mission on Saturday, November 1st. Phantom Three was a routine mission: two helicopter gunships (usually AH-1 Cobras) and a Command and Control Huey would go out and shoot up suspected VC locations. I remember that on that first Saturday, the sun was shining brightly. I had on my new, very green fatigues, and I carried my M-16 with a bandolier of loaded magazines. Bob was very calm, so that helped a great deal. But the effect was to make the war seem commonplace, not exceptional. I remember taking off from Can Tho Army Air Field and flying to Phong Thuan District town to pick up an advisor from the District advisory team. Then we took off and flew low for several kilometers over the closely grouped small Vietnamese houses that were perched on canal lines near Phong Thuan. Many of the houses had roofs of corrugated steel, and I could see men and women in black pajamas looking up at us in a kind of stupefaction. It dawned on me that we were intruding into their backyards; back home people would not have been pleased. I kept thinking that we'd suddenly come upon the VC. Instead we went up to about 1500 feet and watched the gunships roll in on hootches along a canal line and fire their 2.75 inch rockets and miniguns. They pummeled the hootches for a while. I think I remember a secondary explosion—a sign that we were hitting VC weapons caches. Then we went down to about 200 feet, and the door gunner started to shoot his M-60 machine gun at the hootches. Only later on in my tour did I realize that this was singularly ineffective and needlessly dangerous. A machine gun is best deployed when it sets up a killing zone—an impossibility 200 feet up and fairly stupid in a slow-flying Huey. We were making ourselves a target after our gunships had expended their ammunition.

It took me a while to realize that I actually had the authority to stop some of the silly nonsense. On this particular day, as happened all too often, the M-60 jammed after firing altogether too few rounds. We spent the day watching the gunships shoot up VC locations throughout the province. I think we refueled twice and went back out. The VC never shot back.

So my first engagement with the enemy was puzzling. Why were we shooting up hootches? How did we know that it was OK to shoot those particular hootches? Who said we could shoot? All of that was bewildering in an operational sense, but the existential Angst compromised me. I felt like I was in some sort of catatonic state, much like the soldiers in Terence Malick's *The Thin Red Line*. Malick presented soldiers who seemed to feel their non-presence at cataclysmic events in which they had actually participated. I felt like a junkie who is "not there." I had no clear sense of myself as a U.S. Army officer. How would I act if the VC should happen to capture me? Since I had no quarrel with the Viet Cong (as Muhammad Ali said), would I cooperate with them? My soul was in deep distress. Yes, I was worried about my body, but I quickly learned that I would have to be very unlucky not to survive my year. Most advisors on Team 56 did.

But I was troubled by the Phantom III, and later the Phantom Twilight, missions. Even though we were shooting at hootches in areas clearly controlled by the Viet Cong, why was mere residence in an area controlled by the Viet Cong a reason to be shot at or to have one's house blown up? I remember one evening in July 1970 when I was on Phantom Twilight, the gunships rolled in on a few people who were in the box cleared for shooting in Phong Dien District. Before we were finished for the evening, we received a call from one of our MAT teams: we had wounded a few villagers. We swooped down and picked up the villagers we had just shot. I remember feeling horribly guilty as a middle-aged man pointed to his bleeding foot when he was placed on the helicopter floor. He was not wounded seriously, but we took him to the 29th Evacuation Hospital at Binh Thuy Air Base. The local Village Chief stuck up for us: he told his villagers that the wounded people should not have been where they were. But my conscience bothered me. The Agenbite of Inwit or "the again-biting of inner wit." It continues to bite.

I should also point out that we probably would have reported the villagers as KBA when they were barely hit by the rockets and mini-guns on the Cobra gunships. So much for the accuracy of our statistics—and the foolhardiness of McNamara's statistics war.

Nick Turse makes the case that these gunship strikes were targeting civilians, and I must admit that civilians probably lived in some of the hootches we shot at. We thought we were shooting at VC guerrillas in the Phong Dien case, but obviously we were not. The VC may have wanted us to do just we were doing. Colonel Conger told the military historians that the VC would attack an outpost "with a B-40 [rocket-propelled grenade] or small arms fire or harass them [the friendlies] and pull back and watch the houses burn, auspices of the U.S. gun ships." Conger was rather certain that the use of American firepower was counterproductive. When he first arrived in Phong Dinh in February 1968—right in the middle of the Tet Offensive—he found that the U.S. Navy was routinely using a recon-by-fire technique, even as Phong Dinh Sector forces were trying to establish outposts in the areas where the Navy was routinely lobbing shells into the rice paddies and canal lines willy-nilly in the hope of keeping the VC off balance and away from the Navy's patrols along the Bassac River—a major tributary of the Mekong. Conger said, "We were trying to encourage people to move back into this area and that permitting the Navy to recon by fire would really put a death blow to any efforts to move back in." He saw the problem: "So you had a situation whereby you had the air tearing up the area. You had the artillery tearing up the areas around the outposts. You had the troops safe inside the outpost and all you were doing was protecting an outpost for the sake of the outpost itself and the poor friendly civilians that were living in the area were really getting torn up. And so we here on the advisory effort in this Province, made a very, very strong pitch to all military staff and to the Province Chief that we needed a definitely new approach with reference to combat operations."[100]

A few years later in graduate school, I foolishly thought I had the surrealism of Vietnam behind me until I read Joseph Conrad's *Heart of Darkness*. I stopped cold when I read this passage:

> For a time I would feel I belonged still to a world of straightforward facts; but the feeling would not last long. Something would turn up to scare it away. Once, I remember, we came upon a man-of-war anchored off the coast. There wasn't even a shed there, and she was shelling the bush. It appears the French had one of their wars going on thereabouts. Her ensign dropped limp like a rag; the muzzles of the long six-inch guns stuck out all over the low hull; the greasy, slimy swell swung her up lazily and let her down, swaying her thin masts. In the empty immensity of earth, sky, and water, there she was, incomprehensible, firing into a continent. Pop, would go one of the six-inch guns; a small flame would dart and vanish, a

little white smoke would disappear, a tiny projectile would give a feeble screech-and nothing happened. Nothing could happen. There was a touch of insanity in the proceeding, a sense of lugubrious drollery in the sight; and it was not dissipated by somebody on board assuring me earnestly there was a camp of natives-he called them enemies!—hidden out of sight somewhere.[101]

Well, there were camps of enemies in Phong Dinh, but firing into a province was likely to make the entire province into an enemy camp. Conger was talking about the situation in 1968, and clearly he did succeed in restraining some of the worst abuse of fire power, but the Can Tho Arty logs reveal that H&I (Harassment and Interdiction) rounds were fired every day in 1969 and 1970 (except for the periods of truce). But I was stunned to discover that B-52 strikes were made in the province in 1972 and 1973—after Conger was long gone as Province Senior Advisor. (He was killed in a plane crash in Georgia on February 12, 1972.) I do recall that he complimented Bob Burns and me as he signed his intelligence exit form just before he left for departure from Can Tho Air Field. He said he was lucky to have had such good S-2 officers. He was not a man to pass out compliments freely, so we did feel honored. In recent years I have learned to appreciate his desire to control the use of U.S. firepower.

The B-52 strikes must have been a species of the madness Conrad found off the coast of Africa—an expression of the utter futility of the U.S. advisory effort. After years of trying to get the friendly Vietnamese to "close with and destroy the enemy"—the standard World War II vintage, American infantry doctrine—the friendlies remained on the sidelines. On April 19, 1972, the Province Senior Advisor, Colonel Edward J. Porter, discussed "the recent successes of the VC in the province": "Unlike what has happened in other parts of the country, these victories were not won by the NVA forces or other outside help. They were the results of the efforts of the local communist forces."[102] Clearly the local GVN programs, American supported and inspired, had failed: Colonel Porter wrote on December 14, 1972: "As I have stated in my two previous letters, the Phung Hoang [Phoenix] program here is in very bad condition."[103] The Phung Hoang Advisor had written to his Vietnamese counterpart a year earlier, "It should be noted that the PIOCC [Province Intelligence Operations Coordinating Center] has conducted only six (6) operations in 1971 and none since mid-September."[104] No one who worked in Phong Dinh, close to the end of the American withdrawal in 1973, should have been surprised on April 30, 1975.

The U.S. jumped into the void created by the indifference of the GVN forces and programs. It is astonishing that during the week of January 21 to January 28, 1973, the U.S. made 33 B-52 strikes in IV Corps. Two were made in Phong Dinh on January 25, 1973, yet the strikes seem to have been utterly ineffectual. The TOC logs say that the results for both strikes were negligible[105];

the INTSUM for January 25 says the results were unknown.[106] A previous B-52 strike on December 13, 1972, reported "negative results within the target box."[107] Given the intensity of a B-52 strike, it is quite incredible not to be able to claim any kind of military gain by their use. During the same time period, a former ARVN POW reported that the VC always knew when the B-52s are coming. On the day previous to a strike, a Huey would circle the area to be attacked; the VC would move out of the area. An American source stated that the B-52 strikes had become increasingly ineffective after August 1972. Since a B-52 strike can pulverize a target box one-mile-by-two-miles, ground forces should have found it easy to follow up B-52 strikes, but there were no reports of mass VC casualties in Phong Dinh following the 1972–1973 B-52 strikes.

The INTSUM for January 27 and 28, 1973, reports 58 contacts with the VC—just three days after the B-52 strike on January 25. Most of the contacts were VC-initiated. At no time in 1969–1970 did the VC mount such widespread attacks. The most spectacular events on January 28 included the forced march of civilian villagers on an outpost and the firing of 122mm rockets into the center of Can Tho City and into Can Tho Air Field.[108] I cannot recall a single report of the firing of a 122 in Phong Dinh during my year, and I'm fairly certain that the VC would have fired the rockets if they had had them. Their supply channels were obviously in fine working order in 1973. Our bombing suggests our impotence to change the situation on the ground.

The American Black and Tans

Turse does not consider the impossibility of fighting a war when it is a standard enemy tactic to use the civilian population as a shield and to sacrifice any number of civilians in order to alienate the surviving civilians against the GVN and the Americans. There is no resolving this difficulty: we killed civilians, and the VC wanted us to kill them. On February 25, 1970, a MAT team secured a downed U.S. helicopter; in a nearby VC bunker the team found two women and three children.[109] I guess the VC guerrillas had no rear area to safeguard their children. It is hard to believe that they wanted us to kill defenseless members of their families, but there is not much doubt that they would use any such deaths for propaganda purposes. And we were bound to kill some women and children. I found this out almost immediately.

Vo Nguyen Giap, the North Vietnamese general credited with the Communist victories over the French and the Americans, died on October 4, 2013, apparently at the age of 102. The *New York Times* obituary reports that General Giap's "critics said that his victories had been rooted in a profligate disregard for the lives of his soldiers." Giap "is said to have remarked after the war with France": "'Every minute, hundreds of thousands of people die on this earth.... The life or death of a hundred, a thousand, tens of thousands of human beings, even our compatriots, means little.'"[110] While Giap may have been callous about casualties, his attitude should not have been ours.

In fairness I must say that the American soldier was put in an impossible situation. He couldn't identify enemy soldiers except by their behavior: there was no standard VC uniform. Consequently practices such as firing bursts from automatic weapons near VC suspects to test their reaction seem to have evolved. I knew that at least some door gunners thought this was an acceptable practice. As was frequently the case, I translated the situation into Irish terms. I was reminded of my mother's dislike for the Black and Tans, who terrorized Ireland during the Irish War of Independence (1919–21). Technically temporary constables in the Royal Irish Constabulary, the Black and Tans were recruited mostly from World War I veterans, and they were lawless thugs, a coarse lot. My mother told me that the Black and Tans rousted her family out of their house in Sligo one morning and terrorized the family by browbeating her father and her oldest brother. Lieutenant Colonel Gerald Brice Ferguson Smyth, the Black and Tan division commander for Munster, was famous for allegedly issuing the following orders in June 1920:

> If a police barracks is burned or if the barracks already occupied is not suitable, then the best house in the locality is to be commandeered, the occupants thrown into the gutter. Let them die there—the more the merrier.
> Should the order ("Hands Up") not be immediately obeyed, shoot and shoot with effect. If the persons approaching (a patrol) carry their hands in their pockets, or are in any way suspicious-looking, shoot them down. You may make mistakes occasionally and innocent persons may be shot, but that cannot be helped, and you are bound to get the right parties some time. The more you shoot, the better I will like you, and I assure you no policeman will get into trouble for shooting any man.[111]

While Smyth disputed the accuracy of the quotation, the authenticity of the orders was widely believed because there were so many incidents of Black and Tan brutality. The orders closely resemble the American practice of shooting near the VC to test their reaction. Turse points to the obvious flaw in the practice: who wouldn't duck and run if the bullets are flying nearby? On November 19, 1969, Ben Nelson refused to engage in this practice when the pilots on Firefly wanted to shoot near seven sampans that could not be identified as enemies.[112] Ben was virtuous that night, and many lieutenants and captains on Team 56 were virtuous in other situations as well—hard as it was to be virtuous in Joseph Conrad's flabby devil hell.

We encountered corruption and reported it. How can ideals exist in a totally corrupt society? I remember that God told Abraham that he would not destroy Sodom and Gomorrah if even ten righteous people lived there. At times it was possible to think that no one could be righteous in the American-organized, morally bankrupt society that we saw on a daily basis. So it was easy to see that at some point the whole mess would have to come crashing down. Or, actually, Humpty-Dumpty had already had his great fall. And we were creating a bureaucracy to put him back together again. Bureaucracy is a fantasy of control. It divides the world into parts and hopes to make Humpty-Dumpty whole. But there was no sense of wholeness, just a bunch of parts. Bureaucracy is essentially an abstraction, and our war in Vietnam was built on the false consciousness of a subject-object split. Bureaucracy is the attempt of the subject to force order onto the object at the point of a gun while all the while we kid ourselves that we are not part of the object.

The Phong Dinh Daily Mayhem

The confusion and moral compromise I felt before I went to war was of a piece with the confusion of being there. I was given tasks to accomplish, paper to process, Vietnamese to encounter, and missions to fly. I had no choice about most of my duties, but if I had to pitch, I could throw the occasional knuckle ball.

The sun kept shining on my first day of aerial combat. Bob Burns and I went back to the mess hall for dinner. It seemed hardly credible that we could sit at tables, eat a meal, and talk about Notre Dame football after an afternoon of "shoot-'em-up." (Notre Dame walloped Navy on November 1, 1969, 47–0, to the delight of Bob—an Irish-American, South Dakota State Jackrabbit alumnus, but also a prairie "alumnus" of the Golden Dome.) Here I was at war. My only goal was to get back on the airplane and go home. I didn't understand how the air could remain humid after the rockets had whooshed through it. This was not training or a live-fire exhibition. The gunships were hoping to shoot and kill Viet Cong. I can't remember exactly, but I probably listened to the broadcast of the Notre Dame-Navy game on the Armed Forces Radio Network on that Saturday.

Most days were routine: some friendlies or enemy soldiers were killed; some were wounded; the artillery fired away as did the gunships. There were ambushes every night and day—some friendly, most VC. There were many mechanical failures and accidents that created dangerous and sometimes deadly outcomes. Soldiers screwed up routinely. VIPs visited regularly; the IV Corps press office was in our Team House, and reporters frequently ate in our mess hall. Occasionally we'd get a report of an aircraft shooting when no one authorized it to shoot; it was probably freelancing. Bridges would be blown up and re-built. One night a fire in Can Tho burned 100 homes. There was no GVN social welfare net to help out in such cataclysms. There were frequent reports of GVN graft and corruption. The VC controlled key canals, collected taxes, and posted their flag either to annoy the friendlies or to lure them into a booby trap or the killing zone of an ambush. When there would be a report of a VC location, the first instinct would be to send Shotgun, our L-19 pilot, to take a look and a few shots with his rockets at the location. There were no big battles for an entire year, but every day there was contact with the enemy. Aircraft received ground fire from small arms; outposts received 60mm mortar fire.

I picked out a day in my year at random: on November 25, 1969, the Phong Dinh Province Tactical Operations Center log records the following:

1. At 1:15 a.m. a PF outpost, three kilometers west of Can Tho, was under attack by a force of unknown size. The outpost received B40 rocket, automatic weapon, and small arms fire. Four PF soldiers were wounded.

2. At 2:30 a.m. the Firefly lightship reported having received heavy ground fire at 2:05 a.m. It went to the aid of the outpost under attack and directed Cobra gunships to fire upon the attackers at 2:05 a.m., 2:30 a.m., and 3:00 a.m. Contact was broken at 3:30 a.m. Lieutenant Ben Nelson complained about using the Firefly lightship to taxi pilots from Can Tho Air Field to Binh Thuy Air Base.

3. 50 VC from the C-29 unit were sighted at 5:00 a.m. The source of the report was rated as fairly reliable; the report itself was rated as probably true.

4. 60 VC from the C-71 unit were sighted at 7:00 a.m. The source of the report was rated as fairly reliable; the report itself was rated as probably true. A second sighting report located the 80 members of the C-71 unit at 5:00 a.m. in a different area, eight kilometers east of the later location. The second report's reliability was rated slightly lower—as possibly true. (It was possible for the unit to move eight kilometers on the canals in two hours.)

5. At 7:20 a.m. Thuan Nhon District reported observing eight light observation helicopters (LOHs) flying from the northeast to the southwest. (This report seems erroneous: eight LOHs would not usually, if ever, fly together.) One fired 30 to 40 rounds of unspecified ordnance while out of sight. The report suggests that an American helicopter was firing without clearance to shoot. (A guess: the occupant of the LOH doing the shooting was John Paul Vann, who was known for skylarking around the Delta in a LOH.)

6. Several field teams reported c. 7–8:00 a.m. that Americans would be walking on several different RF/PF operations during the day.

7. At 7:45 a.m. a Chinook helicopter dropped artillery rounds that it was transporting. One round landed on Binh Loc School House; another on a 60-foot barge. Three children were killed, three wounded seriously. Some children might have been lost in the river. An Emergency Ordnance Disposal (EOD) team went to the site. (A report in the TOC log for November 26, 1970, the next day, says three children were killed, one seriously injured, and three released after treatment.)

8. By 9:05 a.m. an airmobile operation was on its way, and a U.S. Air Force Forward Air Controller (FAC) was aloft.

9. An ARVN soldier from the 21st Division was medevaced at 10:45 a.m. He suffered shrapnel wounds from a booby trap. Americans on the ground coordinated the medevac.

10. Phong Phu District reported that 30 to 40 Cambodians were demonstrating at 11:15 a.m. with plans to go to the Province House, the seat of local government, in the afternoon. (The reason for the demonstration is not mentioned, but it probably concerned the treatment of Cambodian refugees.)

11. At 11:52 a.m. MAT 117, on an operation with the RF, received automatic weapons fire from 34 VC. (How did they count the number so exactly?)

12. At 12:20 a FAC reported sighting a sampan with two people aboard taking evasive action in Phong Phu District.

13. The Province L-19 pilot reported sighting two sampans with two people in a VC-controlled area at 1:40 p.m.

14. At 2:50 p.m. MAT 57 reported its operation complete. Results: one North Vietnamese Army mask captured (whatever such a mask may have been). MAT 117 also reported at the same time that five hootches had been destroyed on its operation.

15. 150 VC from an unknown unit were reported sighted at 3:00 p.m. The source of the report was rated as fairly reliable; the report itself was rated as possibly true.

16. At 3:40 p.m. the L-19 pilot requested permission to shoot at another location in a VC-controlled area. He received permission to shoot at 4:10 p.m. Results: one VC KBA; one sampan destroyed in Hoa My hamlet.

17. At 7:14 p.m. a FAC was aloft and at 7:25 p.m. he requested permission for an air strike where he spotted four or five lights moving and estimated 50 to 100 VC on the move. The air strike was completed at 9:15 p.m. The FAC reported three structures destroyed.

18. At 7:42 p.m. an outpost in Phong Thuan District was receiving harassing fire from an estimated ten VC. Contact was broken at 8:15 p.m.

19. At 8:05 p.m. the Police Advisor reported the discovery of a mine across the road from Palm Springs—the whimsical nickname for a compound with swimming pool for U.S. CORDS civilians in Can Tho. Explosive Ordinance Disposal (EOD) responded. (John Paul Vann kept a bedroom at Palm Springs for trysts and as cover for his promiscuous sexual escapades.)

20. At 8:25 p.m. Phung Hiep District reported an outpost in contact with

about 20 VC. The outpost returned fire and received artillery support. At 8:47 contact had been broken.

21. An ARVN soldier, delirious with malaria, was medevaced at 10:25 p.m.

In addition to these reports in the TOC log, the Province S-2 reported five sightings of known VC units with a total strength of 250 guerrillas. Four of the sighting locations received artillery; the fifth an air strike. There were two sighting reports from the American 525 MI Group; no response to these sightings was recorded.[113]

So what did we have on this one day in Phong Dinh? Well, quite enough copy for the tabloid *New York Daily News* for at least a week. I can imagine the headlines for a local paper called *The Phong Dinh Daily Mayhem*:

CAMBODIANS to GVN: STOP STEALING OUR FOOD!
OOPS! U.S. CHINOOK DROPS AMMO LOAD: 3 CHILDREN DEAD
VANN LOVE NEST TARGET OF VC MINE
TAXI SCANDAL: PILOTS HITCH COPTER RIDES
VC BLASTED BY ARTY AND AIR—
    ONE DEAD (MAYBE); RICE PADDIES CRATERED
VC MOVE AND ATTACK AT WILL: 250 VC GUERRILLAS SIGHTED
AMERICAN INTEL SCANDAL: 525 MI GROUP IGNORED
FOUR DEAD, EIGHT WOUNDED IN PHONG DINH

How typical was November 25, 1969?

—While a Chinook didn't drop ammo on a school again, a Chinook did drop artillery rounds again on November 30th, this time not on a populated area. (A TOC log entry that I made reports some attempt at a cover-up: the load was dropped between 8 and 9:00 a.m. but not reported to the Vietnamese until 1:30 p.m.[114]) On February 7, 1970, the Firefly lightship dropped a box of flares.[115] A flare was housed in a metal canister about two feet long: it did not weigh a great deal, but it could cause damage if it landed on anyone. One of the flares did discharge when it hit the ground—a fire hazard.

—On November 11, 1969, two weeks prior to the report of unauthorized firing by an unknown helicopter, another unidentified, low-flying helicopter, "loaded with mini-guns" killed a 16-year-old civilian, Trong Van Choi, at 4:30 p.m. Team 56 advisors on the ground in Thuan Nhon District looked "at the body and reported multi-gunshot wounds to the head & chest, left side and both legs."[116] Less than a week after the November 25 incident, on December 1, 1969, at 6:20 p.m. Major Milbank, the District Senior Advisor for Thuan Trung, notified the TOC that a group of three

Cobra gunships and four Hueys flew overhead near Co Do. One chopper "broke away from the group and came within 100 feet of the ground.... Milbank felt it is poor public relations and requested we report it."[117]

—And the VC frequently picked prominent targets (like Palm Springs) in Can Tho for terrorist attacks:

—At 9:15 p.m. on December 1st, the same night as the Thuan Trung incident, a man on a bicycle threw a grenade in the area near the Province Hospital and an American compound in Can Tho.[118]

—On January 30, 1970, a grenade placed in the gas tank of a Vietnamese jeep parked near the USO canteen and the Intelligence Section of IV Corps headquarters in Can Tho exploded at 7:20 a.m. Four ARVN soldiers were wounded.[119]

—On March 30, 1970, an American warrant officer reported that a grenade was thrown at his ¾ ton truck, three blocks west of the main intersection in Can Tho. The grenade bounced off the truck but did not explode.[120]

—On March 9, 1970, a bomb went off at the American Cultural Center at 12:43 p.m. Four civilians were wounded.[121]

—On January 31, 1970, Team 56 advisors at two locations separately reported at 8:33 a.m. that an unknown American helicopter was firing its door guns. No one seems to have identified the chopper, and no aircraft had been given permission to shoot.[122]

—And almost every day, there were friendly and enemy casualties—caused mostly by air strikes, artillery, and accidents. Accidents were very common: on March 4, 1970, an RF soldier accidentally discharged an M79 grenade into the market place in Thuan Nhon. Eight civilians were wounded, four of whom required medevac.[123] And there is even a report in the TOC logs of a VC screw-up: on February 20, 1970, two VC units engaged in a fire fight with one another; blood was later found on the ground by the friendlies.[124]

—The Americans and the Vietnamese crossed signals periodically too. On September 6, 1970, an American L-19 pilot was given permission to shoot at a group he identified as VC. The Vietnamese duty officer, while given the correct grid coordinates, misread them and gave the L19 permission to shoot. The 4th ARVN Rangers reported that they had 8 WIA, 1 KIA as a result.[125]

Then there were non-combat altercations, but since arms were so plentiful [Bulletin to the NRA], the results were often deadly:

—On February 6, 1970, at 2:30 a.m. two PSDF members intentionally fired on one another in Can Tho, but bystanders became the casualties. One civilian was killed; another wounded.[126]

—On March 13, 1970, Lieutenant Dave Heinrich, while driving across a bridge near the red-light district (Ben Xe Moi), was attacked by five ARVN Rangers. He was hit in the head with a rock; his glasses and watch were stolen although he was not hurt.[127]

—On April 20, 1970, the Military Police reported that in the 440th Transportation Company Enlisted Men's Club at Binh Thuy Air Base, an American fired an M-16 and wounded three Americans, one seriously.[128]

And, on December 2, 1969, Colonel Conger called off an air strike because the intended strike area was "highly populated with friendly [people]."[129]

This Can't Be Happening

It's quite singular to have little ambition for an entire year, except to cross off days very similar to November 25, 1969, on my Julian Date Calendar. A Julian Date Calendar assigns a number to each day of the year. January 1st is 001, and December 31 is 365. Much like a prisoner marking off the days to his release, I kept the calendar on the wall next to my desk in the S-2 office. Maybe I was hoping to get the "heart of wisdom" promised in Psalm 90 if I learned "to number our days." So I went through the year, much as I arrived, surprised that I could actually be in Vietnam but clueless about definitive steps to do anything but go there and then serve there. The fog of battle starts at home and never burns off. I did conclude that I would never again allow myself to be trapped into a situation in which my moral choices were foreclosed by my mere existence in the situation. I was in Vietnam. We were there to make war.

The questions never went away: Am I really here? Is this just a dream? Who is going to shoot at us? What is the door gunner shooting at from 200 feet? What happened to John Goggin? In "The Sweetheart of the Song Tra Bong," Tim O'Brien tells the story of a medic who invites his girlfriend to join him on a mountain-top aid station. And, sure enough, Mary Anne Bell gets off a chopper one day, dressed in pink culottes. The basis of O'Brien's story may seem unbelievable, but the unbelievable had a way of happening, much like what happens when a Little League baseball manager puts a guy in right field who can't catch fly balls. The ball always finds the guy.[130]

Well, one day Ben Nelson's wife found him in Can Tho: she spent about a week with us. It sure was bizarre to go to breakfast in the morning with this woman who was quite normal. During the week I'd see her in the green and white Land Rover that Ben used to drive. Very middle-class, the whole thing. I think she even went to our movie one night. What else would a young couple do in Can Tho on a beautiful December evening? Ben actually had to swap Firefly assignments with another guy so as to be with her every night. (To say nothing of what might have happened if Ben had run into trouble with Victor Charles during an evening's sojourn at 100 feet above Can Tho and environs while his wife was in Can Tho.) They stayed at the Palm Springs compound— in retrospect, this is amusing, given John Paul Vann's "residence" there. Then

Ben's wife went back to Hawaii, where she was waiting out Ben's year in Vietnam with their young child. She must have been courageous, to think almost nothing of getting on the plane to pay Ben a visit. It seemed perfectly normal after we got used to the idea. Actually any American could have paid a visit at any time. Maybe we would have gotten the word back sooner about how fruitless the war was.

Some time after Ben's wife visited, he wound up in the hospital at Binh Thuy Air Base—about five miles outside Can Tho. I'm not sure why he was there, but he may have contracted malaria. Well, after yet another night of consuming ten-cent cans of Carling Black Label, Steve Black and I thought Ben must be lonely, and we really ought to pay him a visit. The problem was that our solicitousness for Ben reached its peak about 9:30 p.m. We figured it was our duty to go to the air base immediately. We found an empty cookie tin in which we inserted two cans of cold beer and then loaded up Black's jeep with an arsenal of weapons, just in case we ran into any trouble. Black produced a shotgun somehow, and we grabbed fragmentation, CS (tear gas), and incendiary grenades from the stock that was lying around the Team House. I took my M-16 and a bandolier of magazines, and off we went.

When we got to the hospital, the nurses immediately told us that it was too late to visit, but Black, who was dressed in his flight suit, explained that he had just flown in from Saigon and he had to go back: couldn't he just have a few minutes with his dear friend, Lieutenant Nelson—an old buddy from basic training at Fort Dix. Black, who looked like the boy next door, could be very endearing, so the nurses relented, and they left us alone with Ben in a large, ward-like room in which he was the only patient. We gave him the cookie tin and cautioned him to open it only when no one was around. On the sign above his bed, Black changed Ben's rank from LT to LTC, or lieutenant colonel, so that Ben, as the youngest lieutenant colonel in the army, would get better treatment—a battlefield promotion of sorts.

Finally after giggling for about a half-hour, Black and I set off on the return trip to the Team House. It was getting close to midnight—well after curfew. Only personnel with legitimate military business were allowed on the roads. The road to Can Tho was wide open, and Black was whizzing along. As he drew near a bridge, he slowed down, and I heard him pop a grenade. I couldn't see any reason for alarm, so I was alarmed. But when I looked at Black, I saw a mischievous smile on his face. Now the bridges were heavily guarded by sleeping RF troops, so Black dropped a CS grenade out of the jeep and then took off down the road. As I looked back, I could see a bustle of activity on the bridge, and Black was thoroughly delighted with himself. After all he was being benevolent: he woke the RF soldiers up and gave them something to talk about.

There was a certain peculiar recklessness about our behavior: it was great fun to subvert the enterprise that did not inspire our commitment—morally or politically. We had our fun when we couldn't take the boredom any more although Black was good at avoiding ennui. Probably because he was plagued by the horrors of his combat flying, he couldn't sleep at night, so he devoured books and slept during the day when he wasn't flying. He had been drafted when he dropped out of Harvard for a semester. He was having fun when he would go up in his L-19 and, on many days, break whatever rules he could. One day he decided to fly in low over the Team House, about 25 feet up, just to say hello to everyone. I can't imagine what the control tower at the air field was saying. On another day he even changed his call sign while orchestrating helicopter gunship strikes. He decided that "Shotgun" was worn out, so he re-named himself the "Pro from Pebble Beach" and even managed to have the gun-ship pilots change their call signs too. The VC on the ground had nine irons, golf bags, and caddies. Black would be overjoyed to show me the holes in his airplane's wings whenever he got the chance. One day he absolutely insisted that I come by his plane at the air field to see a fist-sized hole in the right wing very close to the cockpit. He was laughing deliriously. And then he wanted me to go up with him. I was having none of that; I had had enough fun on the road back from Binh Thuy. I couldn't get past the moral emptiness of our lives. Black apparently couldn't either. Why else would he have put himself on mock-trial in Oregon years later?

By the time I reported for active duty in January 1969 just as Nixon was being sworn in as president, I had become decidedly anti-war. I was not alone: I found that many of my fellow lieutenants at the U.S. Army Infantry School shared my skepticism about either the moral rectitude or the political wisdom of the war in Vietnam, i.e., the necessity of opposing the international Communist conspiracy. I don't remember hearing any reason for fighting in Vietnam while at either infantry or intelligence school; support for our nation's war policy was simply assumed although being anti-war is not the same as being insubordinate—a contradictory state of mind that limits a soldier's zeal and sense of purpose. (Being of two minds in a war zone might actually limit the evil one undertakes when the cause is so unclear.) I can remember a lieutenant from Baltimore at the Infantry School who carried a clipboard with the slogan, "Justice in Vietnam"—a riposte to the hordes of Officer Candidate School troops who carried clipboards with "Victory in Vietnam" bumper stickers affixed. (Was anyone defining "victory"? What would victory look like?) Carrying a clipboard with even a modestly anti-war slogan would surely annoy the battalion commander, Lieutenant Colonel Wilbur J. Thiel.

I evolved into opposition to the war without a drastic shift in political attitude. I had been skeptical about wars in general and their moral value from an early age. I actually remember that one day in grade school, Raymond Daugherty said to me, "My father says that there's a war about every 20 years. If that's so, then we might fight in the next one." It must have been about 1958. I felt transfixed, and I do remember the moment with startling clarity. 1965, the year of the major American troop deployment to Vietnam, was 20 years after the end of World War II. I guess Ray's father was pretty smart, and even at age 10 I wasn't keen to go to the next war.

It is true that I moved from simple cowardice, i.e., I didn't want to be killed in any war, to informed opposition by the time I reported for duty. The lack of moral fiber in such an evolution nagged at the edges of my "informed opposition." In some ways the Viet Cong had already won the propaganda war before I left for Vietnam. I was embarrassed to be in the army when it seemed that all the smart and cool people evaded the draft with relative ease. I had no sense of serving my country; my service had no nobility about it. When you convict yourself of lack of character, you don't like yourself very much.

In retrospect I realize now that evading the draft was not impossible, and I might have been able to avoid service entirely when a draft lottery was instituted in 1969. I never checked what number I would have received until 2012. I waited until Easter Sunday 2012 to find out that my birthday, May 2nd, was Number 298: I never would have been drafted had I not joined ROTC and had I been able to delay induction until December 1969. I didn't look up this number until 2012 since I felt the matter was moot in 1969, and a high number would have only depressed me. I'm able now, without rancor, to contemplate 298. I'd have considered myself a dumbass for being in Vietnam when I could have been drinking beer and playing rugby—and other socially useful activities. And I already thought I was an immoral dumbass for being there.

The other strong factor that led me to become more anti-war was the simple fact that every intelligent woo-able young female that I met was anti-war. (The Viet Cong won their hearts too even though the women did not think about it so consciously: they were not Jane Fondas—actively giving aid and comfort to the enemy.) I certainly never met any young woman who would encourage me to go to war and sacrifice for my country. This never happened. Maybe that's proof enough that the war was questionable. Now I was not an advanced wooer of women, but those whom I did manage to get into conversation with were at a minimum skeptical of the war. Many had participated in anti-war demonstrations. I know I turned red in the face whenever a young woman found out in September 1969 that I was on my way to Vietnam. My ticket to Saigon was a real conversation stopper.

I do remember the poster that said, "Women say yes to men who say no." The converse of that statement, "Women say no to men who say yes," was cer-

tainly an implicit threat to my hopes of meeting the woman of my dreams, con-
fused as my psyche was likely to be by my staunch Irish Catholic upbringing
although mine was more liberal than most Catholics of my generation. I've often
thought that the poster was a brilliant stratagem that would cause some draft-
age guys to consider whether they wanted to go to Vietnam or at least give them
misgivings about going.

At Fort Benning (Benning School for Boys) we stood in stands before
periods of instruction and shouted "Kill." But no one ever said why we should
kill. The training cadre members were trying to de-sensitize us to the idea of
taking human life. The army, I later found out, had employed legions of social
and behavioral scientists to solve the problem of getting infantry soldiers in
contact with the enemy to pull the triggers of their weapons. Studies had shown
that an incredible number simply wouldn't shoot. So, as a result, we yelled, "Kill."
I never joined willingly in this stuff: occasionally I might mumble "Kill" so as
to avoid being singled out as a "slacker" of sorts. (I was just filled with moral fiber.)
The army never seemed to understand how to handle politics. The closest it
came to the political was the day I was required to stand in formation when
Eisenhower died (March 28, 1969). A proclamation was read, honoring him
for his role in leading the army in World War II. The proclamation had a political cast to it—the kind that was missing from the Vietnam War.

Almost everyone in Infantry Officers Basic Course–8 (IOBC-8) had a college degree: where was the capacity to think critically? An officer does need
critical thinking skills on the battlefield to make tactical and moral decisions.
Most guys seemed simply to accept that they were headed to Vietnam, yet many
did have doubts about the purpose of the war. The guys seemed to have a grue-
some sense of duty that helped them move one foot after the other while hoping
somehow to luck into an assignment to Korea or Germany. (Officers who did
not go to Vietnam and who served during the peak years of the war seem oddly
to regret not going, like they missed something or performed less valuable service.) It is remarkable that I can't recall a single infantry lieutenant in IOBC-8
who was itching to get to Vietnam to fight those despicable Commie bastards.
(An aside: Paul Woodruff, now a thoughtful philosopher at the University of
Texas, graduated from IOBC-8 as the number one student in our class. I wonder
what he was thinking. What made him studious in, let's say, tactical nuclear
weapons class?) Critical thinking was a luxury for the kids still in college: we
were already compromised. We had to wait until 2012 for the Texas Republican
Party to include a plank against teaching "critical thinking" in its platform.

In 1969 army lieutenants headed to Vietnam merely resisted facing the
inevitability of the trip to Vietnam; now we are militantly opposed to even
thinking about what our country has been doing in Afghanistan. But when we

rode on cattle cars to training, we did sing (to the tune of "My Bonnie Lies Over the Ocean") with heartfelt skepticism about what we were doing:

IOBC sounds like some bullshit.
To me, to me.
They make you a second lieutenant.
They give you a bar of gold.
They make you a forward observer.
You live to be three seconds old.

Buy Bonds or Else...

I only heard overt protest over the war when the battalion commander for IOBC-8, Lieutenant Colonel Thiel, demanded that we buy U.S. Savings Bonds by payroll deduction. Yes, by checking the payroll records of the 200 guys in IOBC-8, he found out who the five were who wouldn't buy bonds. Our personal finances, to his mind, were not personal: they were symptomatic of our shaky patriotism, and, by God, Thiel wasn't losing his Savings Bond flag on the pole outside his office because five smart-ass lieutenants weren't buying bonds. Yes, he got to fly a special Savings Bond flag when 100 percent or thereabouts of his battalion signed up for the bonds. His pursuit of that dumb flag was akin to Lieutenant Scheisskopf's desire to win the parades competition in *Catch–22*. The parades were more important than beating the Nazis, and winning the competition eventually got Scheisskopf (Shithead, in English) promoted to general without hearing a shot fired.

So one afternoon the five of us were jerked from training and told to report to battalion headquarters. Thiel, a man with the wrinkled, angry, weathered stone face of a 49-year-old man who had developed a strong contempt for college boy lieutenants, stood us at attention in his office and then interrogated us about why we sorry unpatriotic bastards were not buying bonds. This was not an occasion when I was embarrassed. Each guy had to explain his reasons. I was fourth on line; John Goggin was second on line—refusing to buy bonds six months before he was killed in Vietnam. Fortunately for me, Thiel completely lost his cool with the third guy—a first lieutenant named Murtha from Green Bay, Wisconsin, who told him that he wasn't buying them because the war in Vietnam was immoral. Thiel nearly had a coronary, and I thought he was going to assault Murtha physically. When Thiel asked Murtha what he was doing in the army, Murtha, who had been studying to become a priest but had decided to leave the seminary, replied that Thiel had a good question.

Thiel completely lost it and moved on to me. I chose my words carefully: "I disagree with national priorities." Thiel then asked me who pinned the bar on my shoulder. I told him I was commissioned at Fordham University although the correct answer to his question was, "My mother, Sir." But he was already so bent out of shape about Murtha who had been much more explicit about his opposition to the Vietnam War that he moved on to the last guy—a Southerner named Harper who told Thiel that bonds were a bad investment. That was really funny because Harper was probably right. It was also funny that all this probably resulted in Murtha's being sent to Korea, where he was promoted to captain and served as an aide to a general. I met him while on R 'n' R in Tokyo in September 1970, and we had much fun in sharing our stories although I was jealous that he had actually figured out how to get off the next plane to Vietnam. Thiel would surely have put him on that plane.

And, by the way, Thiel, despite being our battalion commander, never once spoke to us on any other occasion about any other subject, and I do not recollect his showing up for any training exercise. The motto of the Infantry School is "Follow Me." Thiel was leading us all right: to buy bonds. So much for leadership in the Cold War. I hope the bastard blushes if he ever reads this.

I was fascinated to discover that Thiel participated in a 1970–72 study at Ft. Benning of the shape of a future all-volunteer army. A directive dated November 20, 1970, called upon commanders of the experimental volunteer units to "eliminate coercion in fund drives, savings bond campaigns, and similar activities by establishing campaign organizations which do not parallel existing chains of command."[131] Apparently Thiel's practice in coercing lieutenants was to become taboo in the new army.

The Kaiser: An Irish Hero

Clearly the VC had won the war with the women I knew, including my mother. When she pinned the bars on my shoulder, she was observing an old army custom that a new lieutenant should have the bars pinned on by a woman. The unstated part of that tradition was that the woman endorsed what the man was doing. My mother wanted me to stay at home, for sure. The only war stories I ever heard from her were about the savage treatment of her family by the Black and Tans back in Ireland. My mother loved the fact that her father, John Murphy, kept a picture of the Kaiser up in the house throughout World War I.

I was never in any doubt that my mother would endorse resistance to the Black and Tans. She lived to be almost 101 years old. Even when she was quite disoriented in her last years, she would speak as if she were 12 years old and living in Cloonkeelane. She was greatly concerned that her younger brother John not get into trouble. I wondered if there was some residue of Black and Tan visitations in her final anxieties. History mattered to both my mother and father—Irish history—and American history too. While they both did not ever want to return to Ireland, they remained true to their Irish history and raised me with respect for resistance to British imperialism. That was an un–American upbringing.

I had absorbed the anti-imperialist value of not lording it over the indigenous people by watching Peter O'Toole in the 1962 movie, *Lawrence of Arabia*. When I got to Phong Dinh Province, I posted T.E. Lawrence's principles for dealing with tribal people in the S-2 office in Phong Dinh. They were brilliant pieces of advice about not assuming racial superiority. I remember particularly Lawrence's injunction: "Do not try to do too much with your own hands. Better the Arabs do it tolerably than that you do it perfectly. It is their war, and you are to help them, not to win it for them. Actually, also, under the very odd conditions of Arabia, your practical work will not be as good as, perhaps, you think it is."[132]

My childhood lessons in humility made accepting Lawrence's advice easy, but I was not prepared for the political war into which I was inserted, i.e., the Phoenix Program. My dear friend, Mark Barrett (no shirker he), has said that he had moral qualms about the Phoenix Program while convalescing from

John and Winifred Murphy.

injuries suffered in training at the Engineering School at Fort Belvoir. He said that he thought then that he might not be able to serve in such a program. He was no commie pinko liberal, yet his moral nature was perplexed by the idea of killing civilians.

Fortunately, I was not assigned as a Phoenix officer as most MI lieutenants in MACV were, but I did have to deal with constant discussion of VCI, i.e., Viet Cong Infrastructure—a euphemistic and mechanistic neologism designed to gloss over the fact that Phoenix was an assassination program directed at civilian political leaders. In fairness, it must be said that the VC themselves made no such distinction: everyone was both political and military, but the Geneva Convention was a handy propaganda tool with which to damage American morale and fighting ability. The VC had their own Phoenix Program: they routinely assassinated GVN village and hamlet chiefs. On November 15, 1969, Thuan Nhon District reported that its Vietnamese S-2, dressed in civilian clothes, was assassinated in Chu Thien Village.[133] On February 27, 1970, six VC, the TOC log reports, "broke into Nhon Loc I Hamlet, assassinated the Chairman & Deputy Chairman to the People's Council of Nhon Ai Hamlet."[134] The Province Monthly Report for April 1970 reports that during the past month, "There were ... several assassination attempts directed against local GVN officials."[135] Still there is no getting around the fact that the GVN Phoenix tactics often involved nighttime raids and swift dispatch of VCI by assassination.

It is probably quite true that the nature of the Viet Cong organization required a Phoenix Program—once the battle with the Vietnamese Communists had been joined. There could be no winning the war as long as the VC political structure—the National Liberation Front—remained intact and operative throughout the countryside. (And the very ineffective Phoenix program of 1972 suggests how poorly motivated the friendlies were to win the war.) But to engage in such a program was to violate principles dear to the American heart such as habeas corpus and trial by jury. In his book on the Phoenix Program, Douglas Valentine reports: "Legendary CIA officer Lucien Conein described Phoenix as 'A very good blackmail scheme for the central government. 'If you don't do what I want, you're VC.'"[136] We corrupted our values by promoting such behavior. And it was probably easy to fall into such behavior because the vital interests of the United States were not at stake in the war. We would still have habeas corpus in Knoxville, Tennessee—usually—although some black people might dispute that claim. In a recent conversation with Bob Burns, he wondered whether the drone war in Afghanistan and Pakistan will eventually be seen as the Phoenix Program arisen from the ashes of the Vietnam fiasco— a good question.

The Phoenix Program

Although I was not assigned to the Phoenix Program, I was sent to Phoenix School in Vung Tau for a week of training. I learned all kinds of neat skills such as fingerprinting ("Roll the fingers from left-to-right"). My classmates were mostly American junior officers, but there were a number of enlisted men and a couple of majors. But there were also some gallant allies—a few South Korean lieutenants and some English-speaking Vietnamese. We learned how the communists organized themselves, the roles that various party leaders filled, especially on the village level. But we were free to go to the beautiful beach on the South China Sea every afternoon. It was so odd: we lay in the sun while the war went on. The water was clean. We might have been on Waikiki or Daytona Beach or some other fabled American beach. As a kid I had gone mostly to Orchard Beach in the Bronx where we cavorted in far less splendor. During the evenings in Vung Tau, we all gathered in a room in the barracks and drank beer. Officers fraternized with enlisted men; the usual non-fraternization rules seemed inappropriate for a Shangri-La resort like Vung Tau.

One night a rather free-wheeling discussion arose about the war itself. So here we were in Vietnam, and several guys were expressing anti-war sentiments while attending Phoenix School—being trained for what would become one of the most debated programs of the war. At Congressional hearings on the program in 1971, a former serviceman described it as a "sterile, depersonalized murder program."[137] Yet there was significant skepticism expressed by a number of guys. Finally a Spec 4 from Los Angeles faced off with an MI major who said he was a medical doctor. The major's claim to a medical degree was very odd, but the Spec 4 was not awed. He asked the major how he could have chosen a career in military intelligence, with specific assignment to Phoenix, when he had the capacity to heal people and do all kinds of good in the world. The discussion grew heated, to say the least, and the room began to clear out. Finally the major lost control completely, grabbed the Spec 4, and shoved him against the wall. He screamed at him, "How dare you question me? I was a POW for five years." Before I could interfere to stop the physical confrontation, the major released the Spec 4 and stormed out of the room.

Well, this was quite amazing. The Spec 4 was actually very cool about the

185

whole incident. I told him that the major was out of line, but the Spec 4 did not want to pursue the matter. We started to discuss this major who seemed to have a bizarre story. We were wondering whether he was telling the truth when he re-entered the room and apologized to the Spec 4. They shook hands, and the major left. And I decided that I had had quite enough excitement for the night.

The Wannabes

But in the years since I've wondered about the wannabe syndrome that seems to be rampant, even 40 years after U.S. troops were withdrawn following the Paris Peace Accords. I've been fascinated by the case of Joseph J. Ellis, the eminent historian, who was exposed by the *Boston Globe* on June 18, 2001, as a fake warrior.[138] Ellis actually had the temerity to claim that he was a platoon leader with the 101st Airborne Division at one point and then a member of General William Westmoreland's personal staff at another point. He told these lies, apparently for years, to his students at Mt. Holyoke College. He probably learned the lingo of the Vietnam veteran while teaching for three years at West Point. Then on May 10, 2010, Richard Blumenthal, then a candidate for the U.S. Senate from Connecticut, spoke of his memories of "the taunts, the insults, sometimes even physical abuse" endured by Vietnam Veterans. On another occasion he actually spoke of "the days that I served in Vietnam." When the Blumenthal story broke, Bob Miller at the Danbury *News-Times* called me for my reaction; Miller reported:

> So when told of Attorney General Richard Blumenthal's statements that he served in Vietnam—when he didn't—Hagan laughed sardonically.
> "Another wannabe," he said.
> If the news turns out to be true, Hagan said, Blumenthal would not deserve anyone's vote.
> "Because he's a liar," he said.[139]

Well, the people of Connecticut were not disturbed enough by Blumenthal's lie to elect the Tea Party wrestling magnate, Linda McMahon, and, in retrospect, I guess I would have voted for Blumenthal too if I lived in Connecticut. (What a choice!) But I do worry that facts do not seem to concern anyone too much anymore. We are served up heavy doses of pure fakery called "reality TV," and we swallow it whole. On March 7, 2004, on the HBO show, *Curb Your Enthusiasm*, comedian Larry David actually staged an encounter between reality TV "vets" and a real veteran of Hitler's concentration camps. We don't seem to know any more if there is any difference in the experiences. And I wonder whether we lost the habit of truth in Vietnam. I sometimes think that my students will tell me it's my opinion when I tell them the Yanks beat the Twins on Monday, July 1, 2013. We do not expect truth telling from politicians. The Gulf of Tonkin resolution was the official basis for the U.S. to wage war in Vietnam. Allegedly the North Vietnamese Navy had engaged a U.S. warship on August 4, 1964. President Johnson actually admitted in 1965: "For all I know, our Navy was shooting at whales out there."[140] And he did know better, but who cares about truth? Where were our ideals?

Shoot First; Reform Later

Politics were at the heart of the war, but America had no politics fit for the reality of the situation and worthy of a soldier's blood. More importantly, the emptiness of our politics did not give the soldier the moral imperative to shed his enemies' blood. Without such sanction he is being set up to think of himself as a murderer. Our Communist adversaries were never in doubt about the high ideals of their cause. They knew that Vietnam desperately needed a social revolution, and so did we. How else to explain our own terminology: my advisory team was part of CORDS—an acronym for Civil Operations and Revolutionary Development Support. We were in the revolution business, and we actually promoted land re-distribution schemes. We weren't such bad Communists, were we? Our revolution was very top-down; the VC were revolting bottom-up. The GVN's land reform program did not work well because the people who were supposed to do it were dividing up their own land. The Joint U.S. Public Affairs Office stated on March 20, 1967: "Three-quarters of the farmers in the RVN still do not own the land they till."[141] (Years later, it dawned on me that British colonialism had created much the same situation in Ireland until the twentieth century.) In 1969 Colon Godwin, the Team 56 civilian agriculture advisor, called land reform in Phong Dinh "a real snarled up mess." Godwin was aware that other Americans, probably in Saigon, were fond of pointing to Taiwan and the Philippines as exemplars, but the people doing the dividing in those countries did not have similar vested interests in the outcomes. In Taiwan the dividers came from the mainland, displaced by Mao's revolution. And perhaps their "even-handedness" benefitted the newcomers, who were not sensitive to the concerns of the indigenous Taiwanese.

American schemes for developing Vietnam were often plagued by cultural blindness. Colon Godwin was a forty-something, jovial and ironic North Carolinian, who was referred to as "Farmer Brown." I did not know that he was a Baptist minister who had spent time in Ghana as a missionary and who had been a chaplain at Western Carolina University. In his interview with the military history team in early 1969, Godwin's Evangelical bent shines through his secular talk about the quality of the people sent to work with the Vietnamese. I didn't recognize the Evangelical vocabulary until I listened to the interview recently. He obviously was speaking about troubles he had encountered with co-worker advisors in the past. He said "You're going to need a special breed of man to do this type of thing." He must be "emotionally stable." "Women and drink, alcohol ... these are two of the big problems in Vietnam.... You use a person who can control himself and his habits. You wouldn't let a rum-head get in here. You also use a person who can control himself where women are concerned."[142] Godwin lived in the Palm Springs civilian compound—the den of iniquity that rumor described periodically. He seemed to realize that Americans had botched the nation-building job in Vietnam because of unharnessed sexual license.

Godwin also believed that small civilian and military units, if put in place years earlier, would have been a better solution than the introduction of large American combat forces, in division strength. His statement shows how the window for winning the war with the right tactics had closed long before 1969. Westmoreland's bludgeoning tactics, coupled with insensitivity to Vietnamese culture, had resulted in a loss of years to unsuccessful and bloody big-unit tactics. Those 500-pound bomb holes in the rice paddies were speaking to me and to all the advisors, but I didn't hear them until I was leaving. Godwin argued for a carefully chosen volunteer force of civilians and military who would be culturally sensitive and who would respect the capabilities of the Vietnamese. He had obviously heard enough blanket dismissals of the Vietnamese as incompetents from American idiots.

Godwin was keen to point out that the program to promote the substitution of a hybrid rice, IR8, for the indigenous, traditional strain was highly problematic from a cultural awareness point of view. IR8 rice, in 1969 at least, was a system, not just a crop. To achieve a sixfold increase in yield per hectare, the Vietnamese farmers would need fertilizers and insecticides commonly available in the U.S. So Godwin had serious doubts about the sustainability of the project without the intervention of Monsanto. There were milling problems with IR8 rice that required readjustment of rice mills. Godwin was overseeing the local implementation of an American system in Vietnamese culture, and he could see the problem in what he was doing. Americans believe in technology: the IR8 project grows out of the same mind that promotes the superiority of the M-16 to the AK-47 and sent the troops to the PX to buy stereos and cameras.

Dr. John Baker, a medical doctor assigned as the Team 56 advisor to the Phong Dinh Hospital in the spring of 1969, sharply criticized MEDCAPs, or Medical Civic Action Programs, in terms similar to the problems Godwin cited with IR8 rice. MEDCAPs were usually one-day programs in which doctors, nurses, dentists, and other medical personnel would visit a Vietnamese village or hamlet and run a clinic. No doubt some medical problems could be alleviated by one-time care, but the introduction of Western medicine into the village without follow-up made the whole exercise little more than a psychological operation, according to Baker in his military history interview. He argued that Western medicine is a system—much like what Godwin described. Unless there was some way to implement permanent change in the Vietnamese system, only a few bad teeth would be pulled, and a few sores or other maladies susceptible to quick fixes could be treated on a one-day MEDCAP. Baker does not deny that such a day might have a positive psychological effect, but he was clearly skeptical of showmanship medicine.[143] In short, Baker was probably also skeptical of the headline-producing work of the Irish-American hero of my youth in the 1950s, Dr. Tom Dooley.

The Vietnamese in villages that MEDCAPs visited were probably delighted with the quick fixes, and, as Godwin notes, Vietnamese farmers were happy with increased yield per hectare. But the American system was setting up dependence on international commerce, i.e., Monsanto as supplier of fertilizers and insecticides. Godwin was implementing the theory of modernization espoused most notably by Walter Rostow, a key Lyndon Johnson economic advisor. The modernization idea evolved from the notion that "traditional society" was prevented by custom and beliefs from espousing the value of the individual, and that the transformation of so-called "third world" societies could only come from a Western-educated elite who would promulgate the values of rational thought, management and bureaucracy. Godwin could see the problems with the modernization model, but he kept carrying his M-16, i.e., IR8 rice.

Ga-Ga About Gadgets

I spent a year listening to my fellow G.I.s converse about watches, stereos and cameras—their favorite topic other than DEROS, a verb often deployed to describe their most fervent desire. Everyone seemed determined to DEROS with the best watch and the best stereo and camera equipment available. While I was bored with the talk about hi-fis and fancy Canons and Nikons, I did buy a small portable radio, a Canon Demi 35mm half-frame camera, and a Seiko watch. I bought the watch because the humidity of Vietnam corroded my Uncle Paddy Hagan's New York City Transit Authority gold retirement Gruen watch. Apparently 99 percent of American troops either owned or had access to a radio and listened avidly to AFVN—the armed forces radio network station in Saigon. ("We Gotta Get Out of This Place" by the Animals was very popular.) When the PX at Can Tho Air Field would receive a new shipment of stereos or cameras, the news would circulate quickly, and jeeps would converge on the PX. Nikon F50s and Miranda Gs were popular cameras; soldiers became experts on buying stereo components. The PACEX catalog allowed GIs to buy expensive items, even cars, which would await them when they went home. The troops were mesmerized by the wizardry of the technology and never tired of discussing it. The troops, unrealistically for some, were dreaming of and preparing for post–Vietnam middle-class lives back in the states; the PX prices were a short cut to the good life. I dreamed of a few cold ones and good *craic*, and I admired greatly the most simple piece of American technology—the World War II vintage P38 can opener, which could be carried on a dog tag chain and opened cans cleanly. Otherwise I noticed that the machines kept breaking down, especially the M-60 machine guns on the Hueys. If you asked what the troops believed in, it certainly wasn't the merit of the anti-communist cause: they never discussed it. Their god was technology. I refuse to carry a cell phone with me today: I will not have false gods before the Lord my God. I'd rather be a pilgrim buying a relic at Canterbury or Chartres or Knock.

You might think that the fallibility of technology would make the troops skeptics rather than believers, but the capacity for self-deception, as Saul Bellow said, was immense. I remember that on January 8, 1970, a helicopter gunship fired a rocket when the pilot turned the chopper on at Can Tho Air Field.[144]

The rocket sped down the runway, hit the ammo dump, and blew it up along with the enlisted man who was guarding it. I don't know whether the firing of the rocket was sabotage or just a technological glitch, but most people were keen to label the incident sabotage. Ben Nelson was at the airfield that night and thinks it was simply a technological screw-up. I too doubted the sabotage theory, mostly because I kept getting on helicopters with multiple technological malfunctions. At one point, several of the junior officers and I wrote highly critical descriptions of the technological malfunctions on the Firefly chopper. We cited, among many other matters, the continual non-operation of several searchlight bulbs and questioned the wisdom of flying with a weak flashlight that made us a target but failed to illuminate the ground we were supposed to be searching. Many of the problems were human failings: The chopper was supposed to carry flares to be dropped in support of outposts under attack, but too often the crew had not attached the flare box to the side of the chopper. One report states the chopper had to return to the air field to pick up the flares when an outpost was under attack. The delay must have made the Popular Force troops wonder about American efficiency—the reverse of the usual bad mouthing of the PFs by Americans. On other occasions the chopper could not take off because crew members were missing. But faith in technology abided: despite the frequent non-functioning of the searchlight bulbs, a mini-gun was installed to increase our fire power. No one questioned whether the increased firepower was of any value if we couldn't detect enemy infiltrators on the ground. Surely shooting them with an M-60 was just as effective as shooting them with a mini-gun, but we believed in technology.

Even a thoughtful man like Colonel Conger was given to a certain valueless belief in making the pacification system work. In his military history interview, his primary focus is the military situation: he thinks security must precede "revolutionary development"—that buzz-phrase that undergirded pacification. Revolutionary development implied good government, self-help projects, public order—the conditions for a stable society that Rostow claimed a traditional society lacked. There is a mechanistic quality to this thinking. Coercion precedes commitment; people will accept the Western-style democracy that we were trying to install if we can make them safe. There is not much thought given to suspicions about the value of Western ideas in an Eastern country. Conger actually believes that the hearts and minds will follow after the people have been coerced. He might say "after they have been made secure and safe," but the VC were focused on the history of the previous Western power—France, and clearly that was a smart way to win friends in the populace. Conger, like Rostow, saw society as a machine that needed maintenance by a strong military.

And technology was ideology from a communist point of view. Lenin had argued that the theory that so-called third world countries had not developed stems from their being on the periphery of a world system geared to consumption by metropolitan elites in the West. The Communists knew that our greatest weakness, despite our own revolutionary efforts, was the charge that we were a colonial power, the French with a bit more class and money (as the Vietnamese S-2 staff confided to me one day).

The Epic of
Lieutenant Kennedy

*However serious the situation is, we will always remember
Chairman Ho's advice: "Let's live great lives, and let's die
bravely and gloriously."*—Can Tho City Party Committee, June 5, 1969[145]

So you would think that every effort would be made to avoid occupying
the role vacated by the French in 1954, but hardly anyone seems to have worried
about giving the Viet Cong propaganda victories. Americans, ignorant of and
downright contemptuous of history, never worried that they might be acting
just like the French had. The November 10, 1970, report of Lieutenant Richard
Kennedy of the movement of his MAT to Thoi Long Village in Phong Thuan
District is a gem of a mini-epic. Kennedy writes: "Upon arrival they [the advance
party] encountered numerous communication problems and no physical help
in unloading the team's heavy equipment. Two days later all personnel were
deployed only to find our situation was one of mass confusion. We were to be
living in the Hoa Hao Pagoda, which didn't overly please anyone due to the
French having been there before, plus local beliefs that we would all be killed
if we angered the 'Angel' living inside the Pagoda." While the Hoa Hao were
fiercely anti-communist, it can't have pleased them the Americans were living
in their pagoda—just as the French had. I might suspect that a communist
sympathizer suggested housing the Americans in the Hoa Hao pagoda, but
that is less likely than the very real likelihood that the Americans who picked
out the site lacked cultural and religious sensitivity. I have to think that Lieutenant Kennedy was an Irish-American who understood angels, so MAT 11
survived its sojourn in the pagoda.

Kennedy goes on with his report: "The next few days we were busy trying
to get our house organized as well as making an effort to keep the kids from
stealing our equipment. We failed miserably in the latter effort because our
PSDF guards were just as busy taking our gear as the children were. I then built

a fence to keep the pests at 20 feet distance. That didn't work either because they then changed tactics by throwing rocks, mud, etc. Being a very patient person I merely let them go without any 'Big to do.'"

Kennedy eventually discovered America's most powerful weapon: Hollywood movies. He writes: "Now MAT 11 was ready to begin. A favorite always is movies which we promptly showed to the adults and children. This went well the first night and MAT 11 was in good spirits. The following night they wanted films again but we had none, which brought an instant display of anger from the respectable people of Thoi Long. Two days later we tried again to win them back to our side but to no avail since our generator wasn't in the mood for activity. More rocks, sand and mud were aimed at the Co Vans [Vietnamese for 'advisors']. At this I politely kept my temper within the confines of the pagoda. 'Patience is a virtue.'"[146]

Clearly Kennedy was blessed by that angel with patience although I suspect Kennedy was well aware that virtue can hurt you. I also imagine that the VC had their "yucks" about the dopey Americans in the pagoda with the angel. It is easy to believe that the VC had their claws in the local GVN administration: they never ignored the political. We never considered it, really.

I read Viet Cong documents regularly: the political was never divorced from the military. In his 1968 study of Phong Dinh, Potter reports:

> ... one youth [who had rallied to the GVN's cause] replied that his death as a PF [Popular Force] would bring sorrow to his family, but his death as a guerrilla would bring sorrow to the village. What he meant was that a PF was only a mercenary whose death was of no concern to the village, but a guerrilla was part of the village, and his death would be mourned by all. The NLF has taken great pains to ensure that all its prospective fighters believe that their death will be mourned by all. Before any major battle (usually weeks before) villages are required to construct coffins and a mass ceremony (funeral) is held for the unit going into battle. Then, afterwards, NLF graveyards are conspicuously marked and used for public ceremonies. No such ceremony accompanies GVN preparation for combat, and no public care is taken of the dead. NLF ceremonies have generally supplanted the traditional ceremonies associated with the various phases of the rice cycle, and given them a new "revolutionary" meaning. Likewise communist party holidays and commemoration of major events in the Viet Minh's campaign have replaced many of the Buddhist celebrations. With the exception of the commemoration of the fall of the Diệm regime, the GVN has no national ceremonial events.[147]

A Prayer for the
Kids of Cooper Street

"*There are things a man must not do to save a nation.*"[148]
—John O'Leary, Irish Fenian leader,
quoted by W.B. Yeats

For the VC, there was no shirking. Death was always possible, even likely, but, oh, so worthwhile, or so it has seemed. I suspect that not every VC soldier was brimming with national pride. But a soldier needs to believe in the morality and justice of his war. Our leaders failed to convince us. I was raised to believe in the just struggle for a united Ireland-unlike the war without a cause in which, I blush to admit even today, I engaged. I came home from Vietnam committed to being a pacifist in the future, so Irish Northern Aid, the Provisional IRA support group, did not entice me. I had finally figured out how not to go to war.

Last time I checked, about a year ago, a floor-to-ceiling black metal gate bars the entryway to the alleyway of 10 Cooper Street. I hate to think that grumpy neighbors and a grouchy superintendent have established order and security at the expense of their kids' contemplative growth. The "heavenly hurt" of "a certain slant of light," to borrow Emily Dickinson's phrases, is no longer available in that alleyway for the kids of Inwood. I worry that 10 Cooper Street resembles post–Vietnam, post–9/11 security-obsessed America. Does keeping kids out of the alley substitute for curing the social ills that drive a manic fixation on security—at home, in Afghanistan, and almost everywhere else? I bet the kids do find other spots to escape the blazing summer sun. I hope they're not indoors behind double-locked security doors and locking window gates, texting drivel to one another and updating their Facebook pages with fake friends. Spare them the tyranny of their cell phones. Bless them, O sun, with consciousness of shade and light. May they enjoy many hours of good *craic* on summer days.

Memory of shade and light drives me to wonder what is going on in Can Tho now, so I take a tour via Google maps. A huge statue of Ho Chi Minh has been erected in what appears to be a very modern, bustling city. A new super-highway-type bridge spans the Bassac River. Binh Thuy Air Base is now the Can Tho International Airport. I wonder whether Ho's statue will someday face the same fate as Nelson's Pillar in Dublin. It used to block the light on O'Connell Street. The British hero of Trafalgar was blown up by Irish Republicans on March 8, 1966, 157 years after its erection in honor of the man James Joyce dubbed "the one-handled adulterer." Or will Uncle Ho be handled like the huge statue of Saddam Hussein in Baghdad? An American tank pulled it to the ground on April 9, 2003, just one year after its erection. May no kid from 10, 24, or 30 Cooper Street be in Can Tho when Uncle Ho bites the dust.

Appendix:
Correspondence with
Congressman William F. Ryan, 1970

*(William Fitts Ryan Papers; Seeley G. Mudd
Manuscript Library, Princeton University)*

Advisory Team 56 (S2)
APO San Francisco 96215
May 18, 1970

Hon. William F. Ryan
303 Cannon Building
Washington, D.C. 20515

Dear Sir:

At the present time I am a member of the U.S. Army serving as the Assistant S-2 Advisor for Phong Dinh Province in the Mekong Delta. I am from the Inwood section of your district and also am a member of Assemblyman Jack Walsh's club.

My purpose in writing is to voice my sentiments about what I feel to be the grave and senseless prolongation of this war. Let me assure you that your efforts to end it are met with applause from this quarter.

My capacity as an advisor requires me to work closely with Vietnamese officers. Basically they are characterized by a status conscious self-centeredness which renders them almost entirely ineffective in responding to the needs of the people. Corruption is widespread and more often than not American aid in the form of materiel of all types finds its way into the black market to the benefit of corrupt officers.

I was personally involved in the removal of a corrupt District Chief only to discover that the honest officer who personally detailed to me the extent of his corruption was also relieved (reassigned according to official sources) because he had embarrassed the Vietnamese by reporting what he knew to an American. It is a fact that knowledge of the District Chief's corruption was widespread, but squelched due to the fact that the District Chief was known to have relatives in high places in the Saigon government. I do have a carbon copy of my report to the Province Senior Advisor detailing the particulars of this corruption as outlined to me by the S-2 of this district (Thuan Nhon). This man braved considerable personal risk to himself and his family in order to relay this information to me. At the present time, I find it almost impossible to look the man in the face as I feel a certain guilt about his demise. I do not feel that any effort was expended by the upper echelons of command on this advisory team to see that this man was not transferred. He was acknowledged to be the best officer in Thuan Nhon District. The District Chief was relieved, however.

Another frightening thing about the U.S. Advisory effort over here is that the advisors display almost no sociological awareness. What is a dubious venture to start with, i.e., advising what amounts to be the privileged class, is compounded by the refusal of advisors to even begin to deal with and understand the cultural differences of an Eastern Culture. To many advisors, the Vietnamese are "gooks" and "zips" and little more. It would seem that we are incapable of attaining the goals that we seek simply because we lack the human understanding necessary to even begin to accomplish this dubious end.

As regards the aforementioned particular case, if you are interested in pursuing the matter, I understand that the Province Monthly report of Phong Dinh Province (of which I am the "ghost writer") is available for the information of Congressmen. Back issues of the report should provide sketchy details of the problem. I assure you that there is no real substance to them, but they do give a general idea. I hesitate to send you the carbon copy of my report to the Province Senior Advisor because it could well earn me a term in Leavenworth, if it were to be known that I had done such a thing.

Actually the whole incident becomes somewhat minor when one considers the everyday indifference of the people to our efforts due to their unappreciated and probably unwanted presence. What Vietnam needs is a social revolution and this is a need the Viet Cong have seized upon and the GVN has paid lip service to. It is for this reason and this reason alone that the Viet Cong continue to exist. Whether their panacea is the correct one for Vietnam is highly questionable as evidenced by their continued and very real atrocities, but this matters not as they do offer what the people want to hear and the GVN daily continues to ignore the people's needs. What little the GVN does do for the people is for the most part directly attributable to appeasement of American pressures, not from a real sense of concern for the people's needs.

In closing, please forgive the somewhat sloppy nature of this letter, but I do feel that I had to say what I did. It gets difficult to live with oneself over here.

Peace,
Edward A. Hagan
1LT MI

As the roommate of Lt. Hagan and the Engineer Advisor of Phong Dinh Province, I would like to add my personal affirmation to what he has stated. My personal experiences with the Vietnamese have led me to the conclusion that his statements are entirely apropos in my sphere, as well as his own.

Sincerely,
Benjamin E. Nelson
1LT CE
Engineer Advisor
Phong Dinh Province

May 27, 1970

1st Lt. Edward A. Hagan
Advisory Team 56 (s2)
APO San Francisco 96215

Dear Lieutenant Hagan:

I appreciated receiving your very thoughtful and informative letter which confirms my understanding of some of the conditions under which you are working. I admire you for your dedication and your appreciation of the cultural and sociological factors involved.

I hope the day will not be far away when I have the pleasure of seeing you in Inwood.

With best wishes.

Sincerely,
William F. Ryan
Member of Congress

WFR/sp

P.S. Would you mind if I used quotations from your letter without attribution?

June 16, 1970

The Honorable Melvin R. Laird
Secretary of Defense
Washington, D.C. 20301

Dear Mr. Secretary:

I understand that your Department receives monthly reports from our military advisors in the various provinces of South Vietnam. I believe that these reports are referred to as either the "Hamlet Evaluation System Reports" or "Province Monthly Reports."

I am interested in securing reports for the months of January, February, March and April of this year from the following provinces: Binh Dinh, Quang Nam, Phong Dinh, and Pleiku. I will appreciate your providing me with these reports.

Thank you very much for your assistance.

With kindest regards.

Sincerely,
William F. Ryan
Member of Congress

WFR/scp

Advisory Team 56 (S2)
APO San Francisco 96215
June 12, 1970

Hon. William F. Ryan
1040 St. Nicholas Avenue
N.Y., N.Y. 10032

Dear Congressman Ryan:

I am in receipt of your letter of May 27, and I thank you for your interest as well as your prompt reply. With regard to your request to use quotations from my letter, I now find myself in a difficult position. The Province Senior Advisor has just issued a policy statement on the release of information which would make my position very tenuous if you should release the information I passed to you on the Thuan Nhon District Chief. Even if you did not use my name, it would be a simple matter to trace it to me. To say the least the policy statement is spurious, but I do not believe that it is worth the risk of a term in Leavenworth to release that information. I am enclosing a copy of the policy statement for your information.

However, I do not have any objections to your use of any of the other information I relayed to you. I do not have a carbon copy of my letter, but I don't recall anything else in it that would earn the extreme displeasure of my commanders (other than my distaste for the war).

A few other things have occurred since my last letter that you might find interesting:

a) The President's Committee was here and visited the Province Chieu Hoi (Rallier) Center. The questions they asked were most interesting. While I was not there in person, I was informed by other members of this advisory team that in questioning a VC village guerrilla unit chief who had rallied, there was a definite attempt made to connect him with Cambodia. Questions as to his place of birth, where he received his training, and where he received his arms and munitions were all met with the same answer, i.e., right here in this village. It appears that the Committee was looking for a connection between this VC leader and the NVA infiltration from the North. Thus they would obtain some justification for the foray into Cambodia. I do not believe that this is sheer conjecture on my part, as the people who related the information to me feel much differently about the war than I do. It was they who stated that the committee was attempting to connect the VC leader with the Cambodian base areas.

Our fine senators and congressmen on the committee don't seem to realize the verity that an insurgency movement can only exist with the support or at least the acquiescence of the indigenous populace.

b) The Can Tho University students have also been demonstrating of late. It is interesting to note what they are protesting:

1) The Lon Nol Government in Cambodia;
2) Treatment of Vietnamese nationals in Cambodia;
3) The war;
4) GVN repression of students.

Of course, a good percentage of this may be VC inspired, but most of it is, in all likelihood, not. This information has been stifled by the Province Chief, and was confided to one of our advisors by the Police Chief.

I would appreciate it if you did not quote me on the last two points I made. They are, no doubt, taboo for me to make according to the enclosed policy statement. I only have four months left over here, and after that I will be released from active duty and I won't care how you quote me.

Again, I would like to add my support for your stand against this war and I encourage you to continue to make your voice heard.

Peace,
Edward A. Hagan
1LT MI

July 7, 1970

1st Lt. Edward A. Hagan
Advisory Team 56 (s2)
APO San Francisco 96215

Dear Lieutenant Hagan:

I was glad to have your letter of June 12 and the enclosed policy statement. I was also interested in learning of the visit of the President's Committee and also to have your observations on the protest of the university students.

Thank you again for your encouraging words and I hope that your four months will pass quickly.

With warmest regards.

Sincerely,
William F. Ryan
Member of Congress

WFR/sp

Glossary

AK-47—the standard Communist rifle.

ARVN—Army of the Republic of Vietnam

CORDS—Civil Operations and Revolutionary Development Support—the umbrella organization for the American military and civilian operations in the Mekong Delta Region or Region IV.

COSVN—Central Office for South Vietnam—the control center for coordinating communist insurgent and main force military actions.

Craic—an Irish word, pronounced "crack," meaning the "talk" or lively conversation.

DEROS—Date Eligible for Return from OverSeas—Every GI in Vietnam had a specific date on which he was eligible to go home. Most were immediately discharged once they arrived at a stateside military base.

GVN—Government of Vietnam; South Vietnam—America's ally in the war.

INTSUM—Intelligence Summary—a daily report of enemy sightings and engagements as well as any significant intelligence garnered in the preceding 24 hours.

IRA—Irish Republican Army

KBA—Killed By Air, a term used to claim enemy deaths by visual evidence from U.S. aircraft. The claim is weaker than KIA—Killed in Action.

L-19—a two-seat, fixed-wing aircraft used primarily for aerial reconnaissance and coordination of aerial combat activities in Phong Dinh Province. Sometimes it was called an O-1 Birddog; it resembled a World War I airplane. Eight rockets were mounted on its wings, designed primarily for marking targets but capable also of engaging small enemy units.

L-Z—Landing Zone—an area cleared for landing by a helicopter, usually a place that required removal of brush and trees in order that a helicopter could land.

MAT—Mobile Advisory Team. A unit of about six men, usually two junior officers (captains and lieutenants), three non-commissioned officers (a heavy weapons advisor, a medic and one other sergeant), and an RTO or radio operator (usually a Specialist 4). MATs were assigned to villages and worked to develop local defense forces and to promote civic participation.

M-16—the standard American rifle, also carried by South Vietnamese troops.

M-60—the standard American machine gun; it fired the standard 7.62mm NATO round and was capable of firing 500 to 600 rounds per minute. Two M-60 machine guns were usually mounted on UH-1D (Huey) helicopters.

MACV—(commonly pronounced "Mack-Vee") Military Assistance Command Vietnam.

NLF—National Liberation Front—the political organization of the communists or Viet Cong.

PF—Popular Forces. Local militias intended to be assigned on the village level. In Phong Dinh they were often deployed away from their villages because of the need to secure Binh Thuy Air Base and Can Tho Army Air Field. Americans frequently disparaged RF-PF troops as "Ruff-Puffs."

PSDF—People's Self-Defense Forces. These were local semi-military organizations, composed either of 16- or 17-year-old males or males between 39 and 50, i.e., males not of draft age. They performed the function of local defense against incursions by Viet Cong guerrillas although they generally would back away from confronting large VC units. Their effectiveness varied greatly from locale to locale. PSDF members were armed, often with irregular weapons.

RF—Regional Forces. Local militias that were supposed to be under the command of Province Chiefs. These units were supposed to be raised locally and assigned locally.

RTO—Radio Telephone Operator, essentially the radio operator.

SEATO—South East Asia Treaty Organization—the military alliance that made South Vietnam a military ally of the United States.

TOC—Tactical Operations Center—the nerve center for all combat operations in Phong Dinh Province. The Province S-2 (Intelligence) and S-3 (Operations) were headquartered there. Radio traffic for both the Vietnamese and American nets was based there.

Notes

1. Kevin Powers, *The Yellow Birds* (New York: Little, Brown, 2012), 216.

2. H.R. McMaster, "The Pipe Dream of Easy War," *New York Times*, July 20, 2013, accessed February 10, 2015, http://www.nytimes.com/2013/07/21/opinion/sunday/the-pipe-dream-of-easy-war.html?_r=0.

3. Michael Herr, *Dispatches* (New York: Vintage, 1991), 260.

4. Tim O'Brien, "How to Tell a True War Story," *The Things They Carried* (New York: Broadway Books, 1998), 69.

5. Andrew J. Bacevich, interview by Phil Donahue, *Moyers and Company*, PBS, September 6, 2013.

6. Colonel Harold Van Hout, Phong Dinh Province Monthly Report, July, 1970, Box 893, File 1601–11A, Administrative and Operational Records, 1966-March 1973; Advisory Team 56 (Phong Dinh Province Advisory Team); Civil Operations and Rural Development Support (CORDS) Military Region 4 (MR 4); Office of Civil Operations and Rural Development Support (CORDS); U.S. Military Assistance Command Vietnam (MACV); Records of the United States Forces in Southeast Asia, 1950–1975, Record Group 472; National Archives at College Park (NACP), College Park, MD.

7. Colonel Harold Van Hout, letter to Colonel Le Vang Hung, December 15, 1970, Box 888, File 103.03A, Advisory Team 56 Records, NACP.

8. Colonel Harold Van Hout, Phong Dinh Province Monthly Report, June 1970, Box 893, File 1601–11A Advisory Team 56 Records, NACP.

9. Walt Whitman, "When Lilacs Last in the Dooryard Bloom'd," *poets.org*, accessed February 10, 2015, http://www.poets.org/poets org/poem/when-lilacs-last-door-yard-bloomd.

10. Van Hout, Phong Dinh Province Monthly Report, July 1970.

11. Colonel Lester M. Conger, Phong Dinh Province Monthly Report, January 1970, Box 893, File 1601–11A, Advisory Team 56 Records, NACP.

12. John Paul Vann, a former Army lieutenant colonel, was the second ranking American in the Mekong Delta in 1969–70. By 1972 he had become the senior American in Vietnam. Neil Sheehan won the Pulitzer Prize in 1989 for *A Bright Shining Lie: John Paul Vann and America in Vietnam* (New York: Vintage, 1988).

13. Lieutenant Colonel Jack L. Young, Memorandum, July 23, 1970, Box 888, File 103.03, Advisory Team 56 Records, NACP.

14. Captain Neil Meoni, July 18, 1970, Box 888, File 103.03, Advisory Team 56 Records, NACP.

15. Colonel Lester M. Conger, Completion-of-Tour Report, April 15, 1970, Box 888, File 103.05, Advisory Team 56 Records, NACP.

16. See appendix for full text of my letters.

17. George Orwell, "Politics and the English Language," *A Collection of Essays* (1946, New York: Harvest Books, 1981), 166.

18. 1st Lieutenant Edward A. Hagan, Counterpart Evaluation, July 20, 1970, Box 888, File 103–03, Advisory Team 56 Records, NACP.

19. Major Philip S. Kim, Interview with Captain Joseph P. Saffron, 20th Military History Detachment, March 25, 1969, Vietnam Interview Tape Collection (VNIT 381), U.S. Army Center of Military History, Fort McNair, D.C.

20. Cf., Jerry Lembcke, *The Spitting Image: Myth, Memory, and the Legacy of Vietnam* (New York: NYU Press, 2000). Although his claims have been disputed, Lembcke argues convincingly that there is no documented case of spitting on returning Vietnam veterans.

21. H. Bruce Franklin, "Teaching the Vietnam War in the 1990s," (presentation, Annual Joint Meetings of the Popular Culture Association/American Culture Association, Philadelphia, PA, April 12–15, 1995).

Franklin estimates that 80% of his students were misidentifying the shooter and the prisoner during the 1990s.

22. Jaime Concepcion, Interview with John Albright, 20th Military History Detachment, March 27, 1969, Vietnam Interview Tape Collection (VNIT 381), U.S. Army Center of Military History, Fort McNair, D.C.

23. Sebastian Junger, *War* (New York: Twelve, 2010), 25.

24. John F. Kennedy, Memorandum to the Army, April 11, 1962, *jfklibrary.org*, accessed February 10, 2015, http://www.jfklibrary.org/JFK/JFK-in-History/Green-Berets.aspx.

25. Howard Maxwell Potter, "Provincial Politics in South Vietnam: A Participant-Observer Case Study of Phong Dinh Province" (master's thesis, Ohio State University, 1968).

26. Alfred Lord Tennyson, "The Charge of the Light Brigade," *poets.org*, accessed February 10, 2015, http://www.poets.org/poetsorg/poem/charge-light-brigade.

27. W. S. Gilbert, "When I First Put This Uniform on," *Patience* by W.S. Gilbert and Arthur Sullivan, 1881, accessed February 10, 2015, http://www.public-domain-poetry.com/william-schwenck-gilbert/when-i-first-put-this-uniform-on-16348.

28. Nancy Beth Jackson, "If You're Thinking of Living In/Inwood; Away From Manhattan Without Leaving," *New York Times*, December 15, 2002, accessed February 8, 2015, http://www.nytimes.com/2002/12/15/realestate/if-you-re-thinking-of-living-in-in wood-away-from-manhattan-without-leaving.html.

29. Major Robert Jackson, qtd. in Colonel Harold Van Hout, Phong Dinh Province Monthly Report, May, 1970, Box 904, File 1601–11A, Advisory Team 56 Records, NACP.

30. Captain Robert V. Burns, "Counterpart Report," 20 July 1970, Box 888, File 103–03, Advisory Team 56 Records, NACP.

31. Colonel Lester M. Conger, Phong Dinh Province Monthly Report, February 1970, Box 904, File 1601–11A, Advisory Team 56 Records, NACP.

32. Van Hout, Phong Dinh Province Monthly Report, July, 1970.

33. Colonel Edward J. Porter, "AFRIS—Province Advisor Completion of Tour Report," November 15, 1972, Headquarters, Phong Dinh Province, MR-IV, Advisory Team 56, 2.

34. General Douglas McArthur, Farewell Speech, West Point, New York, May 12, 1962. http://www.americanrhetoric.com/speeches/douglasmacarthurthayeraward.html.

35. Leo Durocher, April 10, 1947, qtd. in Peter Golenbock, "Men of Conscience," eds. Joseph Dorinson and Joram Warmund, *Jackie Robinson: Race, Sports, and the American Dream* (New York: Routledge, 1998), 18.

36. Timothy G. Patton, September 5, 1999, The Vietnam Veterans Memorial—The Wall-USA, http://thewall-usa.com/guest.asp?recid=18952.

37. Colum McCann, *Transatlantic* (New York: Random House, 2013), 190.

38. Private George Braziller, ed., *The 133rd AAA Gun Battalion: Occupied Germany 1945*, (Munich, Germany: R. Oldenbourg, 1945), 81.

39. "Orientation," Report of Operations (April 1, 1946-June 30, 1946), 133rd AAA Gun Battalion, June 28, 1946, Box 13742, Record Group 407, Records of the Adjutant General's Office, 1917-, Entry 427 (NM-3), World War II Operational Reports, 1940–1948, National Archives at College Park, College Park, MD.

40. Phong Dinh Province INTSUM, August 18, 1970, Box 862, File 502–02, Advisory Team 56 Records, NACP.

41. Ibid.

42. Ibid.

43. Ibid.

44. Dale Andrade, "Bring Our POWs Back Alive," *Great Battles*, January 1992, 32.

45. James William Gibson, "About James William Gibson," *James William Gibson*, Description of *The Perfect War: Technowar in Vietnam*, (New York: The Atlantic Monthly Press, 1986), accessed February 2, 2015, http://www.jameswilliamgibson.com/aboutgibson.htm.

46. William Bach, Counterpart Letter, April 15, 1970, Box 889, File 1601–09A, Advisory Team 56 Records, NACP.

47. William Bach, Counterpart Letter, June 15, 1970, Box 889, File 1601–09A Advisory Team 56 Records, NACP.

48. Jaime Concepcion, Memorandum to RF/PF Advisor re: District Senior Advisor Problems—September, October 3, 1970, Box 889, File 1601–01, Advisory Team 56 Records, NACP.

49. Captain Douglass R. Hemphill, Letter to Province Senior Advisor, September 4, 1970, Box 895, File 1603–03A, Advisory Team 56 Records, NACP.

50. Francis J. Connell, *The New Baltimore Catechism No. 3* (New York: Benziger Brothers, 1954), 160.

51. Winifred Murphy, First Papers, December 17, 1929.

52. Lieutenant Governor Malcolm Wilson, Commencement Address, Fordham Preparatory School, Bronx, New York, June 18, 1964.

53. Michael Herr, *Dispatches* (1977: New York: Vintage, 1991), 15.

54. Daily Log, Tactical Operations Center, Phong Dinh Sector, February 24, 1970, Box 843, File 228–09, Advisory Team 56 Records, NACP.

55. General Peckem's communications about cleanliness and procrastination made Major Major feel like a procrastinator, and he always got those out of the way as quickly as he could. The only official documents that interested him were those occasional ones pertaining to the unfortunate second lieutenant who had been killed on the mission over Orvieto less than two hours after he arrived in Yossarian's tent. Since the unfortunate lieutenant had reported to the operations tent instead of to the orderly room, Sergeant Towser had decided that it would be safest to report him as never having reported to the squadron at all, and the occasional documents relating to him dealt with the fact that he seemed to have vanished into thin air, which, in one way, was exactly what did happen to him.

Joseph Heller, *Catch–22: 50th Anniversary Edition*, (New York: Simon & Schuster, 2011), 115.

There was something inherently disreputable about Yossarian, always carrying on so disgracefully about that dead man in his tent who wasn't even there and then taking off his clothes after the Avignon mission and going around without them right up to the day General Dreedle stepped up to pin a medal on him for his heroism over Ferrara and found him standing in formation stark naked. No one in the world had the power to remove the dead man's disorganized effects from Yossarian's tent. Major Major had forfeited the authority when he permitted Sergeant Towser to report the lieutenant who had been killed over Orvieto less than two hours after he arrived in the squadron as never having arrived in the squadron at all. The only one with any right to remove his belongings from Yossarian's tent, it seemed to Major Major, was Yossarian himself, and Yossarian, it seemed to Major Major, had no right.

Heller, *Catch–22*, 126.

56. Junger, *War*, 135.

57. Captain Gary Hoebeke, Interview with Major Charles G. Vemity, 20th Military History Detachment, March 25, 1969, Vietnam Interview Tape Collection (VNIT 381), U.S. Army Center of Military History, Fort McNair, D.C.

58. Major Philip S. Kim, Interview with 20th Military History Detachment.

59. *Full Metal Jacket*, directed by Stanley Kubrick (1987; Burbank, CA: Warner Home Video, 2013), DVD.

60. Colonel Nguyen Van Khuong, Order No. 115/TKPD/CL/ADBT, Phong Dinh Sector, Citation Cross of Gallantry for Edward A. Hagan, 1st Lieutenant, March 12, 1970.

61. Phong Dinh Province INTSUM, January 27 & 28, 1973, Box 863, File 502–02, Advisory Team 56 Records, NACP.

62. Colonel Harold Van Hout, Phong Dinh Province Monthly Report, May 1970, Box 904, File 1601–11A, Advisory Team 56 Records, NACP.

63. Phong Dinh Province INTSUM, December 29, 1972, Box 904, File 228–07, Advisory Team 56 Records, NACP. (VC activity took place on December 27, 1972, but reported on the INTSUM of December 29, 1972.)

64. Phong Dinh Province INTSUM, December 28, 1972, Box 904, File 228–07, Advisory Team 56 Records, NACP. (Document was dated December 8, 1972, but reported on the INTSUM of December 28, 1972.)

65. William Saunders, Interview with John Albright, 20th Military History Detachment, March 27, 1969, Vietnam Interview Tape Collection (VNIT 381), U.S. Army Center of Military History, Fort McNair, D.C.

66. Herbert W. Timrud, Interview with John Albright, 20th Military History Detachment, March 27, 1969, Vietnam Interview Tape Collection (VNIT 381), U.S. Army Center of Military History, Fort McNair, D.C.

67. Robert Musil, *The Man Without Qualities*, Vol. I, trans. Sophie Wilkins (New York: Vintage International, 1996), 95.

68. David H. Hackworth, *About Face* (New York: Simon & Schuster, 1989), 589.

69. Junger, *War*, 132.

70. Saunders, Interview with 20th Military History Detachment.

71. Captain Robert V. Burns, Memorandum to Deputy Province Senior Advisor re: Major Bon, Thuan Nhon District Chief, March 5, 1970.

72. "Mme. Nhu and the Press," *America*, October 19, 1963, 449.

73. Madame Ngo Dinh Nhu, qtd. in "Madame Nhu Given Warmest Welcome Yet," *Fordham Ram* (New York, NY), October 17, 1963, http://digital.library.fordham.edu/cdm/compoundobject/collection/RAM/id/8446/rec/1 .

74. Phan Trong Kim, Interview with John Albright, 20th Military History Detachment, March 26 1969, Vietnam Interview Tape Collection (VNIT 381), U.S. Army Center of Military History, Fort McNair, D.C.

75. Timrud, Interview with 20th Military History Detachment.

76. Hackworth, *About Face*, 743.

77. Captain James Pederson, Interview with Major Charles G. Vemity, 20th Military History Detachment, March 25, 1969, Vietnam Interview Tape Collection (VNIT 381), U.S. Army Center of Military History, Fort McNair, D.C.

78. Major James M. Kraft, Interview with Major Charles G. Vemity, 20th Military History Detachment, March 25, 1969, Vietnam Interview Tape Collection (VNIT 381), U.S. Army Center of Military History, Fort McNair, D.C.

79. Colonel Harold Van Hout, letter to Colonel Le Vang Hung, November 16, 1970, Box 888, File 103.03A, Advisory Team 56 Records, NACP.

80. Potter, "Provincial Politics in South Vietnam," 157–9.

81. Colonel Lester M. Conger, Daily Log, Tactical Operations Center Phong Dinh Sector, September 11, 1970, Box 838, File 228–09, Advisory Team 56 Records, NACP.

82. Colonel Lester M. Conger, Phong Dinh Province Monthly Report, September 1969, Box 904, File 1601–11A, Advisory Team 56 Records, NACP.

83. Potter, "Provincial Politics in South Vietnam," 159.

84. Nick Turse, *Kill Anything That Moves: The Real American War in Vietnam* (New York: Picador, 2013), 249.

85. "Contemporary Geopolitics, Phong Dinh," 1969, Box 877, File 1601–10A, Advisory Team 56 Records, NACP.

86. Daily Log, Tactical Operations Center, Phong Dinh Sector, May 8, 1970, Box 845, File 228–09, Advisory Team 56 Records, NACP.

87. Daily Log, Tactical Operations Center, Phong Dinh Sector, May 14, 1970, Box 845, File 228–09, Advisory Team 56 Records, NACP.

88. Daily Log, Tactical Operations Center, Phong Dinh Sector, January 19, 1970, Box 842, File 228–09, Advisory Team 56 Records, NACP.

89. Ibid.

90. Van Hout, Phong Dinh Province Monthly Report, May 1970.

91. Senator Jacob K. Javits, Testimony, Foreign Relations Committee Hearing on the Javits-Pell Resolution for Disengagement from the Vietnam War, United States Senate, February 4, 1970.

92. In "The Vietnam Solution," Robert D. Kaplan reports on the ability of the Vietnamese to put the war behind them. Then he reports on the difference in the way Vietnamese and Americans remember the war: "'The Vietnamese don't have amnesia regarding the war against the United States in the 1960s and 1970s,' a Western diplomat explains. 'Rather, a certain generation of America is stuck in a time warp.'" *The Atlantic*, June 2012, 56.

93. Colonel Lester M. Conger, Interview with Captain Joseph P. Saffron, 20th Military History Detachment, May 17, 1969, Vietnam Interview Tape Collection, VNIT 381, U.S. Army Center of Military History, Ft. McNair, D.C.

94. Van Hout, Phong Dinh Province Monthly Report, July 1970.

95. Daily Log, Tactical Operations Center, Phong Dinh Sector, January 26, 1970, Box 842, File 228–09, Advisory Team 56 Records, NACP.

96. 1st Lieutenant Edward A. Hagan, "Monthly Counterpart Letter," Box 889, File 1601–09A, August 15, 1970, Advisory Team 56 Records, NACP.

97. Warren E. Parker, Letter to Deputy for CORDS, January 17, 1973, File 1601–03, Box 905, Advisory Team 56 Records, NACP.

98. Dennis Smith, *Report from Engine Co. 82* (New York: Warner Books, 1999 [1972]), 119.

99. Tim O'Brien, "On the Rainy River," *The Things They Carried* (New York: Broadway Books, 1998), 59.

100. Colonel Lester M. Conger, Interview with 20th Military History Detachment.

101. Joseph Conrad, *Heart of Darkness* (New York: W.W. Norton, 2005), 16.

102. Colonel Edward J. Porter, Counterpart Letter, April 19, 1972, Box 904, File 1603–03, April 19, 1972 Advisory Team 56 Records, NACP.

103. Colonel Edward J. Porter, Letter,

December 14, 1972, Box 903, File 228–07, Advisory Team 56 Records, NACP.

104. Major James L. Hetrick, Letter to PIOCC Special Representative, December 1, 1971, Box 904, File 1603–03A, Advisory Team 56 Records, NACP.

105. Daily Log, Tactical Operations Center Phong Dinh Sector, January 25, 1973, Box 860, File 228–09, Advisory Team 56 Records, NACP.

106. Phong Dinh Province INTSUM, January 27 & 28, 1973.

107. Phong Dinh Province INTSUM, December 13, 1972, Box 863, File 502–02, Advisory Team 56 Records, NACP.

108. Phong Dinh Province INTSUM, January 27 and 28, 1973.

109. Daily Log, Tactical Operations Center, Phong Dinh Sector, February 25, 1970, Box 843, File 228–09, Advisory Team 56 Records, NACP.

110. Joseph R. Gregory, "Gen. Vo Nguyen Giap, Who Ousted U.S. From Vietnam, Is Dead," *The New York Times*, October 5, 2013, accessed February 7, 2015, http://www.nytimes.com/2013/10/05/world/asia/gen-vo-nguyen-giap-dies.html?pagewanted=1&_r=0.

111. Lieutenant Colonel Gerald Brice Ferguson Smyth, qtd. in T. Ryle Dwyer, *The Squad: and the Intelligence Operations of Michael Collins* (Cork: Mercier Press, 2005), 115.

112. Daily Log, Tactical Operations Center, Phong Dinh Sector, November 19, 1969, Box 840, File 228–09, Advisory Team 56 Records, NACP.

113. Daily Log, Tactical Operations Center, Phong Dinh Sector, November 25, 1969, Box 840, File 228–09, Advisory Team 56 Records, NACP.

114. Daily Log, Tactical Operations Center Phong Dinh Sector, November 30, 1969, Box 840, File 228–09, Advisory Team 56 Records, NACP.

115. Daily Log, Tactical Operations Center, Phong Dinh Sector, February 7, 1970, Box 842, File 228–09, Advisory Team 56 Records, NACP.

116. Daily Log, Tactical Operations Center, Phong Dinh Sector, November 11, 1969, Box 840, File 228–09, Advisory Team 56 Records, NACP.

117. Daily Log, Tactical Operations Center, Phong Dinh Sector, December 1, 1969, Box 840, File 228–09, Advisory Team 56 Records, NACP.

118. Ibid.

119. Daily Log, Tactical Operations Center, Phong Dinh Sector, January 30, 1970, Box 842, File 228–09, Advisory Team 56 Records, NACP.

120. Daily Log, Tactical Operations Center, Phong Dinh Sector, March 30, 1970, Box 843, File 228–09, Advisory Team 56 Records, NACP.

121. Daily Log, Tactical Operations Center, Phong Dinh Sector, March 9, 1970, Box 843, File 228–09, Advisory Team 56 Records, NACP.

122. Daily Log, Tactical Operations Center, Phong Dinh Sector, January 31, 1970, Box 842, File 228–09, Advisory Team 56 Records, NACP.

123. Daily Log, Tactical Operations Center, Phong Dinh Sector, March 4, 1970, Box 843, File 228–09, Advisory Team 56 Records, NACP.

124. Daily Log, Tactical Operations Center, Phong Dinh Sector, February 20, 1970, Box 842, File 228–09, Advisory Team 56 Records, NACP.

125. Daily Log, Tactical Operations Center, Phong Dinh Sector, September 6, 1970, Box 848, File 228–09, Advisory Team 56 Records, NACP.

126. Daily Log, Tactical Operations Center, Phong Dinh Sector, February 6, 1970, Box 842, File 228–09, Advisory Team 56 Records, NACP.

127. Daily Log, Tactical Operations Center, Phong Dinh Sector, March 13, 1970, Box 843, File 228–09, Advisory Team 56 Records, NACP.

128. Daily Log, Tactical Operations Center, Phong Dinh Sector, April 20, 1970, Box 844, File 228–09, Advisory Team 56 Records, NACP.

129. Daily Log, Tactical Operations Center, Phong Dinh Sector, December 2, 1969, Box 840, File 228–09, Advisory Team 56 Records, NACP.

130. Tim O'Brien, "The Sweetheart of the Song Tra Bong," *The Things They Carried* (New York: Mariner, 2009), 85–110.

131. Brigadier General Willard Latham, *The Modern Volunteer Army Program: The Benning Experiment, 1970–1972* (Washington, D.C.: Department of the Army, 1974), 111.

132. T.E. Lawrence, "Twenty-seven Articles," *Lawrence of Arabia*, PBS.org, accessed February 2, 2015, http://www.pbs.org/lawrenceofarabia/revolt/warfare4.html.

133. Daily Log, Tactical Operations Center, Phong Dinh Sector, November 15, 1969, Box 840, File 228–09, Advisory Team 56 Records, NACP.

134. Daily Log, Tactical Operations Center, Phong Dinh Sector, February 27, 1970, Box 843, File 228–09, Advisory Team 56 Records, NACP.

135. Colonel Harold Van Hout. Phong Dinh Province Monthly Report, April 1970, Box 904, File 1601–11A, Advisory Team 56 Records, NACP.

136. Douglas Valentine, *The Phoenix Program* (New York: Morrow, 1990), 13.

137. K. Milton Osborn, Testimony, Congressional Hearings, 1971, qtd. in Jeffrey Hays, "Phoenix Program Facts and Details," *Facts and Details*, last modified 2013, accessed February 3, 2015, http://factsanddetails.com/southeast-asia/Vietnam/sub5_9b/entry-3358.html.

138. Walter V. Robinson, "Professor's Past in Doubt; Discrepancies Surface in Claim of Vietnam Duty," *Boston Globe*, June 18, 2001.

139. Robert Miller, "Area Vietnam Veterans Hold off Condemnation of Blumenthal," *News-Times* (Danbury, CT), May 18, 2010, accessed February 7, 2015, http://www.newstimes.com/news/article/Area-Vietnam-veterans-hold-off-condemnation-of-491591.php#photo-183768.

140. Lyndon Johnson, qtd. in Robert Jewett and John Shelton Lawrence, *Captain America and the Crusade against Evil* (Cambridge, UK: Wm. B. Eerdmans Publishing, 2003), 102.

141. Joint U.S. Public Affairs Office, "Psyops Aspects of GVN Land Title and Land Tenure Programs," Guidance Paper #34, March 20, 1967.

142. Colin Godwin, Interview with Captain Joseph P. Saffron, 20th Military History Detachment, May 16, 1969, Vietnam Interview Tape Collection (VNIT 381), U.S. Army Center of Military History, Fort McNair, D.C.

143. Dr. John Baker, Interview with 20th Military History Detachment, April 5, 1969, Vietnam Interview Tape Collection (VNIT 381), U.S. Army Center of Military History, Fort McNair, D.C.

144. Daily Log, Tactical Operations Center, Phong Dinh Sector, January 8, 1970, Box 841, File 228–09, Advisory Team 56 Records, NACP.

145. Captured Viet Cong Document, Can Tho City Party Committee, "1969 Plans," June 5, 1969, Box 875, File 502–03, Advisory Team 56 Records, NACP.

146. Lieutenant Richard Kennedy, Report of Lessons Learned by Mobile Advisory Team 11 in Deployment to Thoi Long Village, November 10, 1970, Box 890, File 1601–09A, Advisory Team 56 Records, NACP.

147. Potter, "Provincial Politics in South Vietnam," 155–6.

148. John O'Leary, qtd. in W.B. Yeats, "Poetry and Tradition," August 1907, *readbookonline.net*, accessed February 10, 2015, . http://www.readbookonline.net/readOnLine/53220/

Index

Abrams, Gen. Creighton 86
Afghanistan 4, 7, 10, 13, 30, 31, 36, 41, 54, 57, 110, 124, 131, 178, 184, 197
Agent Orange 14
AK-47 rifle 131, 144, 152, 161, 190, 207
Alderson, 1st Lt. Robert 27, 43
Ali, Muhammad 162
Allen, Woody 156
An Giang Province 132
Andrade, Dale 88
Apfel, Pfc Robert 107
Army of the Republic of Vietnam (ARVN) 1, 19, 35, 36, 86, 87, 106, 128, 131, 165, 170, 171, 172, 173, 207

Bacevich, Andrew 13
Bach, William 90
Baker, Dr. John 190–191
Ball, John M. (Mac) 23
Barrett, Mark 182–184
Beckett, Samuel 116, 124
Behan, Brendan 85
Bellow, Saul 7, 192
Berra, Yogi 83
Bien Hoa 40
Binh Thuy Air Base 63, 107, 146, 147, 149, 162, 169, 173, 175, 176, 198, 208
Black, Capt. Steven 104, 105, 107–108, 111, 122, 175–176, 182
Black and Tans 166–167, 182
Blumenthal, Sen. Richard 187
body count 8, 42, 56, 61, 89, 106, 126, 135
Boer War 4, 64
Boko Haram 4
Bon, Major 20, 132
Bonhoeffer, Dietrich 13
Boorda, Jeremy 123
Brackman, Arnold 30
Brennan, John 58
Briggs, John 99
Brophy, Brendan 94
Buddhism 16, 17, 35, 37, 39, 76, 90, 132, 137, 196
Bund, American 82

bureaucracy 11, 14, 23–25, 32, 47, 74, 91, 123, 141, 144, 151, 167, 191
Burns, Capt. Robert V. 24, 25, 61–62, 108, 111, 125, 127, 129, 132, 140–143, 161, 164, 168, 184
Bush, Sfc Arthur 22
Bush, George W. 9, 10, 135

Caesar, Julius 27
Cambodia 17, 21, 91, 106, 170, 171, 205
Caputo, Philip 1, 41
Can Tho Army Air Field 15, 63, 84, 87, 103, 104, 114, 135, 146, 149, 161, 164, 165, 169, 192, 208
Can Tho City 14–16, 17, 18, 24, 28, 35, 55, 73, 74, 104, 106, 115, 117, 126, 132, 133, 137, 139, 141, 143, 150, 152, 158, 165, 168, 169, 170, 172, 174, 175, 197, 198
Canada 92
careerism 72, 73, 77, 116, 119, 121–123, 185
Carlyle, Thomas 11
Carpenter, Lucas 54
Carroll, Jim 102
Catholicism, Roman 1, 47, 48, 50, 51, 68, 69, 76, 80, 84, 89, 94, 95, 97, 118, 132–133, 178
Central Office for South Vietnam (COSVN) 106, 151, 207
Chamberlain, Wilt 119
Chau, Dai-uy [Captain] 25
Chau Thanh A (VC unit) 134
Cherbourg, France 81–82
Chieu Hoi Program 21, 204
China 16, 30, 34, 35, 88
Cimino, Michael: *The Deer Hunter* 41–42, 119
Civil Operations and Revolutionary Development Support (CORDS) 117, 119, 141, 170, 189, 207
Clinton, Hillary Rodham 30
Clinton, William Jefferson 9, 18, 47
Cochrane, Mickey 49
Coen Brothers 78
Colby, William E. 20, 154, 158
Cold War 35, 96, 181